CYBERGHETTO
OR CYBERTOPIA?

Race, Class, and Gender on the Internet

Edited by Bosah Ebo

 PRAEGER

Westport, Connecticut
London

ZA4150
.C93
1998

Library of Congress Cataloging-in-Publication Data

Cyberghetto or cybertopia? : race, class, and gender on the Internet /
   edited by Bosah Ebo.
      p. cm.
   Includes bibliographical references and index.
   ISBN 0–275–95993–7 (alk. paper)
      1. Cyberspace—Social aspects—United States.   2. Internet
(Computer network)—Social aspects—United States.   3. Minorities—
United States—Social conditions.   I. Ebo, Bosah L. (Bosah Louis)
ZA4150.C93   1998
303.48'33—dc21   97–23881

British Library Cataloguing in Publication Data is available.

Library of Congress Catalog Card Number: 97–23881
ISBN: 0–275–95993–7

First published in 1998

Praeger Publishers, 88 Post Road West, Westport, CT 06881
An imprint of Greenwood Publishing Group, Inc.

Printed in the United States of America

The paper used in this book complies with the
Permanent Paper Standard issued by the National
Information Standards Organization (Z39.48–1984).

10 9 8 7 6 5 4 3 2

To my inspiration,
    Chineze, Noni, and Dumebi

Contents

Preface   ix

1. Internet or Outernet?
    Bosah Ebo   1

Part I: Class on the Net

2. Exposing the Great Equalizer: Demythologizing Internet
    Equity
    Alecia Wolf   15

3. Ensuring Social Justice for the New Underclass:
    Community Interventions to Meet the Needs of the
    New Poor
    John G. McNutt   33

4. The Challenge of Cyberspace: Internet Access and
    Persons with Disabilities
    Mark Borchert   49

5. Cyber-Soldiering: Race, Class, Gender, and New Media
    Use in the U.S. Army
    Morten G. Ender and David R. Segal   65

6. How the Web Was Won: The Commercialization of
Cyberspace
James L. McQuivey   83

Part II: Race on the Net

7. Challenging the Mandarins: Comparing City
Characteristics and Nationwide Newspaper Coverage of
the Internet, 1993–95
John C. Pollock and Elvin Montero   103

8. Domination and Democracy in Cyberspace: Reports
from the Majority Media and Ethnic/Gender Margins
Meta G. Carstarphen and Jacqueline Johnson Lambiase   121

9. Equity and Access to Computer Technology for
Grades K–12
Paulette Robinson   137

10. On the Electronic Information Frontier: Training the
Information-Poor in an Age of Unequal Access
Rebecca Carrier   153

Part III: Cybergendering

11. Democratizing Internet Access in the Lesbian, Gay, and
Bisexual Communities
Nadine S. Koch and H. Eric Schockman   171

12. Communicative Style and Gender Differences in
Computer-Mediated Communications
Kevin Crowston and Ericka Kammerer   185

13. Netsex: Empowerment Through Discourse
Charlene Blair   205

14. Embracing the Machine: Quilt and Quilting as
Community-Building Architecture
Andrew F. Wood and Tyrone L. Adams   219

Index   235

About the Editor and Contributors   237

Preface

Technological innovations tend to engender debates about social justice. The arrival of the automobile raised questions about the impact of mobility and urbanization on close communal enclaves. The advent of nuclear technology generated debates about the impact of the radical transformation of production techniques on corporate social responsibility. The introduction of the communication technologies of telegraph, radio, and television raised concerns about the decentralization of communal linkages and social isolation. The arrival of the Internet is now raising questions about social justice.

The Internet is undergoing such a fast-paced metamorphosis that any attempt to examine its profile flirts with some risk. There is still a debate whether electronic communities are really tangible communities bound by traditional communal criteria such as explicit group demarcations, governing rules, participatory membership, recognition by external authority, and mechanisms for monitoring behaviors and conflict resolutions. Some have suggested that at best there are only partial manifestations of traditional characteristics in electronic communities. Yet, the evidence indicates that the Internet is dramatically changing the nature of social relationships. Whether cyberspace will simply retain vestiges of traditional communities with similar hierarchical social linkages and class-structured relationships or create new egalitarian social networks remains an open question. Put another way, are we headed toward a cyberghetto or a cybertopia?

Essays in this anthology use a variety of methodological and theoretical perspectives, including historical overview, philosophical speculation, sociological projection, cultural introspection, virtual ethnography, discourse, and quantitative analysis to explore the implications of the Internet for social justice. An eclectic assortment of contributors, including political scientists, sociologists, and communications and information systems scholars bring a rich multidisciplinary approach to examining how issues of race, class, and gender will be manifested on the Internet.

Some of the specific issues the chapters address include whether electronic networks will accommodate marginal constituencies within the notions of economic, social, and political empowerment. What is the potential of the new cyberculture to encompass the cultural forms of marginal constituencies? How will commercial imperatives of the Internet redefine the relationship between elite and marginal constituencies in terms of production and access to knowledge? Will the Internet be the great equalizer by bringing universal socialization or will it create hedonistic isolations that will depreciate the sense of community? Will the Internet consign certain groups to the margins of cyberculture if their skills are not suited to the technology or will the technology promote diverse skills? What impact will the Internet have on rural and urban life? How will electronic commerce shape class and gender structures?

Addressing these questions is a daunting task, and I thank the contributors for their dedication and commitment to tackling this enormous assignment. I thank my colleague and good friend Professor Frank Rusciano of the Department of Political Science at Rider University for many valuable thoughts. I thank Elisabetta Linton, acquisitions editor at Greenwood Publishing Group, for making this project a pleasant experience. I would also like to thank Terri Jennings, production editor, and Frances Rudner, copyeditor, for their work. Finally, I thank my family for their support and encouragement.

Internet or Outernet?

Bosah Ebo

New technological artifacts often challenge existing social structures by introducing new rules for social relationships. Legal, ethical, cultural, and political infrastructures of society must adjust to the impositions of new technology. Regulatory agencies, legislators, legal institutions, and consumers must adapt to the prescriptions of new technology. Technological innovations also dislocate routine processes and create anxieties for people. Society is forced to redefine old rules or identify new rules for sustaining social relationships. Besides introducing an appreciable level of social comfort, new technology raises important questions about social justice.

Twenty years ago there were 50,000 computers in the whole world; today 50,000 computers are sold every ten hours (Gonzalez 1995). The number of American households that own personal computers grew by 15 percent in 1995 (*Investor's Business Daily*, April 23, 1996: A8). Thirty-eight and a half percent of American homes now have one or more personal computers. A survey of teens in homes that have video game machines and personal computers indicates that 54 percent of the teens spend more time with the personal computers, and 88 percent would rather have a personal computer if forced to choose between the two (*Investor's Business Daily* April 23, 1996: A8). The influence of computer technology extends beyond the home; 54 percent of Americans use a computer at home, work, or school. Sixty-two percent of employed Americans use a computer at the workplace (*Philadelphia Inquirer* November 19, 1995: D3). Experts predict that the Internet and Web will make electronic commerce the dominant mode of economic mediation as the number of virtual communities grows.

The $500 billion worth of goods American companies buy electronically a year is a small percentage of their total purchases, but it indicates an emerging trend toward electronic commerce (*Business Week* June 10, 1996: 110).

The Internet is also redefining communities and reordering society into new forms of social networks. New values and terms for private and professional relationships are emerging (Buck 1996; Gates 1995; Baym 1995). The *Los Angeles Times* (June 17, 1996) stated: "People in all types of career categories need to know how to use this tool in order to get ahead . . . starting now." An article in *Time* magazine points out:

Access to the information highway may prove to be less a question of privilege or position than one of the basic ability to function in a democratic society. Access to the cyberspace may very well determine how well people are educated, the kind of job they eventually get, how they are retrained if they lose their job, how much access they have to their government and how they will learn about critical issues affecting them and the country. (Ratan 1995: 25)

Access to cyberspace becomes even more important as new notions of social identities develop, and the measurement of a good life assumes new dimensions (Shields 1996; Shapiro 1995; Besser 1995). Social and professional relationships are being redefined as loyalties to reference groups move from the domain of close-knit family groups, physical communal neighborhoods, and schools and professional environments to virtual communities and online relationships (Negroponte 1995; Schuler 1996; Rheingold 1993). The new cyberculture is emerging as a fundamental avenue for the formation of economic and social associations (Gumpert and Drucker 1992). As the Internet, Web, and other components of cyberspace become the dominant mediator in ordered life and social relationships, issues of race, class, and gender become germane. If the next generation of commercial transactions, professional enhancement, social interfacing, and group socialization will be developed on the information superhighway, those who have access to the new cyberculture will inevitably stand to benefit the most.

Two conflicting and yet reasonable perspectives are emerging about the impact of the Internet on society. Proponents believe that the Internet could create a cybertopia because of its potential to generate new egalitarian social networks. But critics argue that the potential for a cyberghetto is real because the Internet will retain vestiges of traditional communities with similar hierarchical social linkages and class-structured relationships.

THE CYBERTOPIA PERSPECTIVE

Proponents of the Internet see the technology as a great equalizer because virtual communities do not use disenfranchising criteria for community-building. The Internet deemphasizes hierarchical political associations, degrading gender roles and ethnic designations, and rigid categories of class relationships found in traditional, visually based and geographically bound communities. The management of identities and relationships in virtual communities is not moderated by the traditional elitist social contract that is involuntarily binding and unfairly maintained by regulatory institutions. The Internet is not inhibited by the inherent biases manifested in sexism, racism, and classism found in face-to-face encounters. Instead, the Internet presents a forum that encourages broad participation and emphasizes merit over status. Virtual communities allow isolated individuals to communicate in a manner that protects them from the social expectations and sanctions associated with physically defined communities (Turkle 1995). Virtual communities are cohesive and meaningful social aggregations that allow people to engage in sufficient interactions to form personal and group relationships (Rheingold 1993).

Proponents point to the potential of the Internet to disrupt gender-induced biases in communication as one of its strengths. Research on women and technology indicates that men have traditionally dominated discourse in communication technologies that reveal gender characteristics (Herring 1994; Matheson 1992). The interaction between sex and power is culturally tilted toward the male and may even be repressive for women (Coates 1993; Jansen 1989). For proponents, cyberstealth or physical invisibility on the Internet becomes an important attribute because it invalidates visual or auditory cues that betray a speaker's gender. Cyberdiscourse undermines physical augumentations that are routine components of inter-gender interactions in visually moderated relationships. Women may be able to co-opt the technology of the Internet to create alternative platforms that subvert the patriarchal hierarchy in the social and economic structure of society.

Also, the Internet has the capacity to redefine dominant relationship patterns that are culturally instigated, such as the role of semantic hegemony in sexual relationships. The Internet potentially creates a leveling effect because the two primary tenets of the medium, discourse and anonymity, give women a unique opportunity, maybe even an advantage, in cybersex (see Charlene Blair's Chapter 13 in this volume). Women who could master the unique tactics of online discourse could achieve satisfaction from cybersex and control the direction of their sexuality in this medium. Cybersex gives women a new empowering avenue in sexual relationships with men because it allows for a truly skills-based exchange of pleasure between men and women since it is moderated by the ability to create the text or control the story.

For the proponents of the Internet, cyberstealth also could create self-liberating identities for groups that have been isolated or ostracized from mainstream discourse, such as fat, disabled, or gay constituencies. The Internet could allow groups that have traditionally been dislocated from mainstream social linkages or deprived from participating in physically structured relationships to develop communal bonding (see Mark Borchert's Chapter 4 in this volume). The Internet also is an inexpensive and viable information dissemination avenue for fringe groups, such as militia and religious groups, or other groups that traditionally have been shut off by elite media. The Heaven's Gate cult that committed mass suicide in April 1997 effectively used the Internet to recruit members and to circulate its messages.

The Internet has the ability to create a platform for distance learning and virtual education that could reduce class inequity in formal education caused by physical inaccessibility. Members of marginal constituencies who ordinarily may not have the opportunity to get formal education from good schools because of the expense of physical relocation may be able to do so because of the Internet. The Education Network of Maine has a program that sends lectures and learning materials to students all over the state from classrooms in various campuses outfitted with cameras and computers. The broadcast goes to eighty locations from four channels through microwave and fiber-optic cables (*Chronicle of Higher Education* May 31, 1996: A16). Northern Arizona University has a distance-learning program that delivers education to the Navajo Indian reservation in the northeast corner of the state. The Virtual University established by the Western Governors Association provides an example of a more elaborate model of higher education designed primarily around the Internet (*Chronicle of Higher Education* June 14, 1995: A30).

Some proponents have suggested that because it is unmediated, the Internet has the potential to infuse disenfranchised voters into the political process when it becomes widely available. The Internet could allow for more voter participation and feedback because it is unmediated. The role of the press in the electoral process is actually being redefined by the Internet. Traditionally, the Western libertarian political philosophy recognizes the importance of an informed citizenry in a democratic process. As has the annointed watchdog, professional media have had the primary responsibility for maintaining an informed citizenry. But many critics argue that the media have fallen short of this responsibility because of the increasing pressure of commercial imperatives. For instance, the exorbitant cost of television advertisements does not allow political candidates to have meaningful contacts or dialogue with the electorate. Some studies have suggested that voters are beginning to see the Internet as a viable source of information. A poll sponsored by The Freedom Forum indicates that the news appetite of the American people has been growing at the same time their trust in the news media has been declining. The poll found that while 70 percent find news helpful in decision-making, only about half of the 1,500 surveyed trust the news media (*USA Today* March 3, 1997). There is evidence that the Internet may be usurping some of the responsibilities ordinarily reserved for the press. All the major presidential candidates during the 1996 elections used home pages to circulate policy statements.

Proponents argue that whatever socioeconomic gap currently exists in access to computers will eventually be closed by market forces. Competition will drive the price of personal computers down, making them more affordable. Some supportive evidence indicates that access to computer technology is transcending gender and class barriers. The new buyers of computer technology are less affluent, making between $10,000 and $30,000, and older, in the over-60 years category (*Wall Street Journal* May 21, 1996: B10). In 1995, families headed by someone with high school education constituted 39 percent of new computer owners, the largest proportion (*Philadelphia Inquirer* November 19, 1995: D3). A larger percentage, 46 percent, of Americans living in the remote rural areas of Iowa, Nebraska, Kansas, Minnesota, and North and South Dakota use personal computers, faxes, and e-mail than the rest of the population, at 33 percent (*Wall Street Journal* June 29, 1996: A1). Trend analyses of the electronic games industry indicate that the self-correcting measures of market competition are closing the gender gap in that industry. Video game companies, which initially ignored the young female market and instead targeted young boys with their macho theme programs, are beginning to invest in the young-girl market. Sega of America's Girls Task Force has had dramatic success developing products for girls, and the use of Sega Genesis by young girls grew from 3 percent in 1993 to 20 percent in 1995 (*Digital Kids* June 1995: 15). Texas-based Girl Games and Los Angeles-based e-Girl Interactive companies started marketing online and interactive services exclusively for girls in 1996 (*Digital Kids* June 1995: 15).

Proponents of the Internet also note that community efforts will redress unequal access to the Internet. The city of Santa Monica in California has installed public access computer terminals in groceries, banks, and other public places (Ratan, 1995: 26). Atcom/Info, based in San Diego, has installed public access cyberbooths at airports, hotels and convention centers. Women in Technology International (WITI) sponsors an annual "Take Your Children on the Internet Week" (TYCOTI) with the support of Microsoft, Intel, The Family Channel, Sun, Futurekids, Safesurf, the United Federation of Childsafe Web Sites (UFCWS) and the Center for Children in Technology. The program uses fun and educational activities such as online scavenger hunts, raffles, building home pages and constructing digital time capsules to help young girls explore the Internet. For proponents of the Internet, we may be heading toward cybertopia.

THE CYBERGHETTO PERSPECTIVE

For many critics of the Internet, virtual communities are just another dimension of traditional communal relationships with the same built-in biases of race, class, and gender. Visual identities may be de-emphasized on the Internet to some extent, but the same codes of conduct moderate social relationships in the medium. Virtual communities fulfill the same traditional essence of associations and bonding, and invariably promote social relationships that are orchestrated by inherent inegalitarian tendencies in society. As long as communities on the Internet allow participants to engage freely in the creation of social realities, economic and social classifications rooted in race, class, and gender statifications will invariably influence relationships in virtual communities (Civille 1995).

Some critics argue that the idea that the Internet is an emancipatory technology is untenable because the architecture of the technology harbors an innate class bias and other nuances of power entitlements. Computers are designed and programmed by members of the elite culture and may reflect their cultural orientations and biases. For instance, the wordsmithing and semantic skills required to operate computers do not accommodate the cultural orientations of some marginal constituencies.

Critics argue that access to cyberspace seems currently to be concentrated in the hands of the wealthy and educated, and this has created a techno-illiteracy that has been reified in class, race, and gender stratifications. Telecommunications companies and online providers tend to locate their services and information networks in affluent communities, bypassing inner cities and less affluent rural areas (Squires 1995; Center for Media Education 1994). Seven million American homes, mostly poor, do not have phones and cannot access online services (Ratan 1995: 26). This practice of information apartheid or electronic red-lining dislocates the integration of peripheral groups into mainstream cultural interactions and creates a cyberghetto.

The bulk of the 30 percent of American households that own computers is made up of wealthy and upper middle-class families. Affluent suburban school districts tend to have more and better computer resources than do urban schools (Ratan 1995: 25; Kozol 1992; Piller 1992). Top-notch colleges are making computer technology a routine component of the educational experience. For example, in a bold initiative introduced in the fall of 1996 called "Plan for the Class of 2000," Wake Forest University began giving laptop computers to incoming freshmen (*Computer World* May 27, 1996). The disparity in access to technology in education has serious ramifications. One study indicated that college students who used online text and electronic homework assignments in a virtual classroom tested 20 percent better on exams than students who learned the material in a traditional classroom (News.Com January 17, 1997).

There also is disparity in communal access to computer technology because smaller and rural communities generally cannot afford to buy computers for their public facilities (Irving 1995). In a report titled "The 1996 National Survey of Public Libraries and the Internet," the National Commission on Libraries and Information Sciences noted that libraries serving communities of under 5,000 people are significantly less likely to use the Internet than libraries serving communities of over 100,000 (Bertot, Mc-Clure, and Zweizig 1996).

An ambitious study of the demographic and psychographic characteristics of Internet and Web users by SRI International also revealed elitist tendencies of the technology. The "Upstream" crowd, about 50 percent of Web users but only 10 percent of the U.S. population, consists of the active, upscale, technically and professionally oriented users that drive media coverage and stereotypes of the Web. The problem is with a group the study called the "Other Half," about 90 percent of the U.S. population. This is a diverse group made up of information-intensive consumers who have not found the Internet all that appealing. Obviously, the Web is not yet a mainstream medium and will likely not be until the "Other Half" embraces it. The study also revealed that education is the primary limitation of the information have-nots, those who do not use the Internet at all. Ninety-seven percent of the "Upstream" crowd and 89 percent of the "Other Half" have some college education (SRI International 1996).

Some critics argue that the Internet will not change gender-induced biases because the constructive philosophy and covert tendencies of the medium are male-centric (Miller 1995; McGaw 1987). One reason for this is that women have not played a significant role in designing technological innovations (Jansen 1989). Also, males are generally socialized to be more interested in computers and to use them more than women at a younger age. Parents are more likely to buy computers and video games for their sons than for their daughters. In formal educational settings, educators tend to nudge boys toward computers. Even the messages from video games and media programs portray computers as a male artifact by overindulging in the aggressive and competitive themes of the male culture. The ramifications are obvious. Males make up 66 percent of Internet users and account for 77 percent of its usage (Nielsen Media 1996). This has serious ramifications because there is a positive correlation between time spent on computers and results on achievement tests. Other studies confirm class bias in technological socialization. Twenty-five percent of the users of the Internet make over $80,000, 50 percent occupy professional or managerial positions, and 64 percent have at least college degrees (Nielsen Media 1996).

For many critics, race, gender, and class biases on the Internet are inevitable because the medium is conducive to the philosophy of a class-structured economy (Dawson and Foster 1996; Kleiner 1995). In fact, many critics argue that the debate on the political economy of the Internet has been driven by commercial imperatives more than anything else. Advertisers and marketers have been quick to incorporate the hierarchical consumption patterns of a mass culture into the Internet. Thus, the heavy commercial traffic on the information superhighway, manifested in the strong consumer-oriented profile of the Web, for instance, compromises the potential of the medium to provide universal socialization. For many critics the Internet ultimately will accommodate the hegemonic tendencies of the larger society because it will simply be an extension of the mass consumer culture. The integration of commercial imperatives and economic incentives into the Internet will structure virtual communities as economic enclaves much like the market-segmented class divisions of contemporary society. In that sense, electronic communities will still be structured by socioeconomic interests that reflect race, class, and gender considerations.

Critics note that information technology may actually be depreciating social bonding by creating artificial terms for interactions, and usurping human ability to think. Electronic commerce, for instance, does not accommodate the social and cultural attributes of communal bonding. The agora-oriented community commerce had social relevance beyond trade because it gave the community a place to interact and developed lasting communal ties. Electronic shopping eliminates physical contacts and communal linkages, and may be encouraging isolationism.

A trustworthy profile of the Internet has not yet emerged because the technology is still evolving. Some cultural observers have suggested that the technology is merely a fad that will dazzle and disappear. Indeed, actual use of the Internet has not matched the hype. A poll found that of the 70 percent who knew about the Internet, only 20 percent have used it from their homes (*Los Angeles Times* November 25, 1996). The heavy media coverage of the Internet may be driving the hype instead of actual acceptance of the medium by the public. Nevertheless, enough significant characteristics and attributes of the Internet have emerged to warrant serious examinations of the social relevance and impact of the technology.

There is little doubt that the Internet will have a significant foothold in moderating social relationships. The question is whether the Internet will be the great equalizer or an elitist medium. Will the Internet create universal and inclusive modes of socialization or become the domain of the elite, exacerbating tensions between elite and marginal constituencies? "In an era in which success is increasingly identified with the ability to use computers and gain access to cyberspace, will the new technology only widen the gap between rich and poor, educated and uneducated, blacks, whites, and Hispanics?" (Ratan 1995: 25). Initial evidence suggests that access to cyberspace will be a necessary element in economic and political empowerment, and cultural representation in society. Generally, workers who are able to use computers earn 15 percent more than those in similar jobs who could not use computers (Ratan 1995: 25). While proponents gloat over the potential of the new technology and critics remain skeptical and suspicious, a fundamental issue is one of social justice. Is the Internet a windfall of publicly accessible information and a barrier-free terrain of social associations or just another social revolution with an innate bias that reinforces the marginalization of the underclass, the subliterate, minorities, and women? Will the Internet create a cybertopia or will it exacerbate class divisions by creating a cyberghetto?

Part I of this book examines how class stratification could play a vital role in defining the profile of the Internet. Alecia Wolf uses demographic statistics to examine how the cost of personal computerization may be a prominent inhibitor access to the Internet for marginalized constituencies. In Chapter 2, John G. McNutt points out that information poverty will be important in conceptualizing a new underclass, and that information technology could be a key for social intervention. For Mark Borchert, the Internet may prove to be an important liberating medium for the disabled if government policies and regulations that guide the development of the information superhighway accommodate consideration of social justice. Morten G. Ender and David R. Segal examine the way information technology is reshaping family interactions and social trends in the military culture in the context of race, class, and gender. They observe that unlike in the larger society, the gap in access and use of information technology in the military is moderate. James L. McQuivey argues that the commercialization of the Internet is more a factor of social preconditioning of users than corporate conspiracy. The implication is that users may not be taking full advantage of the potential of the World Wide Web.

The focus of Part II is on how racial identities and attributes will moderate social justice on the Internet. John C. Pollock and Elvin Montero's observation that the higher the percentage of college students in a city, the less likely a city's newspaper is to cover the Internet favorably raises important questions about the role of the Internet as a tool for democratization. Meta G. Carstarphen and Jacqueline Johnson Lambiase examine the potential of the Internet to allow competing cultures to negotiate new power relationships through the collision of language and ideas, and argue that the Internet may be emulating hierarchies of power structures in traditional society. Paulette Robinson discusses the issue of redirecting public policy focus in dealing with computer illiteracy, pointing out that despite government efforts, access to computer technology continues to be unequal for minorities and the poor. Along the same line, Rebecca Carrier's chapter discusses the implications of institutional access to computer technology. She argues that while well-endowed schools will meet the challenges of the new information age, schools that have limited financial resources will be unable to provide their students with a rich technological heritage to compete.

Part III presents competing perspectives on the ways gender and social empowerment will be manifested on the Internet. Nadine Koch and H. Eric Schockman examine how the Internet is leading to a new digital sexual identity in the gay and lesbian community, and the potential for a collective empowerment to reshape the established political order. In their chapter, Kevin Crowston and Ericka Kammerer examine how gender interacts with communicative style to affect decisions to participate in electronic communities. Charlene Blair argues that the Internet has the potential to provide gender leveling because its text-based characteristic redefines empowerment in sexual relationships. Andrew F. Wood and Tyrone L. Adams use a case study to examine how the World Wide Web (WWW) could be used as a protest vehicle to circumvent traditional norms of communication that marginalize feminist voices.

REFERENCES

Atlanta Journal-Constitution, April 30, 1996, p. B1.

Baym, N. K. 1995. The emergence of community in computer-mediated communication. In S. G. Jones, ed., *CyberSociety: Computer-Mediated Communication and Community*. Thousand Oaks, Calif.: Sage Publications, pp. 138–63.

Bertot, J. C., C. R. McClure, and D. L. Zweizig. 1996. National Commission on Libraries and Information Sciences: The 1996 national surveys of public libraries and the Internet. Online. Available: 96NatSur <http://istweb.syr.edu/Project/Faculty/McClure-NSPL96/NSPL96_T.html>

Besser, Howard. 1995. From internet to information superhighway. In James Brooks and Iain Boal, eds., *Resisting the Virtual Life: The Culture and Politics of Information*. San Francisco: City Lights, pp. 59–70.

Blumenstyk, Goldie. 1995. Western states continue to plan "virtual" college. *Chronicle of Higher Education*, June 14, pp. A30–31.

———. 1996. Learning from afar. *Chronicle of Higher Education*, May 31, pp. A15–16.

Buck, K. 1996. Community organizing and the Internet. *Neighborhood Works*, 19, 2, p. 2.

Business Week, June 10, 1996, p. 110.

Center for Media Education. 1994. Electronic redlining. Washington, D.C.: Center for Media Education.

Civille, R. 1995. The Internet and the poor. In B. Kahin and J. Keller, eds., *Public Access to the Internet* Cambridge: MIT Press, pp. 175–207.

Coates, J. 1993. *Women, Men and Language*, 2nd edn. London: Longman.

Computer World, May 27, 1996.

Dawson, M., and J. B. Foster. 1996. Virtual capitalism: The political economy of the information superhighway. *Monthly Review* 48 (3):40.

Digital Kids, June 1995, p. 15.

Gates, B. 1995. *The Road Ahead*. New York: Viking.

Gonzalez, Emilio. 1995. Connecting the nation: Classrooms, libraries and health care organizations in the information age. *NTIA* (June):4.

Gumpert, G., and S. J. Drucker. 1992. From the agora to the electronic shopping mall. *Critical Studies in Mass Communication* 9(4) 186–200.

Hayles, N. Katherine. 1993. The seductions of cyberspace. In V. Anderman, ed., *Rethinking Technologies*. Minneapolis: University of Minnesota Press, pp. 173–90.

Herring, S. 1994. Gender differences in computer-mediated communication: Bring-

ing familiar baggage to the new frontier. On line: http://www.cpsr.org/cpsr/
    gender/herring/html

Hill, G. Christian. 1996. Tally of homes with PCs increased 16% last year. *Wall
    Street Journal*, May 21, p. B10.

Investor's Business Daily, March 21, 1996, p. A8.

———. April 23, 1996, p. A8.

Irving, Larry. 1995. The connected and disconnected in rural and urban America.
    Online: http://ntiaunix2.ntia.doc.gov:70/0/speeches/naruc727.html

Jansen, S. C. 1989. Gender and the information society: A socially structured si-
    lence. *Journal of Communication* 39:196–215.

Kleiner, K. 1995. Sweet sound of cash registers on the Internet. *New Socialist* 2
    (June 3):146, 147.

Kollock, P. and M. Smith. 1995. *The Sociology of Cyberspace: Social Interaction
    and Order in Computer Communities*. Thousand Oaks, Calif.: Pine Forge
    Press.

Kozol, J. 1992. *Savage Inequalities: Children in America's Schools*. New York:
    HarperCollins.

Kramer, L. 1991. *The Sociology of Gender*. New York: St. Martin's Press.

Los Angeles Times, June 17, 1996.

Los Angeles Times, November 25, 1996, p. 1. Online: <http://www.latimes.
    com/>

Matheson, K. 1992. Women and computer technology: Communicating for herself.
    In M. Lea, ed., *Contexts of Computer-Mediated Communication*. New
    York: Harvester Wheatsheaf, pp. 67–88.

McGaw, J. A. 1987. Women and the history of American technology. In S. Harding
    and J. F. O'Barr, eds., *Sex and Scientific Inquiry*. Chicago: University of
    Chicago Press, pp. 47–77.

Miller, L. 1995. Women and children first: Gender and the settling of the electronic
    frontier. In J. Brook and I. A. Boal, eds., *Resisting the Virtual Life: The
    Culture and Politics of Information*. San Francisco: City Lights, pp. 49–57.

Negroponte, Nichola. 1995. *Being Digital*. New York: Alfred A. Knopf.

News.Com, January 17, 1997.

Nielsen Media. 1996. Nielsen Internet Surveys. Online: <http://www.nielsenmedia.
    com/demo.htm>

Ostrom, E. 1990. *Governing the Commons: The Evolution of Institutions for Col-
    lective Action*. New York: Cambridge University Press.

People need news but many don't trust the media. *USA Today*, March 3, 1997.
    Online: <http://www.usatoday.com/elect/eq/eq179.htm>

Philadelphia Inquirer, November 19, 1995, p. D3.

Piller, C. 1992. Separate realities: The creation of the technological underclass in
    America's public schools. *MacWorld*, (September):218–30.

Plugged-in on the prairie: Rural residents prize telecommunications tools. *Wall
    Street Journal*, May 21, 1996, p. B10.

Ratan, S. 1995. *Time* (Spring):25–26.

Redd, L. N. 1988. Telecommunications, economics and black families in America.
    Journal of Black Studies 19 (1):111–23.

Rheingold, H. 1993. *The Virtual Community: Homesteading on the Electronic
    Frontier*. Reading, Mass.: Addison-Wesley.

Schuler, D. 1996. *New Community Networks: Wired for Change*. New York: ACM Press.

Shapiro, Andrew. 1995. Street corners in cyberspace. *The Nation*, July 3, pp. 10–14.

Shields, Rob. 1996. Introduction. In R. Shield ed., *Cultures of Internet: Virtual Spaces, Real Histories and Living Bodies*. London: Sage Publications, pp. 1–10.

Squires, R. (1995). High tech redlining. *Utne Reader* 86:73.

SRI International. (1996) Exploring the World Wide Web population's other half. Online: <http://future.sri.com/vals/vals-survey.results.html>

Turkle, Sherry. 1995. *Life on the Screen: Identity in the Age of the Internet*. New York: Simon & Schuster.

USA Today. 1996. People need news but many don't trust the media. May. Online: 96NatSur: <http://istweb.syr.edu/Project/Faculty/McClure-SPL96/NSPL96_T.html>

Wilson, David L. 1996. Campus computing officials plan the next generation of networks. *Chronicle of Higher Education*, November 1, pp. A25–26.

PART I

Class on the Net

2

Exposing the Great Equalizer: Demythologizing Internet Equity

Alecia Wolf

Computer users in diverse areas of interest tout the Internet as the "Great Equalizer." Proponents of this view maintain that offline barriers to successful communication dissipate in the ethers of cyberspace (Polly 1992; Engleman 1995; Webster 1995; Bleier 1996). This optimistic position maintains that the absence of face-to-face communication erases the prejudices associated with assorted "isms": sexism, racism, and classism. This chapter challenges these claims by examining a host of demographic statistics regarding Internet users. The author contends that the conclusions derived from available statistics are incomplete or misleading and often blind researchers to other relevant factors. The limited presence of certain groups on the Internet may be the result of factors ignored by the interpretations of research findings.

This chapter addresses the possibility of incomplete, misleading, and biased interpretations of Internet users by analyzing statistics on World Wide Web and Internet use. These statistics are compared with U.S. Census social and demographic data. The chapter employs the use of charts to contrast the generally accepted profile of the typical Internet user with that of the rest of the population. These comparisons demonstrate the interpretive biases.

The author proposes that, in addition to other variables, the chasm between average salaries of the typical Internet user and the rest of the population suggests that the initial cost of getting online (computer, modem, access fees) may contribute to the "unwillingness" of women and others to "actually personally *pay* for Internet access."

The findings of this chapter are significant if true because a belief in the Internet as a Great Equalizer dismisses the need to work toward equality in this area. Accepting the assumptions and the stereotypes perpetuated by deficient interpretations results in an incorrect profile of Internet users. A misinterpretation on this scale negatively affects those who seek equality for themselves and others. From an economic position, these misinterpretations also adversely affect the business seeking accurate profiles on which to base their marketing strategies.

Judy Michaud, director of WebWriters, . . . refers to the Internet as the *"Great Equalizer"* offering opportunities that are a way out of the pink ghetto. (A Woman's [Net] Work is Never Done 1996; emphasis added)

One of the most interesting things about telecommunications is that it is the *Great Equalizer*. It lets all kinds of computers and humans talk to each other. The old barriers of sexism, ageism, and racism are not present, since you can't see the person to whom you're "speaking." You get to know the person without preconceived notions about what you THINK he [*sic*] is going to say, based on visual prejudices you may have, no matter how innocent. (Polly 1992; emphasis added)

The Web is the *Great Equalizer*. It will help to usher in a new renaissance of global entrepreneurship and the benefits that follow naturally: innovation, productivity, and freedom. (Christensen 1995; emphasis added)

Just as the arrival of the PC in the early 1980's—and the subsequent networking of them in the late 1980's—allowed the smaller "boutique" law firms to match the largest firms stride for stride, in terms of research and productivity the Internet is yet another *"Great Equalizer"* in neutralizing the advantages of geographic location. (Bleier 1996; emphasis added)

The Web really is the *Great Equalizer* of the Internet. The consumer/browser who just reads and clicks, now has the same access to information resources that only Unix gurus once had. Further, the Web allows small businesses to compete against large businesses. For a small investment of money and creative time, a site can be available to everyone to browse; from Albany to Albania, from Boston to Botswanaland. And a small business or organization can be just as slick and visible as a Fortune 500 company. Isn't it nice to hear that the Web is fair? (Webster 1995; emphasis added)

One finds optimistic quotations extolling the "fairness" and "equality" of this new technology springing up all across the Internet. A certain appeal exists to embrace this new world of Internet equality and to view prejudice and inequality as an offline problem. The advocates of the Internet as Great Equalizer maintain that the barriers to equality associated with race, age, sex, and the other isms dissipate in the ethers of cyberspace (Polly 1992). As Linda Engelman (1995) writes: "Equality on the Net is a given."

The promoters of the Great Equalizer claim that the information previously available only to an elite few now lies within the grasp of all consumers and that small businesses currently enjoy an equal footing with larger corporations (Webster 1995; Bleier 1996). No shortage exists of studies revealing the demographics and use patterns of Internet users. The lure of the Internet as a new market for businesses drives much of this research. The research results are in, but the interpretation of the data masks the inequalities that still exist, while simultaneously providing a deficient profile of some online users that simply reproduces the stereotypes of offline society. So before breaking out the champagne and party hats to celebrate the long-awaited equality for all, brought to us courtesy of the Internet, the demographics of a typical Internet user warrant further examination.

DEMOGRAPHICS

Surveys conducted by businesses and other research teams (CyberAtlas, Cybercitizen, ETRG, among others) describe the typical Internet user as overwhelmingly white, male, and well educated, with a higher than average income in a white-collar professional career. These statistics make quotes like the following all the more puzzling:

There is no type of demographic group not found in cyberspace [sic]. While certain kinds of people are more likely to be found, every sort of person is represented to some degree in cyberspace. *There is nothing inherently disenfranchising about cyberspace for people with any one or another sort of demographic characteristic.* (Cybercitizen Key Findings 1995; emphasis added)

To determine how equal the Great Equalizer is, this study contrasts the demographic characteristics of educational attainment, income, race, and sex for both Internet users and the general population of the United States. Data from the 1995 Statistical Abstract of the United States are compared with data from several online sources, relying heavily on survey data syn-

Figure 2.1
Comparison of Educational Attainment for Internet and General Population

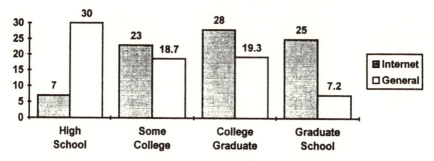

Source: Adapted from U.S. Bureau of the Census, *Statistical Abstract of the United States 1995.*
Table 242. Educational Attainment: States 1990; and e-land e-stats 1996 Net User Demographics www.e-land.com/e-stat_pages/net_user_demo_frames.html.

thesized by e-land, a Web site dedicated to Web marketing. These synthe-
sized data are used to avoid potential biases in Internet demographics. The
wide divergence of survey results suggests that an element of truth exists
in the claims alleging the duplicity of Internet demographics. This unreli-
ability stems from the potential biases of research. The tendency exists to
inflate or minimize numbers depending on the interests of the firm conducting the research. Where possible, results from available sources are
averaged to minimize this possible bias. In addition to comparing demographic data, this chapter also discusses the role of barriers to equal technological access in contributing to the level of inequality online.

EDUCATION

The overwhelming majority of Internet users own college degrees, in
contrast to the general population. The following figures represent the educational attainment of Internet users and the general population by percentage. Figure 2.1 gives a side-by-side comparison of the educational levels
of Internet users and the general population. The disparity indicates that
in terms of educational attainment, the Internet fails to earn the status of
the Great Equalizer.

Table 2.1 presents a more detailed account of educational attainment of
the general population broken down by race and sex. The statistics on
educational attainment clearly demonstrate that the Internet has yet to earn
the name Great Equalizer. In the general population, the largest percentage
of people hold a high school diploma, the category least well represented
on the Internet. The data in Table 2.1 demonstrate that even among white
males, the typical Internet user is not representative.

Table 2.1
Educational Attainment of General Population by Gender and Race

Level of Education by Percent	High School Graduate	Some College	Associate Degree	Bachelors Degree	Advanced Degree
Male	32.3	17.3	6.3	15.9	9.2
Female	36.2	17.4	7.5	13.7	5.9
White	34.5	17.5	7.1	15.1	7.9
African-American	36.2	17.5	6.3	9.5	3.4
Hispanic	26.2	13.3	4.7	6.2	2.9
Other	26.0	14.3	6.3	22.0	10.4

Source: Adapted from U.S. Bureau of the Census, *Statistical Abstract of the United States 1995.* Table 240. Years of School Completed by Selected Characteristic 1994.

INCOME

The initial investments associated with going online coupled with monthly access fees prohibit some members of society from gaining access to the Internet. The following Figures, which contrast the median levels of household income of Internet users with those of the general population, clarify why certain groups lack equal representation online. Again, one finds a gap in the income data available from survey results. The reported income levels of Internet users range from below $30,000 to over $100,000. Inflated income figures suggest the research bias mentioned earlier. Convincing potential advertisers that wealthy customers abound on the Web drives income figures higher. Other survey results are based on self-reporting and the anonymity of cyberspace lends itself to hyperbole.

Household income levels of Internet users are presented in Figure 2.2 while Figure 2.3 shows the median household income levels of families by race. Even allowing for overstatement of income levels, the data in Figures 2.2 and 2.3 show that very few of the general population approach the average income level of Internet users.

Figure 2.2
Income Level of Internet Population

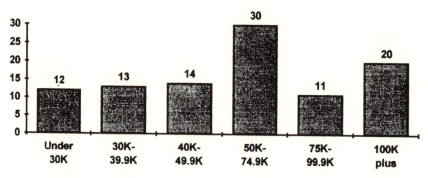

Source: Adapted from e-land e-stats 1996 New User Demographics www.e-land.com/e-stat_
pages/net_user_demo_frames.html.

RACE

Figure 2.4 represents the breakdown by race of Internet users and of the general population.

The categories shown in Figure 2.4 (white, African-American, Asian, Hispanic) represent the four categories for which most surveys collect data. The comparison of the two sets of data offers no evidence of the Great Equalizer as a legitimate metaphor in terms of racial equality. Instead, the comparison suggests that the Internet serves to maintain the status quo, favoring society's dominant white population. The e-land data neglected to address race, and instead simply reported that males constitute 65 percent to 75 percent of all net users (e-land 1996). This leaves one to wonder whether in this case "male" is understood as "white male." The data examined in this chapter leave unmentioned any participation by Native Americans, resulting in no comparable data. Figure 2.4 illustrates that African-Americans and Hispanics experience the greatest disparity in terms of equal representation on the Internet. No surveys examined differentiate by sex within the category of race, so again, no comparable data exist.

Surveys reveal that in the demographic categories of educational attainment, income, and race the Great Equalizer is somewhat of a misnomer. Gender is the final demographic variable analyzed by this chapter to gauge equality on the Internet.

GENDER

The goal of Internet equality still eludes women as illustrated by the breakdown of gendered participation on the Internet. As Figure 2.4 dem-

Figure 2.3
Median Household Income by Race for the General Population

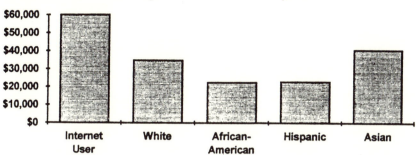

Source: Adapted from U.S. Bureau of the Census, *Statistical Abstract of the United States 1995*. Table 728. Many Income of Households 1993.

onstrated, whites constitute the bulk of Internet users. Table 2.1 shows that in terms of educational attainment and race, only a small percentage of the total population of white males find their way online. Therefore, the white male presence on the Internet represents the elite of the advantaged racial and gendered class. Figure 2.5 shows the breakdown by sex of Internet users and of the general population.

The Woman Question

The presence of women online remains a hotly debated topic. Gender estimates for online use range from 20 percent to 43 percent female participation. Several societal forces and external factors discussed below play a role in the unequal representation of women on the Internet. Evidence suggests at least some research fails to take these factors into account, as in the following quote from the *American Internet User Survey* (1995):

Additionally, women are more likely than men to use the Internet *exclusively* from work or academic locations, while men are more likely to use the Internet from multiple locations, including afterhours use from home. Behind this finding is the related finding that men are significantly more willing than women to actually personally *pay* for Internet access. Thus, men are more than twice as likely as women to access the Internet from home.

The assumptions made by this type of interpretation fail to recognize, among other things, the very real phenomenon of a woman's "double day." Ellen Israel Rosen describes the double day of work for women as "to come home from paid jobs to dinner, dishes, cranky children, and tired husbands; to work all week and spend much of the weekend doing laundry and cleaning the house" (Kramer 1991). When one contrasts the discretionary time

Figure 2.4
Breakdown by Race of Internet Users and the General Population

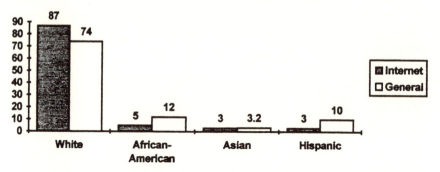

Source: Adapted from U.S. Bureau of the Census, *Statistical Abstract of the United States 1995*. Table 18. Resident Population by Race; and The American Internet Survey 1995. New Survey Highlights http://etrg.findsvp.com/features/newinet.html.

available to most working women with the patterns of Internet usage, the underrepresentation of women online gains a sharper focus. Estimates of time spent per week online ranges from thirty minutes a day to twenty hours per week. Given the time constraints that confront many women, finding even thirty minutes a day to explore the Internet presents a daunting challenge. While some may argue that the Internet actually saves time in the long term, others may find the initial investment in time impractical. Selecting the hardware and software that best suits one's needs, locating an access provider, learning the basics of logging on and setting up the computer so that it operates effectively represent only the initial investment in time Internet users must expend to stay current. Software updates, access-provider changes, new formats on Web pages all mean that users must engage in a continual learning process or get left behind.

Time constraints represent only one of the barriers to the Internet for women; financial constraints serve as an additional hindrance. While time and financial constraints can exist independent of one another, they are often concomitant. The combination of the gendered wage differential with the explosion of single mothers as heads of households and the double shift women work better explain the reasons behind the low numbers of women on the Net. This suggests a more complex explanation for the absence of women online than simply "an unwillingness to pay" for Internet access. This is not to deny that many people find the initial investments associated with getting online prohibitive. In addition to hardware and software costs, access requires a monthly fee paid to the provider of an access service. Further, successful use necessitates spending time and money on some form of training to familiarize not only women, but all new users with the ins and outs of the information superhighway (Bauman 1995).

Figure 2.5
Gender Breakdown for Internet Users and the General Population

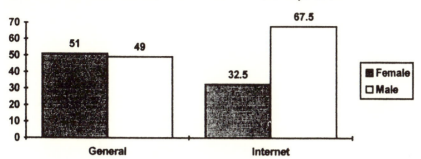

Source: Adapted from e-land e-stats 1996 Net User Demographics www.e-land.com/e-stat_ pages/net_user_demo_frames.html.

One reason this element of training and education is so crucial for women lies in the socialization of young girls in our society. They are systematically, if unintentionally, discouraged from a wide range of academic pursuits, particularly in math and science (*AAUW* 1992). *The AAUW Report: How Schools Shortchange Girls* reveals how young girls receive an inferior education to boys in America's schools. The results of the report indicate that American education dissuades girls from pursing math-related careers in proportion to boys. Additionally, the study shows that the gender gap in science continues to increase. In terms of race, teachers overlook African-American girls more often than white girls. The report also shows that curricula ignore or stereotype women and that elements of gender bias show up in many standardized tests. Such gender bias serves to undermine the self-esteem of young girls, effectively channeling them away from careers in math and science (AAUW 1992).

In analyzing the demographic data and their simplistic interpretation regarding the type of person online and why they do or do not have a presence on the Net, one finds that the assumptions researchers make about women (or the lack of women) online reproduce the same stereotypes that prevail offline. The perception of women's interest in stereotypically female domains informs the following attempt to explain the recent influx of women on the Internet via online services like Prodigy and America Online: "Online services, with their user-friendly graphics and popular news and chat groups centered around 'communities of interest' appeal to women at least as much as men, and maybe even more" (e-land 1996).

While certainly not disagreeing that these features provided by online services may indeed appeal to some women (as well as to some men), this type of interpretation fails to recognize the broad range of Web sites and news groups created for and by women. Some of these Web sites and news groups do address stereotypically female interests appealing to the homebody-housewife-mother triad—newsgroups like alt.recipes, alt. sewing, and various support groups for the "caring nurturer." What one loses in the interpretation of the data is the opposite end of the female spectrum—the Web sites and news groups created by and appealing to a very different type of woman. News groups like alt.feminazis almost certainly appeal to a different sort of woman than does alt.sewing. WWWomen.com represents an excellent example of a Web site that successfully blends women's interests. This Web site incorporates traditionally feminine interests like fashion, beauty, and mothering with links to sites for and about women in business, science, technology, computers, government, sports, and education. As demonstrated by the demographics presented earlier, the women currently online represent a very small portion of the population and cannot be considered representative of the stereotypical woman. Clearly, the presence of these women on the Internet illustrates that they are not conventional women, something businesses need to know to attract them as customers.

Inaccurate user profiles explain in part the complaints that Internet users do not make online purchases (O'Keefe 1995). Businesses that strive to make the Internet a profitable enterprise need an accurate profile of Internet users. To do otherwise is to miss an entire untapped market, not only of women but of other minorities as well. The demographics illustrate that these groups lack a representative presence on the Internet. However, to effectively create a demand, those businesses (particularly access providers) trying to attract women and minorities must know why these groups are not online. Other businesses need accurate profiles to create appropriate advertising campaigns. This information is crucial for effectively marketing products and services. Designing an advertising strategy to persuade women to "actually personally pay" for Net access that only stresses low price or affordability will be ineffective at inducing technophobic women who must wrestle with time constraints to go online. Additionally, a promotion stressing features like chat rooms lacks appeal to the woman searching (and able to pay) for a research tool.

Of the women online, some discovered in navigating the Internet that contrary to the rhetoric, cyberspace is a gendered space. Researchers note that computer-mediated conversation (CMC) neutralizes such social status clues as appearance, voice, organizational hierarchy, and often gender (Shade 1993). However, even if one assumes the Internet is sex-, race-, or class-blind, it is still not the same as an equitable environment in that the prejudices and discrimination are assumed to be absent only to the extent that the differences can be concealed. Further, research in CMC illustrates that the gendered styles of communication translate to CMC and are recognizable as male or female styles, negating the erasure of gender differences online (Herring 1994). Shade explains:

[T]he new "electronic frontier" is unfortunately still a very masculine dominated space, one in which many women may feel uncomfortable at the best of times. Ensuring equitable gender access to the Internet should be a prerogative of this information age. This means that *we must pay close attention to the metaphors that people will use* and see in this new world, so that they won't exclude women, or include them in undesirable ways. It means making the Internet easily accessible to all people; making networking an attractive communications tool for women, by creating tangible and viable information and resources; and by encouraging young girls and women to become involved in the development and deployment of the technology. (Shade 1993; We 1993; emphasis added)

Some research that exposes the gender inequality on the Internet has an unsettling effect. Often in the process of struggling to make the Internet more accessible to women, the opposite occurs. The findings of such research suggest that the Internet is a threatening place for women—pornography, mail bombs, online sexual harassment and flames lurk behind each click of the mouse (Shade 1993; We 1993; Herring 1994). Give this warning to the technophobic woman and she will not likely embrace the idea of sacrificing time and money to go on the Internet. While certainly evidence abounds detailing stereotypical types of male behavior (swearing, hostility, aggressiveness) to women and newcomers, these traits take on a lesser threat of physical harm in cyberspace. Gladys We points out that some women feel safer communicating online for that reason (We 1993). CMC participants harboring fears of this sort use anonymous log-ins and gender-neutral names. Shade's research indicates that in response to male behavior some women prefer participation in women-only conferences and mailing lists (Shade 1993). While certainly this anonymity and restriction to certain lists leaves much to be desired in terms of equality, this trend toward warning women about the evils of the Internet comes dangerously close to constructing women as victims and discouraging their participation. Such research helps to create what it attempts to overcome by instilling apprehension in women. This is not to deny the very real disparity of gendered presence online or the aggression some people experience. The problems of male domination after women gain Internet access and the problems of unequal access are real, but constructing any groups as victims serves no positive function.

BUSINESS

Several of the quotations in this study suggest the introduction of the information superhighway leveled the playing field. The assumption, and indeed the rhetoric, implies that everyone can get access to the Internet. Business owners must simply sign up and log on to make a profit. No difference exists between the Web presence of small family-owned business and a major corporation. This view of course fails to account for the very real distinction between the core and periphery firms in terms of resources available to commit to the Internet. Combining lack of resources with the concomitant lower caliber of personnel employed in the periphery sector clearly places it in a disadvantaged position.

The more technologically experienced employees in the core firms produce more professional and polished Web sites than periphery workers. In view of the rapid pace of change on the Internet, effective presence requires awareness of current trends in software, Web site creation, and the market. Core firms utilize available resources to hire system administrators responsible for upgrades, patching bugs in software programs, maintaining and updating Web sites, and providing secure connections. Further, they employ staff members to respond promptly to online customer orders or requests. Core firms are advantaged by their ability to provide their personnel with the necessary resources to gain familiarity with the size and composition of the Internet market.

Many periphery firms lack the financial, human, or technical resources to take advantage of what is available. Jumping online too soon without sufficient familiarity with the Internet produces negative implications for the credibility of a business. Rather than the positive corporate image businesses hope for, potential customers grow disenchanted with a Web site that takes too long to load due to overenthusiastic use of graphics or motion, or a company that runs out of free online offers, or when subjected to delayed shipping or response times. Averting such hazards takes research and research takes money, a resource in shorter supply in periphery firms. However, some companies will enjoy a profit from using the Great Equalizer metaphor, specifically those businesses selling computers. Calling the Internet the Great Equalizer helps to sell more computers. The metaphor masquerades as a quick fix to social inequality while ignoring the factors that lead to inequality.

EQUALITY OF ACCESS

Equality of access necessarily affects Internet equality. While a standard telephone line can be an individual's pathway to the riches of the Information Age, a personal computer and modem are rapidly becoming the keys to the vault (Irving 1995). The elite's access to the Internet increases rather than decreases inequality since the ability to deploy one form of power often tends to facilitate access to other forms of power. Tom Soto (1995) makes the claim that we are standing on the threshold of two technologically separate societies. He writes: "One will be driven by increased utilization of computer networks, the other shaped equally by lack of access, with a further increase in unemployment and dead-end service jobs. The best and the brightest will be skimmed off as an information elite."

Figure 2.6 shows the access to computers by race for the general population.

Based on the demographic analysis in this chapter, the information elite Soto speaks of is composed of the already advantaged class in the United States. Online statistics indicate the replication of the offline standard that privileges white, middle-class males over the rest of the population. The response to this trend led to the interest in universal access to technology.

Availability of universal access, either in homes or at public access centers (libraries or public kiosks), denotes one of the major concerns in bringing equality to the Internet. A large segment of the population lacks both affordable access to the Internet and a voice in the development of its content. While the number of people speaking for and about low-income and other disenfranchised individuals continues to rise, little is being done to encourage these disenfranchised individuals to speak for themselves to shape the debate and policies in ways beneficial to them. In the long run, empowering affected populations to speak for themselves will be essential (Disenfranchised Communities 1995). O'Connor (1995) expands this line of reasoning:

The people who attend . . . conferences at which the weighty questions of technology arise, discuss using computers to improve the lives of the technological "have nots" by giving them access to computing. But, as the panel pointed out, what those people really do not have is any voice in how the systems are designed or in the development of the rules that govern their use. . . . Until the people *inside* the industry really do offer those outside it a seat at the table, and not just some conscience-assuaging mindshare, the "have nots" will never become "haves."

What goes unnoticed in speaking for these "others" is that without their input they are assigned the "proper," "correct," values of the middle class, the class that writes, publishes, and surfs on the Internet. The assumption that everyone desires access to the Internet and the presumed similarity of the information everyone wants and needs reveal the danger in refusing the "others" the chance to voice their opinions. This assumption obscures the reality that not everyone shares the same core values as the people speaking for and constructing the information for "others." A very real possibility exists that at least a portion of the "have nots" may indeed be "don't wants":

The coming evolution of the financial services markets and the payments mechanism are seen as the prophetic signs of the end of society and life as we know it. The book of Revelation in the Bible is held closely by Christians as the prelude to the end of the world brought about by the great battle of Armageddon where good (God/Jesus Christ) will overcome evil (Satan). To many the cashless society and the mark of the beast are represented by smart cards and the information superhighway. To some of the Christian faith, electronic funds transfers are the ultimate expression of the Devil himself. This issue will continue to proliferate especially

Figure 2.6
Access to Computers by Race

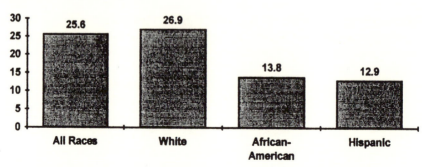

Source: Adapted from U.S. Bureau of the Census, *Statistical Abstract of the United States 1995*. Table A. Level of Access and Use of Computers: 1984, 1989, and 1993 http://www.census. gov/p...o/computer/compusea.txt.

among those *who are not or who choose not to be technologically literate.* (Philosophical Issues 1996; emphasis added)

O'Connor (1995) presents yet another reason why some may choose not embrace access:

[C]omputer technology—far from being the great populist equalizer and agent of social benefit that many insiders believe it to be—is one of the greatest tools for centralization of power ever created. With computers, governments have the means for tighter control of their citizens. The computer and instantaneous communication make it possible to concentrate economic power in the hands of large multi-national corporations and world financial institutions whose interests often are divorced from any individual community of people. With the explosion of technology, individuals count for less, not more.

Bringing about equality necessitates identifying the "information poor" or the "have nots." To that end, a 1995 study conducted by the U.S. Department of Commerce examined variables like age, race, education, income, and region, but curiously left sex absent from the investigation. One wonders why the Department of Commerce places emphasis on these other variables, while overlooking roughly 50 percent of the population. "Falling Through the Net" identifies the information "have nots" as the poor in central cities and rural areas, rural and central city minorities, the less-educated in central cities, young households (under 25 years) in rural areas, and rural senior citizens (Falling Through the Net 1995). These results stand in stark contrast to the demographics of the Great Equalizer's typical online user. The rural and inner-city poor who desire online access face the uncertainty of information redlining.

Information redlining refers to the threat of exclusion from access to the new information superhighway faced by low-income, minority, or rural communities. This exclusion stems from factors such as a lack of physical infrastructure (e.g., fiber optic cables), exorbitant costs, irrelevant information, or a lack of information useful to people in those communities (Information Redlining 1994). A large body of information stresses that the Internet must not leave these communities behind, that unequal access to information and services would exacerbate disparities that already disadvantage low-income, minority, and rural communities. The goals of the Internet to reinvigorate democracy, facilitate communication, educate our children, provide access to affordable health care, and create economic opportunities can only be achieved if communities are "connected" in a non-discriminatory manner (Action Alert 1994).

Evidence indicates that the elite presence on the Web wants to keep disadvantaged groups "disconnected." Peter Huber argues in an essay for *Forbes* magazine that universal service "will do more harm than good by increasing the TV-induced stupefaction of lower-class households. The have-nots inhale low-grade information like greasy hamburgers" (Goldsborough 1994). Through arguments like Huber's, the elite presence on the Web works against reaching the ostensibly achieved goal of Internet as Great Equalizer. His statement represents the uninformed or naive position of the "culture of poverty" advocates, who argue that the values of the poor differ from those of the middle class. Their concern surrounding the realization of universal access is that the poor will bring these different (read lower) values to the Internet. The elite fear that allowing the poor access will sully the Internet. One need only navigate through the astonishing number of sex, erotica, incest, and child pornography sites to uncover sufficient evidence to counter the position of the elites on this particular issue. The elite managed to establish these sites without input from the information "have nots." However, if the elite simply want to reserve the Internet as a place to associate with other elite members of their class, then the Great Equalizer metaphor serves to further such a goal. The Internet as it stands creates a distance between the elites and the lower classes, while the "Great Equalizer" proclaims that anyone can join the club.

In looking at the statistics in this chapter one finds that the Internet falls far short of earning the name The Great Equalizer. This is not to deny that the Internet represents an exciting potential. However, at this stage in its evolution it remains just that—only the potential to move us toward a more egalitarian society. The Great Equalizer metaphor is based on a functionalist perspective that places all responsibility for joining the new technologically elite class squarely on the shoulders of the individual, while serving to legitimate the status quo. This perspective assumes that rational people will invest in their human capital, but fails to consider the external social forces at work that prevent some rational people from making such investments.

CONCLUSION

The data presented in this chapter clearly fail to substantiate the legitimacy of the Great Equalizer metaphor. This metaphor contributes to the maintenance and reproduction of the status quo. At this point in its evolution it appears that the Internet serves only to equalize the differences among young, college-educated, middle-class, white males. In using a metaphor like the Great Equalizer the tendency persists to dismiss the very real problems of inequality not only as solvable, but as solved. Gaining insight into the ideologies or the forces driving these Great Equalizer proclamations requires careful consideration of those who promote it and why, and which members of society the metaphor serves to advantage and disadvantage.

All members of society must participate in the Information Age to carry forward the promise of democracy in the United States. As more of society's essential functions relocate within the new information infrastructure, effective access will determine whether one engages in the Information Age or remains at the margin. Thus, the guarantee of access to the Internet represents the opportunity for all to participate in the main discourses of society, and so stands well within the spirit of democratic participation (Schement 1996).

The opportunity to participate ought to include everyone. Drawing on the liberal formulation of "equal respect," Davina Cooper's starting point in exploring an ethics of power is "the normative judgment that people should have an equal capacity to make an impact—whether in the home, workplace, or community" (Cooper 1995). The essence of the call for maximum participation in the new information infrastructure stems from the basic assumption that all members of society contribute to its wealth. The opportunity to contribute denotes a right that society should deny no member (Schement 1996).

Solving the problems of online inequality, including access to the technology, requires input from all members of society, regardless of age, sex, race, or class. Other challenges to Internet equality include overcoming technophobia, socialized patterns of aversion to sciences and math, and steering underrepresented groups toward technology, if they so desire. The analysis of Internet users indicates disparity in levels of educational attainment and income, inequality in gendered and minority participation and access, and disproportionate opportunities for periphery and core firms. Careful attention to these areas allows everyone the opportunity to participate in shaping the still young and pliant Internet into a truly Great Equalizer.

REFERENCES

The AAUW Report: How Schools Shortchange Girls. 1992. Online: http://www. aauw.org/2000/resinit.html#J2

Action Alert—Info Redlining on the Info Superhighway. 1994. Online: http:// .rtk.net/E5847T8

The American Internet User Survey—New Survey Highlights. 1995. Online: http:// etrg.findsvp.com/features/newinet.html

Bauman, Patricia. *Chapter Eleven: Capacity Building: A Partnership for Government and the Nonprofit Sector.* 1995. Online: http://cdinet.com/Benton/Jadded/Bauman/eleven.html

Bleier, Brenton. 1996. *Cruising the Information Superhighway: Law and the Internet.* Online: http://www.bleier.com/Inr/cruising.html

Christensen, Dane. 1995. *The World Wide Web: The Great Equalizer.* Online: http://webz.com/theweb/

Cooper, Davina. 1995. *Power in Struggle: Feminism, Sexuality and the State.* New York: New York University Press.

CyberAtlas Website. 1996. Online: http://www.cyberatlas.com/

Cybercitizen Key Findings: Cybercitizen: A profile of online users. 1995. Online: http://www.yanelovich.com/cyber/FINDINGS.HTM

Disenfranchised communities and the information superhighway. 1995. *Computer Underground Digest* 7 (34). Jim Thomas and Gordon Meyer, eds. Online: http://sun.soci.niu.edu/~cudigest/CUDS7/cud734

e-land Website. 1996. Online: http://www.e-land.com/

Engelman, Linda J. 1995. *The Great Equalizer.* Online: http://www.iw.com/1995/07/foundit.htm.

Falling through the net. 1995. Online: http://www.ctcnet.org/na6net.html.

Goldsborough, Reid. 1994. *Straight Talk about the Information Superhighway.* Indianapolis: Alpha Books.

Herring, Susan. 1994. *Gender Differences in Computer Mediated Communication: Bringing Familiar Baggage to the New Frontier.* Online: http://www.cpsr.org/cpsr/gender/herring.html

Information Redlining and Sustainability. 1994. Online: http://www.rtk.net/E6902T264

Irving, Larry. 1995. *The Connected and the Disconnected in Rural and Urban America.* Online: http://ntiaunix2.ntia.doc.gov:70/0/speeches/naruc727.html

Kramer, Laura. 1991. *The Sociology of Gender.* New York: St. Martin's Press.

Netschay, Natasha. 1996. A women's (net) work is never done! *Internet News* 2 (1). Online: http://www.express.ca/Internet_ News/vol1iss2/womvan. htm

O'Connor, R. 1995. *Hey Insiders: Technology Fails as the Great Populist Equalizer.* Online: http://www.sjmercury.com/special/reprints/oconnor.htm

O'Keefe, Steve. 1995. *Internet Demographics.* Online: http://www.olympus.net/okeefe/pubnet/cosmep5.html.

Philosophical Issues. 1996. Online: http://www.trumbull.kent.edu/wwphil/

Polly, Jean Armor. 1992. *Surfing the Internet: An Introduction Version 2.0.2.* Online: uniwa.uwa.edu.au:70/0/compnet/intro/verbose/polly.jnl

Report on NTIA's "Falling Through the Net." 1995. Online: http://www.ctcnet.
org/na6net.html

Schement, Jorge Reina. 1996. *Transcending Access Toward a New Universal Service.* Online: http://www.cdinet.com/benton/Retrieve/povich-etal.txt

Shade, Leslie Regan. 1993. *Gender Issues in Computer Networking.* Online: http://
www.mit.edu:8001/people/sorokin/women/lrs.html

Soto, Tom. 1995. *Tom Soto on the NII: California Could Open the Information Superhighway to All Segments of Society.* Online: http://www.well.com/user/
pse/time_nii.htm

United States Bureau of the Census. *Statistical Abstract of the United States: 1995,*
115th edn. Washington, D.C.

———. *Home Page.* 1996. Online: http://www.census.gov

We, Gladys. 1993. *Cross-Gender Communication in Cyberspace.* Online: http://
cpsr.org/cpsr/gender/we_cross_gender

Webster, Clay. 1995. *The World Wide Web—The Great Equalizer of the Internet.*
Online: http://www.pcinews.com/business/pci/hp/columns/equalizer.html

WWWomen.com Website. 1996. Online: http://www.wwwomen.com

3

Ensuring Social Justice for the New Underclass: Community Interventions to Meet the Needs of the New Poor

John G. McNutt

This chapter discusses information poverty and the future underclass in American society. The nature of information poverty, the factors that contribute to this problem, and the relationship between this problem and current types of poverty are discussed. The potential of social intervention based on information technology is also examined.

INTRODUCTION

American society has never been kind to the plight of the poor. From the poor laws to welfare reform, considerations of social and economic justice have never been paramount in the way that policies intended to deal with poverty have been constructed (Trattner 1995). The dispossessed of our industrial and agricultural economies have been stigmatized, harassed, and punished for their poverty. Now comes the Information Age, promising a host of benefits for all segments of the population (Dillman 1991, 1985). These benefits include instant access to information and entertainment, health care innovations, and freedom from location as a constraint to human activity. The age also promises to incorporate into the economy some of those who are not currently working or working at capacity, such as the physically challenged (Bowe 1993) or those who live in remote areas. While the Information Age may help some of those in the current underclass, it will also add to their numbers. Fortunately, the same technology that propels the information economy can also help those facing a life of poverty. This chapter will discuss the future of poverty and explore how social interventions that use information technology can improve the life chances of the future underclass.

The chapter is divided into four major sections. First, a discussion of the relationships between the current and future underclass will be presented and, based on this discussion, a model of social and economic justice in an information economy will be presented. Next, the potential of technological interventions for achieving social and economic justice for the new poor will be explored. Finally, implications for training social practitioners and the design of service delivery systems are presented.

POVERTY: NOW AND IN THE FUTURE

Poverty has become an important item on the American agenda. The recent passage of welfare reform has led to major changes in how society responds to those who are suffering from economic hardships. It will eliminate most entitlement programs for low-income people, return control of public welfare to the states, impose new requirements on recipients, and reduce the level of expenditures (Bane 1997; Marchetti 1996; Mannix et al. 1997). This is not to say that previous conditions were generous. In comparison with other industrialized nations, the United States has lagged behind in providing for the poor of its industrial and agricultural economies.

Not all of the poor are eligible for or take advantage of social welfare programs designed to help them in their time of need. The working poor manage to attain a limited existence from the margins of the current economy (Bluestone and Rose 1997). Many of the limited programs available for these workers and their families were also eliminated or reduced in the recent welfare reform legislation (Bane 1997; Mannix et al. 1997).

Poverty, in the United States, is determined by falling below an income level called the poverty line. While this measure has been criticized, it has proved difficult to replace (Dolgoff and Feldstein 1980). In 1995, the poverty threshold was $15,569 for a family of four (Weinberg 1996). Currently, about 36.4 million Americans fall below the poverty line (Weinberg 1996). According to a recent report (Weinberg 1996), "Children are 40 percent of the poor, although they are but 27 percent of the total population." Children from single-parent, female-headed households are especially at risk. Poverty disproportionately affects minorities of color, women, new immigrants, those without a high school education and residents of rural areas and the inner cities (Haveman 1994).

For some, the experience of poverty is a short-term phenomenon. This group has suffered a drop in income because of a job loss, divorce, illness, or some other crisis that has pulled them away from the work force. More troubling are the long-term poor. Often called the underclass, members of this group have less chance of ending their poverty (Haveman 1994). Limitations of inner city and rural education, lack of appropriate role models, structural and geographic barriers to employment, and economic restructuring are among the reasons that the long-term poor will find it difficult to escape from poverty (Haveman 1994).

Most of the current poor are the victims of the agricultural and industrial sectors of the current economy. There is a large sector, however, of people who might be considered the initial casualties of the information economy (Huey 1994). These groups include factory workers whose jobs were eliminated by economic restructuring or technological innovation and middle managers who became unnecessary as a result of downsizing (Harrison and Bluestone 1988; Bluestone and Rose 1997; Huey 1994). These are people who, on the whole, were well-off in the past. Now they face an uncertain future with inappropriate skills. They will not, however, be alone.

POVERTY IN THE INFORMATION AGE

The growing dominance of the information sector of the economy will change the structure of wealth and poverty in American society, much in the way that industrial and agricultural revolutions altered the balance of earlier stratification systems. McNutt (McNutt 1996a, 1996b, November 1995; see also Doctor 1994) argued that issues such as physical and mental challenges and geographic isolation will become less important, while education, computer and information literacy, and access to communication networks and information technology will become more crucial to inclusion in the new economy.

POTENTIAL BENEFICIARIES AMONG THE CURRENT UNDERCLASS

Some of the current poor will benefit from the transition. Geographic isolation will become moot for many people. In an information economy, many economic activities can be geographically decentralized, eliminating some of the impact of physical isolation (Huey 1994; Mitchell 1995). Rural areas, for example, will no longer suffer the limitations of poor roads or air transport facilities, so long as they have adequate information infrastructure. The same is true for the inner cities. Information work is easily transferred over communications systems from remote sites to central processing sites (Gurstein 1996; Huey 1994). On balance, those areas that do not have adequate information infrastructure will not benefit and may decline further as the information economy grows. This is especially significant when one considers electronic red-lining (Squires 1995). This means denying certain areas access to network connections and information infrastructure, much in the way that traditional red-lining denied these areas access to insurance and credit. The impact of electronic red-lining is isolation from the economic institutions of society.

Another group that may benefit is the physically and mentally challenged (Bowe 1993). Assistive technology could allow many persons who are currently too impaired to work limited or full participation in the economy. Issues such as mobility, physical dexterity, appearance, and even social skills can be unimportant in a properly designed information work situation (Schoech, Cavalier, and Hoover 1993; Bowe 1993). While there will always be people who suffer from obstacles that even the most clever technological interventions cannot remove, the range of possible accommodations will be greatly expanded.

FACTORS LEADING TO INFORMATION POVERTY

The information economy is a ray of hope for some groups, but not others. Information economy labor markets will favor those who have access to information technology (particularly communications networks), the education and skills necessary to use the technology, and those who have knowledge skills that are economically valuable (see McNutt 1996a, 1996b, November 1995; see also Doctor 1994). The new poor, then, will include people who lack access to these things. Many of the current poor will also fall into this category, so that the size of the underclass will grow. In fact, due to the infiltration of information technology into the industrial and agricultural sectors of the economy, many workers will find their currently adequate skills obsolete and will not be able to maintain their jobs (see McNutt 1996a, 1996b, November 1995).

Access to education is problematic for many of today's poor (Haverman 1994). Problems with public education are well documented, especially in low-income areas. This reduces the chance that children growing up in these areas will be able to participate in the Information Age. Access to higher education is becoming problematic for both low- and middle-income families.

Three aspects of education are crucial to this discussion (see McNutt 1996a, 1996b): basic skills education, computer literacy, and economically viable job skills. Basic skills education includes the ability to read and write and to do simple mathematics. People without basic skills have little chance of developing any of the other skills that are needed to become economically viable in an information society. Computer and technological literacy builds on this foundation. This should, ideally, include the ability to use computers and networked communications and information literacy—the ability to access, evaluate, and synthesize information (Shapiro and Hughes 1996; McNutt February 1996). An important part of this area is an understanding of technology and its potential as a means of gaining access to information. The last part, education for marketable skills, is more difficult to define. They could be as simple as data entry or word processing skills or as complex as legal and medical skills. Education does not necessarily impart these skills, but it may make it more likely that the person possesses them.

Education, then, is an important determinant of success in future labor markets. This is a classic human capital problem, but it is also a structural problem. Human capital theorists (McConnell 1981), point to the need to provide education, training, and retraining for the labor force and explain poverty as a deficiency in human capital among low-income groups. Human capital interventions would provide the means for workers to participate in the economy up to the level of their ability. Evidence suggests that workers will need continual retraining during their work lives in order to remain up to date (Huey 1994). The need for basic information technology and knowledge work skills appears to fit well into human capital analysis, but also present are structural dimensions. Inequities in the present system of education reinforce the current class system (Haveman 1994). Wealthier people have better access to quality private education, and public education varies widely depending on the affluence of the school district. In an era of declining financial aid and increased costs, post-secondary education is becoming a difficult goal for many students.

A more important dimension affects on-the-job training and lifelong education (Huey 1994). Much of this training has traditionally come through the workplace, but may no longer be available. The move toward downsizing has reduced the size of training departments (Huey 1994) and the growing trend toward employing part-time and temporary workers (Bluestone and Rose 1997) has eliminated much of the need for companies to make this kind of investment (Huey 1994). If the trend continues, the training that workers will need to remain current will be at their own expense.

An individual's access to information technology, particularly networked communications, is primarily a structural issue (Doctor 1994). Since information technology is, by and large, a consumer item or one associated with employment, those without an adequate income or employment will probably not have access.

Access to Information Technology

Having adequate access to information technology is a logical prerequisite to participation in the information economy. This would include computers and other essential peripherals. Many Americans have access to these tools at school or work and others purchase them for home use (Civille 1995). African-Americans, low-income people, Native Americans, Hispanics, and other traditionally oppressed groups appear to have less access to technology, according to studies performed by the Census Bureau (Civille 1995). This suggests that current patterns of inequality may be re-created in the future information society (George, Malcolm, and Jeffers 1993; Civille 1995; Doctor 1994).

Access to Communications Networks

Information networks are a key part of information infrastructure. Much of one's ability to participate in the information sector of the economy is dependent on this access (McNutt 1996a, 1996b; Doctor 1994; Mitchell 1995; Kahin and Keller 1995). While access is more complex than just a connection to the network (Kahin and Keller 1995), some basic access is essential. Even that might not be enough. Access to sufficient network capacity (usually specified as bandwidth) may be essential for the new worker. Mitchell (1995:17) notes that "the bandwidth disadvantaged are the new have nots. It's simple: if you cannot get bits on and off in sufficient quantity, you cannot benefit directly from the net." He goes on to observe that high bandwidth network access is the equivalent of location in our current economy.

The changing nature of the labor force presents a potential barrier to access for many workers. If, as Bridges (1994) has predicted, jobs become a thing of the past, workers will depend on network access to identify and obtain information work. Bridges (1994) argues that formal jobs were essential in the industrial era to support the factory system and the assembly line. Since knowledge work is different, and can be done on a more piecework basis, formal jobs are unnecessary.

At the same time, the usual route to network access may be eliminated. This places workers in the undesirable position of obtaining their own access or being closed out of the labor market. Civille (1995) observes that for many current workers, losing Internet access is regarded in the same vein as losing health insurance. This is a structural problem and the logical solution is to guarantee universal access to networks (Doctor 1994; Kahin and Keller 1995).

The right to universal access was a key aspect of the debate concerning the Telecommunications Act of 1996 (PL 104–104). The Clinton administration's original plan (U.S. Commerce Department 1993; Healey May 14, 1994) included rigorous provisions for ensuring universal access. Conservatives in Congress sought to eliminate or greatly reduce these provisions (Healey September 16, 1995, January 15, 1995), but a compromise was reached that allowed a certain level of universal access (Healey February 17, 1996). How these provisions will weather future revisions of the legislation is unclear. Even so, universal access can be a deceptive term. While universal telephone service has been public policy since the passage of the Communications Act of 1934 (Bowe 1993), many homes still lack telephones (Hennelly 1996). One might expect that even more homes will lack network access and that poor homes will be more likely to have this deficiency.

Access to network connections and information technology are primarily structural issues. They involve societal resources that have been inequitably distributed (Doctor 1994). In order to have a just information society, it is essential that everyone be able to participate in the economy (McNutt 1996a, 1996b; Doctor 1994).

SOCIAL AND ECONOMIC JUSTICE ISSUES

The preservation of social and economic justice has concerned many who deal with American social policies and programs (Beverly and McSweeney 1987). Currently, we consider a just society one that is fair, that meets the basic needs of all before the preferences of some, and that guarantees a certain level of well-being (Beverly and McSweeney 1987; Goulet 1971; Rawls 1971). While this thinking reflects an industrial society bias, much of it is directly transferable to an Information Age (Doctor 1994).

Doctor (1994) argues that social and economic justice in an information society would require access to the network and information technology and access to learning opportunities. If these basic tools of participating in the economy are not available to everyone, society cannot be just. We have identified these as structural problems and noted, as Civille (1995) and others have, that the current distribution of these resources is reflective of the inequalities in society. The unjust arrangements in industrial society seem destined to re-create themselves in the Information Age. Only meaningful social intervention can forestall this plight. Fortunately, technological solutions can help redress these problems.

TECHNOLOGICAL TOOLS FOR A JUST INFORMATION SOCIETY

Information technology presents society with a host of new social challenges and provides opportunities for new interventions to help the information poor. This section will explore some of these possibilities for new forms of social interventions. The poor of the information sector face two types of issues: human capital problems that require education and training, and structural issues that require the reallocation of power and resources. Since access to human capital interventions is often a structural issue as well (such as access to training), the lines between the categories are blurred. Within these two general areas, issues occur in access to education, information technology, and the network. Table 3.1 describes this relationship. Table 3.1 allows us to organize potential interventions in a meaningful way.

Human Capital Issues

While Human Capital Theory (McConnell 1981) also deals with investments in health, its principal concern is education. Network and informa-

Table 3.1
Human Capital and Structural Issues in Information Poverty

	Access to Education	Access to Information Technology	Access to Computer Networks
Human Capital Issues	Training Needs	Training Needs	Training Needs
Structural Issues	Barriers to Education	Barriers to Access	Barriers to Access

tion technology can provide high-quality education to all who have access to the system (Jensen 1993; Cleveland 1985). Basic education can be provided through a host of instructional media interventions. The network can make this education available on demand in many places and times where traditional models of instruction are unavailable or too costly (Schuler 1996, 1994). Even without access to a network, education can be provided by stand-alone devices such as tutorial or multimedia programs (Hunter 1995). There is also evidence that information technology can be more effective in teaching certain areas of knowledge and skill than a human teacher (McNutt February 1996).

Information technology can also train new users in using the applications programs. Tutorials are available for most commercial software, including those needed to use the network. Expert systems can be taught to learn a user's style of operating and to make the user more proficient at performing tasks with a program (Butterfield 1995; Schoech 1990).

Perhaps the most fertile area in which information technology can benefit training and education is in lifelong learning and the development of marketable information work skills. Not only are degree programs possible through networked communication and distance education, but short courses, workshops, and related educational interventions are possible (Jensen 1993). In addition, the network provides one means of remaining current in the field and many discussion groups and e-mail lists contain considerable content (McNutt 1996b, February 1996; Hunter 1995).

Information technology can make education relevant, accessible, and (eventually) affordable. Given the number of times workers will need retraining, it may be the only way that many workers will be able to keep up with the volume of information that they will need to stay economically viable.

Structural Issues

Most of the training issues are within settled ground in education. More complex are the structural issues. Structural issues confront the distribution of power in society and deal with situations that are created by the way society is organized. In this case, we can identify two general strategies that address these structural issues: building parallel structures and changing the system.

Parallel structures strategies. This type of structure endeavors to meet needs by creating an alternative means of delivery. This would incur less resistance than a strategy that directly confronts the power structure. Part of this logic is the rationale behind privatization strategies that use the nonprofit sector as an alternative to state bureaucracies (Smith and Lipsky 1993). Changing the system is more difficult. This involves altering resource-allocation patterns and changing structures and relationships (Doctor 1994). Considerable resistance can be expected, depending on the degree of change.

The community computer network movement creates a parallel structure for access to information technology and networks (Schuler 1996, 1994; McNutt November 1996; Civille, Fidelman, and Altobello 1993; Odasz 1995; Molz 1994; Doctor 1994). These networks, also called FreeNets,[1] create free (or low-cost) public access (Schuler 1996). They provide network access to those with computers who lack it and often provide public-access terminals for those without computers. A user with a computer and a modem makes a connection to the community computer networks over standard telephone lines. Those who need a public-access terminal may find them in schools, libraries, and community centers. In some communities, kiosks house a public-use computer in a public place (Schuler 1996; Civille, Fidelman, and Altobello 1993).

A number of the community networks offer extensive training for users. This is often provided by a group of volunteers who understand the computer system. They provide individual training for low-income residents and often answer questions for those who require additional help.

Community networks are also valuable for other reasons in addition to access. They facilitate community building, public discussion, and so forth. By encouraging interaction among community members (via e-mail and discussion groups), they provide the opportunities to strengthen communities ties and networks of relationships (Schuler 1996; Doheny-Farina 1996). They often provide extensive local information, a forum for discussion of community issues, and even social-services interventions (Schuler 1996, 1994; McNutt November 1996; Civille, Fidelman, and Altobello 1993).

While this is an excellent approach, it will not solve the access problem. Even an extensive system of community networks would not have the capacity to be able to provide access to everyone. The problem is just too massive. In addition, the networks are typically small and vulnerable to destruction (Schuler 1996; Cisler 1993). These programs are typically nonprofit and are often run by volunteer boards. Funding comes from memberships, grants, usage charges, and donations (Schuler 1996, 1994; Cisler 1993).

System-Changing Strategies. System-changing strategies should focus on changing the power equation in society. This might include creating new legislation, modifying current legislation, removing barriers in the community, creating access for oppressed groups, and advocacy of public interest considerations (Fitzgerald and McNutt 1997). This type of activity can create considerable resistance from those who have a stake in the existing structure. Access issues (education, network, information technology) are, by definition, structural issues. Structural issues are usually confronted on multiple levels. New applications of technology can help advocates succeed in dealing with these issues. For the sake of clarity, policy change issues will be considered as separate from community change issues.

Policy Changes

The policy framework for telecommunications issues, educational issues, and issues that concern industrial policy can be very problematic for the poor of the Information Age (McNutt 1996a). Powerful interests attempt to mold these policies in such a way as to maximize their own benefit. Those fighting for the poor must guarantee that their voice is heard as well. Technologically based interventions can assist advocates in this task.

Large-scale policy changes require the orchestration of support and political pressure. Activists can organize broad-based coalitions, gather information for organizing, and attract supporters with technology (Buck 1996; Dowling et al. 1991; Fitzgerald and McNutt 1997). Communications networks can facilitate the task of contacting a broad range of stakeholders. Electronic mail is cheaper and faster than conventional mail and requires less employee time to implement. Political organizations have started to use the Internet and it is likely that many lobbying and negotiation efforts will take place in cyberspace (Fitzgerald and McNutt 1997).

Computer conferencing can facilitate negotiation and strategy development involving political actors in diverse geographic areas. This would permit the creation of national coalitions in a brief time period.

Perhaps the most significant application of technology is in the area of policy research. Challenges to policy must be supported by relevant information. Online databases make the tasks of reviewing research, collecting statistics, and performing legal research much more feasible. In addition, analysis, communication, and presentation can be facilitated with computer-based tools.

In a world of devolution, making policy can only be so effective. Intervention at the community level is also needed.

Community Changes

Currently, many relevant decisions are made at the local level. This is especially important in the areas of education and cable regulation, but is true of other areas as well. With devolution, many of the decisions will be made at local and regional levels.[2] As Fitzgerald and McNutt (1997) have argued, many traditional power change strategies will be frustrated in such a diffuse power network.

Community organizing involves the researching of community issues, the involvement of stakeholders, and the implementation of strategies to pressure actors to make local changes. Much of this activity requires a considerable investment of time and effort. Technological aids can make this process more effective (Buck 1996; Dowling et al. 1991).

Much of the day-to-day work that community activists face can be made more efficient through information technology and communications networks (Dowling et al. 1991). Desktop publishing can help produce fliers, newsletters, and reports. Databases can facilitate a host of research efforts. Computer conferencing can make meeting for multicommunity efforts possible and accessible. Database programs can store information about supporters that organizers can use to staff committees and develop action groups. All of these tools can free organizers to focus on the interpersonal activities that are essential for a successful effort.

Macro- and Micro-Level Coordination

It is likely that a multilayered strategy will be needed to address the problems of information poverty in the coming information society. Policy issues and community issues must be carefully articulated so that positive results can be achieved. Technology can provide some of the tools necessary to address some of the problems that will be encountered, but, more important, it can facilitate the coordination between different levels of activity. With a coherent strategy that uses each tool in the strongest possible context, the problem of information poverty can be alleviated if not eliminated.

CONCLUSIONS

As we enter the new millennium, we are faced with new challenges and opportunities. We can have a larger underclass and one that sees very little hope of inclusion. This could have devastating effects on social stability and could make further progress unlikely.

On balance, we can use the tools that information technology provides us. These tools might chip away at the size of the underclass and bring many workers back to productive lives.

If we are to use these tools in a meaningful way, two things must happen. First, we must develop intelligent, coordinated, and comprehensive delivery systems (Schoech 1990). These systems must use all of the elements of the available technology together. Second, community professionals must be trained about information poverty and the means to address it. This would require additional preparation in information technology and related areas (McNutt February 1996, November 1996; Schoech 1991).

In addition to the technical things we can do, we must have the commitment to work on behalf of the new poor. We must be ready to use what it provides to create a new life for all in our society.

NOTES

1. The term FreeNet is a registered trademark of the National Public Telecommunications Network.

2. Devolution is the principle of moving government activity to lower levels of government or to the private sector. It is a major part of the new welfare reform legislation and a guiding principle for many conservative thinkers.

REFERENCES

Bane, M. J. 1997. Welfare as we might know it. *American Prospect* 30:47–53.

Beverly, D. and E. McSweeney. 1987. *Social Welfare and Social Justice.* Englewood Cliffs, N.J.: Prentice Hall.

Bluestone, B. and S. Rose. 1997. Overworked and underemployed. *American Prospect* 31:58–69.

Bowe, F. 1993. Access to the information age: Fundamental decisions in telecommunications policy. *Policy Studies Journal* 21 (4):765–74.

Bridges, W. 1994. The end of the job. *Fortune* 129:62–74.

Buck, K. 1996. Community organizing and the Internet. *Neighborhood Works* 19 (2).

Butterfield, W. H. 1995. Computer utilization. In R. Edwards, ed., *Encyclopedia of Social Work,* 19th edn. Washington, D.C.: NASW Press, pp. 594–613.

Cisler, S. 1993. Community computer networks: Building electronic greenbelts. Online: http://bcn.boulder.co.us/community/resources/greenbelts.txt

Civille, R. 1995. The Internet and the poor. In B. Kahin and J. Keller, eds., *Public Access to the Internet.* Cambridge, Mass.: MIT Press, pp. 175–207.

Civille, R., M. Fidelman, and J. Altobello. 1993. *A National Strategy for Civic Networking: A Vision of Change.* Charlestown, Mass.: Center for Civic Networking.

Cleveland, H. 1985. Education for the information society. *Change* 14:13–21.

Dillman, D. 1985. The social impacts of information technologies in rural North America. *Rural Sociology* 50 (1):1–26.

————. 1991. Information society. In E. Borgetta and R. Borgetta, eds., *The Encyclopedia of Sociology*. New York: Macmillan.

Doctor, R. D. 1994. Seeking equity in the National Information Infrastructure. *Internet Research* 4(3):9–22.

Doheny-Farina, D. 1996. *The Wired Neighborhood*. New Haven, Conn.: Yale University Press.

Dolgoff, R. and R. Feldstein. 1980. *Understanding Social Welfare*. New York: Harper & Row.

Dowling, J., R. Fasano, P. Friedland, M. McCollough, T. Mizrahi, and J. Shapiro, eds. 1991. *Computers for Social Change and Community Organization*. New York: Haworth Press.

Fitzgerald, E. and J. G. McNutt. 1997. *Electronic Advocacy in Policy Practice: A Framework for Teaching Technologically Based Practice*. Paper read at the 1997 CSWE Annual Program Meeting, March

George, Y., S. M. Malcolm, and L. Jeffers. 1993. Computer equity for the future. *Communications of the ACM 56* (5):78–81.

Goulet, D. 1971. *The Cruel Choice*. New York: Pantheon.

Gurstein, P. 1996. Planning for telework and home based employment: Reconsidering the home/work separation. *Journal of Planning Education and Research* 15 (3):224.

Harrison, B. and B. Bluestone. 1988. *The Great U Turn*. New York: Basic Books.

Haveman, R. 1994. The nature, causes and cures of poverty: Accomplishments from three decades of policy research and poverty. In S. H. Danziger, G. D. Sandefur, and D. H. Weinberg, eds., *Confronting Poverty: Prescriptions for Change*. Cambridge, Mass.: Harvard University Press, pp. 438–50.

Healey, J. May 14, 1994. Special report: The information area information network—Congress tries to merge public goals with industry interests. *Congressional Quarterly* 52, S9–18.

————. November 26, 1994. Sides fielding new teams in legislative battles. *Congressional Quarterly* 52:3406–08.

————. January 15, 1995. With democrats at a distance, GOP details its own plan. *Congressional Quarterly* 53:153–54.

————. September 16, 1995. Faith in the market meets the fear of monopoly. *Congressional Quarterly* 53:2787–88.

————. February 17, 1996. Telecommunications highlights. *Congressional Quarterly* 54:406–20.

Hennelly, R. 1996. Forget computers: Kids without phones. *Educational Digest* 61 (5):40–43.

Huey, J. 1994. Waking up to the new economy. *Fortune* 129 (13):36–46.

Hunter, B. 1995. Learning and teaching on the Internet: Contributing to educational reform. In B. Kahin and J. Keller, eds., *Public Access to the Internet*. Cambridge, Mass.: MIT Press, pp. 85–114.

Jensen, R. 1993. The technology of the future is already here. *Academe* 80 (July–August):8–13.

Kahin, B. and J. Keller, eds. 1995. *Public Access to the Internet*. Cambridge, Mass.: MIT Press.

Mannix, M. R., H. A. Freedman, M. Cohan, and C. Lamb. 1997. Implementation of the temporary assistance for needy families block grant: An overview. *Clearinghouse Review* (January/February):868–902.

Marchetti, D. 1996. Reeling from welfare overhaul. *The Chronicle of Philanthropy* 8 (22):38–43.

McConnell, C. 1981. *Economics*, 8th edn. New York: McGraw-Hill.

McNutt, J. G. 1995. *The Development of a the National Information Infrastructure and the American Welfare State: Implications for Nonprofit Human Services Agencies.* Paper read at the 24th annual meeting of the Association of Nonprofit and Voluntary Action Scholars, Cleveland, November.

———. February 1996. *Social Work Education in an Information Society: What Must We Do to Prepare?* Presentation prepared for the 1996 CSWE Annual Program Meeting, Washington, D.C.

———. November 1996. *Community Computer Networks and the Nonprofit Social Services Delivery System.* Paper read at the 25th annual meeting of the Association of Nonprofit and Voluntary Action Scholars, New York.

———. 1996a. Teaching social policy in the information age: Innovations in curriculum content and instructional methods. *Tulane University Studies in Social Welfare* 20:71–85.

———. 1996b. National information infrastructure policy and the future of the American welfare state: Implications for the social welfare policy curriculum. *Journal of Social Work Education* 6 (3):375–88.

Mitchell, W. J. 1995. *City of Bits: Space, Place and the Infoban.* Cambridge, Mass.: MIT Press.

Molz, R. K. 1994. Civic networking in the United States: A report by Columbia University students. *Internet Research* 4 (4):52–62.

Odasz, F. 1995. Issues in the development of community cooperative networks. In B. Kahin and J. Keller, eds., *Public Access to the Internet.* Cambridge, Mass.: MIT Press, pp. 115–37.

Rawls, J. 1971. *A Theory of Justice.* Cambridge, Mass.: Harvard University Press.

Schoech, D., A. Cavalier, and B. Hoover. 1993. A model for integrating technology into a multi-agency community service delivery system. *Assistive Technology* 5 (1):11–23.

Schoech, R. 1990. *Human Services Computing: Concepts and Applications.* New York: Haworth Press.

———. 1991. Human services: Stages and issues in teaching computing. *Social Sciences Computer Review* 9 (4):612–23.

Schuler, D. 1994. Community networks: Building a new participatory medium. *Communications of the ACM* 37 (1):39–51.

———. 1996. *New Community Networks: Wired for Change.* Reading, Mass.: Addison-Wesley.

Shapiro, J. J. and S. K. Hughes. 1996. Information literacy as a liberal art. *Educom Review* 31 (2).

Smith, S. R. and M. Lipsky. 1993. *Nonprofits for Hire.* Cambridge, Mass.: Harvard University Press.

Squires, R. 1995. High tech redlining. *Utne Reader* 86, p. 73.

Trattner, W. 1995. *Poor Law to Welfare State*, 5th edn. New York: Free Press.

U.S. Department of Commerce. 1993. *The National Information Infrastructure: Agenda for Action*. Washington, D.C.: Department of Commerce.

Weinberg, D. H. 1996. *Press Briefing 1995 Income, Poverty and Health Insurance Estimates*. Washington, D.C.: U.S. Bureau of the Census. [Online:http://www.census.gov/Press-Release/Speech/htm1.]

4

The Challenge of Cyberspace: Internet Access and Persons with Disabilities

Mark Borchert

In the past, persons with disabilities have been isolated in many ways from the mainstream of American life. The computer-mediated communication of cyberspace offers these individuals the potential of greater access to social, educational, and vocational resources and interactions. The structure and accessibility of this emerging realm, however, depend in large measure on government policies and regulations that guide developments. This chapter examines the policy framework within which the information superhighway is being created. It suggests that in this context, issues relating to disabilities, universal service, and communication as a social right are important considerations.

INTRODUCTION

Jason is a successful, college-educated consultant. When he is not involved in his consulting business, he enjoys talking with friends, whether it is about last night's game or their plans for the future. He is an avid chess player who has won a regional competition and an active community volunteer. Recently, Jason became the leader of an organization that works for environmental concerns. He acknowledges that it is a time-consuming commitment but one that is well worth the effort. Although Jason has a disability that makes it difficult for him to leave his home, or even his bed, affordable access to a national telecommunications network, offering high-quality two-way voice, data, graphic, and video communication, has removed the barriers that once would have limited his opportunities. His story reflects what the emerging global information infrastructure might mean for members of the disability community in the future.

For persons with disabilities, cyberspace is a realm of incredible potential. The Internet, for example, has created "virtual communities" in which persons, regardless of physical limitations, can enter and interact. Distance learning and telecommuting, also associated with computer-mediated communication, offer many new possibilities to individuals for whom leaving home is a challenge. While telecommunications systems of the past like the telephone excluded many persons with disabilities, new computer technologies provide a means of accessing information based on the users' needs and abilities. The evolving information superhighway appears poised to enhance the lives of countless individuals who previously were excluded from many of the benefits of modern society. The final structure and accessibility of this arena, however, will depend to a large extent on the policy decisions made by legislators, and so it is prudent to consider this context before celebrating possibilities that may or may not materialize.

THE EMERGING RIGHTS OF PERSONS WITH DISABILITIES

On July 26, 1990, President George Bush appeared before legislators, the press, and more than 3,000 disability-rights activists to sign a law that he labeled "the world's first comprehensive declaration of equality for people with disabilities." He announced, "I lift my pen to sign this Americans with Disabilities Act and say, let the shameful walls of exclusion finally come tumbling down" (President's Committee 1990: 11). This legislation passed in both the House and Senate by a large majority, and it was hailed as a bipartisan effort to protect the rights of 43 million Americans with mental and physical disabilities. As a leader in the deaf community, I. King Jordan (1993:xxx), the first deaf president of Gallaudet University, describes the law as "our license to access, which is the birthright of every citizen."

The Americans with Disabilities Act (1990) begins with a description of society's tendency "to isolate and segregate individuals with disabilities" (p. 328), preventing their full participation in American life. Unlike persons experiencing discrimination based on other factors like race, gender, or religion, individuals with disabilities often have had no legal recourse for addressing inequalities. Based on this history, the law seeks "to provide a clear and comprehensive national mandate for the elimination of discrimination against individuals with disabilities" (p. 329). It strives to establish consistent standards and a central role for the federal government in enforcing these standards. By guaranteeing access to employment, transportation, public accommodations, and telecommunications services for citizens with disabilities, the Americans with Disabilities Act (ADA) endeavors to create a more just and equitable society. While earlier legislation prohibited organizations that received federal funds from discriminating against individuals with disabilities, this law extends these standards into the private sector, regulating businesses regardless of the sources of their income.

For disability-rights activists, the ADA is considered a victory in their efforts to redefine societal understandings of disability. In contrast with the dominant view of disabilities as infirmities or disorders afflicting certain individuals and relating to medical problems, this legislation addresses disabilities in relation to civil rights concerns. The ADA presents disabilities as the creation of a society that has not yet modified its structures, policies, and attitudes in light of the needs of persons who are physically or mentally different. Haller (1996:2) writes: "The Americans with Disabilities Act represents a point in U.S. history in which the categorization of people with disabilities is shifting. The ADA acknowledges the full citizenship rights of people with disabilities, just as the Civil Rights Bill for people of color did in the 1960s."

In many ways, the rights guaranteed by the ADA are very different from the rights associated with traditional notions of citizenship. Berlin (1969) discusses two understandings of rights based on two distinct interpretations of liberty. He argues that a "negative" understanding of liberty implies freedom from governmental intervention. Citizens' rights begin when state powers are restricted and individuals are allowed noncoercive choice. Berlin explains that a person with a negative notion of freedom asks, "How far does government interfere with me?" (p. 230). Although personal choice may be limited at times for the sake of justice or the common good, such sacrifices are considered to be the relinquishing of freedoms. Berlin labels an understanding of rights that implies "the absence of interference" as "negative" liberty, though he does not use this term in a normative sense (p. 127). In fact, he presents a defense of this perspective.

Negative liberty can be associated with the freedom of the marketplace. The call for a halt to government intervention, as is evident in contemporary demands for deregulation, can be viewed as the appeal for freedom in terms of the free reign of competition. As Marx and later Marxist scholars note, the problem with this perspective is that the free market is one realm of inequalities and striking disparity. Marx (1844/1972) characterizes the marketplace of industrial capitalism as the sphere of self-estrangement, in which persons are alienated from their lives as producers. Marx argues that communism, grounded in equality and rejecting private property, transcends this alienation and better serves humanity.

Berlin (1969) describes writers like Marx and Hegel as asserting that "to understand the world is to be freed" (p. 142), and he presents these philosophies as emphasizing self-realization. Liberty in this context is not "freedom from" but "freedom to," a perspective that Berlin describes as a "positive" notion of freedom. He writes that this "positive" understanding of liberty has lent itself to distinguishing "a 'real' nature" or "a 'true' self" and to justifying coercion of some persons "in order to raise them to a 'higher' level of freedom" (p. 132). Rather than rights guaranteed by government nonintervention, freedom can be associated with rights secured through the activity of the state. Regulations, by which the government restricts the activity of the free market in order to achieve particular goals, can be seen as a small step in this direction. While some individuals might view the ADA as an encroachment on their rights by the government and its regulations, others—with more "positive" understandings of liberty—might see it as securing rights by providing greater equity within society, by leading society toward a higher goal of the liberation of all.

In approaching policy with a "positive" understanding of freedom, one might argue that the principles within the ADA and related legislation should be extended to guide the emerging information superhighway. Computer-mediated communication promises to create many new opportunities for persons with disabilities. For instance, individuals who are deaf or hearing-impaired have begun using electronic mail and online chat sessions as a convenient means of communicating with others in professional and social situations. With a computer and a modem, persons with health impairments can minimize the isolation created by lengthy hospitalizations. Computers with Braille print-outs, refreshable Braille displays, and voice outputs offer people who are blind or who have low vision greater access to information.

Technological advances in communication, however, have not always benefited persons with disabilities. Individuals who were deaf or hearing-impaired, for example, were quickly cut off from mainstream American culture, occupational opportunities, and access to goods and services when sound films and the telephone were developed. As a new communication marketplace emerges, policymaking will play a role in determining the emancipatory potential of the technology (Calabrese and Borchert 1996) and the liberation or isolation that it creates for people with disabilities.

In his examination of the evolution of the notion of citizenship within Western democracies, Marshall (1950) addresses the various understandings of liberty described by Berlin. According to Marshall, during the eighteenth and nineteenth centuries, citizens were given freedom (in a "negative" sense) to participate in the marketplace. For lower classes, however, inexperience and a lack of resources restricted the exercise of these privileges. Poverty and injustices barred many people from entering the realm of freedom. Marshall records that trade unionism was the initial mechanism through which the lower classes expanded notions of citizenship to include "social rights," entitlements based on a more "positive" understanding of liberty. He is careful to distinguish this development in capitalism, associated with the formation of modern welfare states, from Marx's communist vision for society. Although new social rights activists challenge inequalities and can be more closely associated with "positive" notions of liberty than civil or political rights activists, they ultimately do not threaten the underlying causes of disparity related to capitalism. On the contrary, they stabilize a capitalist society by addressing its most blatant contradictions and the needs of those persons most disadvantaged within the existing social order.

As Barbalet (1988:6) indicates in discussing Marshall, rights to "the prevailing standard of life and the social heritage of society" have in this century joined rights associated with the rule of law and political participation in defining the privileges of citizenship. Rather than limiting government involvement, these social rights call for the government's action in securing certain liberties for all individuals, especially those persons who have been excluded from the benefits of a society. The guarantees associated with the ADA can be seen as an expression of these rights for persons with disabilities. Among its provisions, the ADA guarantees persons with disabilities access to the nation's telecommunications network. This portion of the law represents a redefinition of the traditional understanding of rights and more specifically the right to communication, and it has important implications for the future access of persons with disabilities to the realm of cyberspace.

COMMUNICATION AS A RIGHT

During Congress' final consideration of the ADA, Iowa Sen. Tom Harkin, a Democrat and one of the chief sponsors of the bill, conveyed a message to his deaf brother in American Sign Language. He announced to the Senate, "I told him that today Congress opens the doors to all Americans with disabilities" (*Congressional Quarterly Almanac* 1991: 461). This gesture was appropriate considering that more than half of the persons served by the law, an estimated 24 million Americans, are deaf or hearing-impaired. Although the ADA is often associated with issues of mobility access, the law's regulation of "communication access" is the crucial concern for these millions of Americans. It affects their lives by requiring employers to make "reasonable accommodations" for deaf and hearing-impaired employees, by compelling public accommodation to provide similar goods and services to all consumers, regardless of their disabilities, and by mandating that all telephone common carriers establish telecommunications relay services (Bebout 1990). This law presents communication as a right in which all persons, including individuals with disabilities, should share. This understanding is very different from earlier conceptions of the right to communicate.

Based on Enlightenment notions associated with Bacon and Descartes and with the rise of the scientific method, the drafters of the American Constitution held an optimistic faith in reason. These early American libertarians believed that "truth" could be determined through rationality and that it arose from a context of competing ideas or opinions, rather than from ancient or divine authorities. "Truth is great and will prevail," Jefferson wrote. "She is the proper and sufficient antagonist to error and has nothing to fear from conflict" (quoted in Altschull 1990: 118). The freedom of speech and of the press offered channels for debate from which it was believed that truth would emerge. Based on this perspective, the freedom to communicate and citizenship were closely connected. The rights to free expression were viewed as fostering a marketplace of contesting ideas vital to the new nation, and these concerns culminated in the inclusion of press freedom in the Bill of Rights, ratified and in effect by 1791.

Viewing the freedom of the press as safeguarding the communication essential to democracy, early libertarians entrusted its operation to another institution kindled during the Enlightenment: the free-market economy. Based on arguments proposed by Locke, libertarians believed that—along with life and liberty—the acquisition of property was a "natural right" of persons. They saw the defining purpose of society as the fulfillment of the individual and maintained that through the free-market system, this purpose was served. Libertarians posited that as the business of private media institutions benefited individuals, the public good was also served. The principles of a free-market system and the marketplace of ideas suggested that by removing the barrier to free expression, seen as interference by the government, democracy would flourish. "Open the doors to truth," Jefferson announced in his second Inaugural Address, advocating a laissez-faire government approach to communication rights (quoted in Siebert 1963: 47).

A number of government moves in the United States to restrict expression have met with resistance. For example, the Alien and Sedition Law of 1789, which attempted to curb unwarranted criticism of the government, was quickly abandoned. In fact, with the exception of obscenity and libel regulations, a laissez-faire perspective continues to guide policy concerning forms of communication that existed in the eighteenth century. Pool (1983: 2) argues for this perspective, writing that in issues of publishing, canvassing, and public speech, "the First Amendment truly governs." He, however, questions extensive limitations on freedom in other media. For instance, he proposes that the licensing of radio spectrum users, beginning in 1912, breached "a tradition that went back to John Milton against requiring licenses for communicating" (p. 3). This critique suggests what Berlin (1969) would label as a "negative" understanding of liberty in regard to communication as a right. Pool, as an advocate of libertarianism, views freedom of communication in terms of the nonintervention of the government in the affairs of the market.

Challenging this understanding, Fiss (1990:142–43) calls attention to powerful forces and the limits to freedom within the "free market." He writes: "The power of the FCC is no greater than that of CBS. Terror comes in many forms. The power of the FCC and CBS differ—one regulates whereas the other edits—but there is no reason to assume that one kind of power will be more inhibiting or limiting of public debate than the other" (pp. 142–143).

Examining the writings of Jefferson, Locke, Madison, and others, Holmes (1990) raises some similar concerns. He maintains that although these early libertarians advocated many laissez-faire policies, they did not overlook the threat to liberty posed by private powers and the necessary role of government in addressing this threat. He writes, "Lockean rights are not merely shields against governmental involvement; they include explicit entitlements to affirmative state action" (p. 23). In Madison's affirmation of justice as the aim of government and Locke's insistence on universal access to the power of the state, Holmes finds a basis for a more "positive" understanding of liberty. As Holmes and Fiss suggest, arguments for government nonintervention are not the only basis on which communication has been viewed as a right.

In developing policies governing the radio and television airwaves, the notion of democratic communication, traditionally related to the rights guaranteed by the First Amendment, was faced with new concerns. Beliefs that the spectrum was a "scarce" resource led to the argument that the government had a responsibility to allocate and regulate the airwaves, and to license broadcasters, ensuring that the interests of the general public were served (Horwitz 1989: 120). Entities that received licenses were seen as trustees of public resources. In broadcasting, the rights of listeners and viewers, as well as the rights of persons who originated messages, were matters of concern. Communication as a freedom was viewed as carrying with it public obligations, and the government was seen as a legitimate enforcer of those responsibilities. As Horwitz (1989: 262) describes, *Red Lion Broadcasting Co. vs. FCC* was the "highwater mark" of judication that emphasized the individual's right to have his or her position represented. This case established the right of reply in broadcasting and validated the Fairness Doctrine, the FCC's position that stations must cover controversial issues of public importance and must present contrasting viewpoints in their coverage. Within the context of a more deregulatory atmosphere, later decisions, such as *CBS vs. DNC*, moved to refocus issues on the First Amendment rights of broadcasters. The concerns raised in relation to communication via the electromagnetic spectrum, however, suggest what Berlin would describe as more "positive" interpretations of freedom.

In relation to common carrier communication, the issue of rights was defined differently than in publishing or broadcasting. Horwitz (1989: 90) records: "In order to create a nationwide, efficient, and rational telegraph service for commerce and the national defense, the government would encourage a monopoly, so long as regulatory oversight compelled the extension of service, prevented the abandonment of service, guaranteed fair rates, and guaranteed the consolidated company a fair rate of return."

Telegraphy, in which it was believed that the public interest was best served through a regulated monopoly, established the model that would later govern telephony in the United States. Unlike publishers or broadcasters, common carriers were not allowed editorial control over communication. In the telegraph and telephone industries, communication as a right was not associated with government nonintervention. On the contrary, regulation by the government was viewed as serving an important role in ensuring that the vast majority of Americans would have access to mechanisms for the exchange of information. The right to communicate was understood as a basic standard of life or—to use Marshall's phrase—a "social right." It was seen as an entitlement that all Americans shared.

The right to communicate via the telephone came to be associated with the ideal of "universal service." It was thought that the government had an obligation, through protecting and regulating a monopoly provider, to ensure that even those persons unable to afford telephones or those living in isolated areas received service. Practices like rate averaging and cross-subsidization were mandated by law. Profits from business, urban, and enhanced services were used to support the less profitable rural, residential, and basic services. In terms of the development of telecommunications policy, the right to communicate was identified with providing individuals access to a national communication network. These policies defined citizens as consumers, entitled to certain benefits of modern society.

Although universal service has been the stated goal of legislative rhetoric for decades, until recently the national telephone system has remained inaccessible to millions of Americans with disabilities. In 1990, the government sought to address this oversight by expanding the notion of universal service to include persons with hearing losses or impairments or speech impediments. The passage of the Americans with Disabilities Act, specifically Title IV of the law, amended the Communication Act of 1934 to require that all common carriers provide "communication access" for hearing-impaired Americans. This mandate established telecommunications relay services, providing mediated two-way phone conversations between users of Telecommunications Devices for the Deaf (TDD) and non-users at a cost shared by all consumers. Based on government regulations and offering a group in society access to the "prevailing standard of life," the liberties safeguarded by the ADA can be related to "the social element of citizenship," to use Marshall's phrase. Title IV of the law, focusing on telephony, defines the right to communicate, in particular, as an individual's social right.

Following the passage of this law, disability-rights and public-interest organizations have worked to extend equal-service obligations to incorporate new means of communication and to include individuals who did not benefit from the ADA because of the nature of their disabilities. The World Institute on Disability, for example, strives to ensure that access to America's telephone system is available for disabled persons whose needs and abilities are not addressed by TDD technology, like those with cerebral palsy and certain learning disabilities (Bowe 1993). The organization also pushes for the accessibility of emerging computer-related systems of communication. The Alliance for Public Technology (APT) is another group that lobbies for the accessibility of emerging forms of communication. The APT contends that the distinctions within media policy noted above must be reconsidered and that universal-service obligations—most closely associated with common carriers—should be extended to encompass all industries offering new interactive network systems. Members argue that public-interest aspects of new communication networks must be protected and that finances for these considerations could be furnished through taxes on equipment and service providers, spectrum allocation auctions, and universal-service funds. These groups work to ensure that contemporary understandings of universal service keep pace with the communication marketplace.

UNIVERSAL SERVICE AND ITS FUTURE

Although the origins of universal-service standards are often associated with the Communications Act of 1934, the law has little relation to modern practices connected with this notion. The phrase "universal service" does not appear in the legislation, and nowhere in the Act is there a reference to subsidized telephone penetration. The original meaning of "universal service" focused on considerations other than communication as a social right. As Dordick (1990:23) contends, for Theodore Vail, the first general manager of Bell Telephone Co., the phrase implied "everywhere rather than everyone." Vail's efforts to maintain monopoly control of telephony led him to seek "one policy, one system, and universal service" (p. 23). Mueller (1993) concurs, arguing that "universal service" was Vail's competitive strategy, aimed at ending "dual service" and establishing the company's control of American telephony. Mueller states that for industry officials, regulators, and consumers alike, "universal service" meant "a unified, interconnected monopoly, not regulatory subsidies to promote household penetration" (pp. 355–356).

AT&T as a legal monopoly became the dominant force in American telephony. It was fostered through government regulation for the purpose of serving the "public interest." Prior to President Lyndon Johnson's Great Society era, however, the fulfillment of this public-service mandate was often measured in terms of the health of the corporation itself. Horwitz (1989:135) writes, "It is not difficult to see that the protection of the public interest in telephony for the most part became equated with the successful operation of the Bell System." Only in the 1960s did consumers gain a voice before regulatory agencies, and rights—other than the "civil rights" of market players—began to be considered.

Wilson (1992:359) argues that before this time, the beneficiaries of regulation were a "class of corporate users who, were it not for regulation, would have been the targets of a less controlled form of price discrimination." With the rise of regulatory activism, the interests of local organizations and residential consumers began to take center stage. In the legislation of the Great Society period and with the rise of the welfare state, the notion of communication as a social right emerged. During this period, in which a safety net of social policy was fashioned, the objective of universal service was crystallized.

Although the Great Society era generated regulations addressing the needs and interests of the general public, in its wake an "undertow of neolibertarian, deregulatory thinking" began to emerge, as Rowland (1983) notes. The rise of regulatory activism promoted countervailing forces to emerge, especially within the business community. During the mid-1960s, corporate users recognized that with reforms in telecommunications, the benefits of regulation had shifted to residential and small-business users. Wilson (1992:359) writes, "At this point the corporate sector withdrew its support for the regulation of telecommunications." The call for the return of a "free-market approach" to policy began to be heard.

Federal Communications Commission (FCC) activity in the 1970s reflected a return to a position associating the right to communicate with a "negative" concept of liberty. By the 1980s, Mark Fowler, the Reagan-appointed chairman of the commission, advanced a neolibertarian approach to telecommunications policy, favoring a laissez-faire attitude toward the private sector (e.g., Fowler and Brenner 1983). In the 1990s, efforts toward regulatory reform continue. In fact, Mosco (1990:36) describes deregulation as "central to current American mythos." In communication policymaking, concern focused on issues of convergence, technological innovations and the promises of the free market and the First Amendment, and the discussion of communication as a social right became much more muted.

Browning (1994:105) expresses a perspective not uncommon in the current environment. He writes: "Universal service is a 1930s solution to a 1990s problem. It is time to bury it—slowly and with great care to preserve both its spirit and its many achievements, but bury it nonetheless."

Without a commitment to universal service, however, there is the threat of the creation of a dual society of the information-rich and information-poor. In such a context, some individuals would have access to commercial, educational, and health care services through multimedia telecommunications, while others would remain excluded. Persons unconnected to cyberspace would be deprived—at least to some degree—of what Marshall (1950) labels "the prevailing standard of life." In fact, if one understands emerging communication networks as conduits for governmental information, mechanisms for organizing citizens, and even vehicles of political expression, the infringement on freedom due to the abandonment of universal-service obligations is more profound than merely the denial of social rights. If financial and other inequalities deny individuals access to communication services that are essential for democratic participation, all persons do not share in the promises of liberty. Political freedoms are enjoyed by those people admitted to these new networks, while others are excluded from this sphere of influence. Since persons with disabilities are often disadvantaged in the marketplace, if cyberspace develops as an elite realm without the guidance of principles associated with universal service, the disabled are especially vulnerable to exclusion.

BLUEPRINT FOR CYBERSPACE: THE TELECOMMUNICATIONS ACT OF 1996

The Telecommunications Act, signed into law on February 8, 1996, by President Clinton, is the most significant reworking of national telecommunications policy since the Communications Act of 1934. The Act provides the framework for the emerging information superhighway. As its full title suggests, this legislation focuses on curtailing federal regulations in order to promote competition within and among communication industries. It is based on the contention that the marketplace, freed from restrictive government intervention, is the best mechanism for ensuring the rapid and successful development and use of new communication technologies. The eighteenth-century ideal of the free marketplace of communication— with, of course, some new restrictions—provides a policy apparatus for the development of this new arena. Ultimately, the law rejects the regulated monopoly associated with common carriers as the guideline for emerging cyberspace.

This law is primarily deregulatory in nature, advancing freedom in terms of the lifting of government interference. The legislation, however, is complex and at points even contradictory. It includes provisions that promote and advance new regulations, for example in regard to universal-service standards. Rather than "burying" universal service, as Browning (1994) suggests, to a limited degree this legislation presents universal service as a guideline for the development of new communication networks. In addition, it advances some of the initiatives first addressed by the ADA. For instance, it includes guidelines ensuring closed captioning in video programming and requires the FCC to investigate the possibility of regulations regarding video description services for persons who are blind or have low vision. For disability-rights activists, these aspects of the new law offer means of ensuring greater access to the communication networks of the future.

The Telecommunications Act presents an understanding of universal service not in terms of a particular mode of communication but in relation to an evolving standard that takes into account continual advances in telecommunications technology. Potentially, universal service could involve affordable access to two-way, voice, data, and video communication networks for all citizens, including persons with disabilities. In fact, the law establishes funds for universal service and telecommunications development to which all providers are required to contribute. These resources will be used to ensure equitable access and the continued development of new capabilities for communication networks. According to the law, universal-service standards are only created after the majority of consumers begin to utilize a service. Without advanced networks, however, these services have no means of reaching the general public. Rather than following the marketplace, policies relating to universal service should promote advancements in telecommunications and lead the development of the information superhighway.

Perhaps even more significant for persons with disabilities is Section 255 of the Act. This section requires that telecommunications service and equipment providers make their goods and services accessible to individuals with disabilities. In continuing the policies advanced by the ADA, this law addresses the freedom to communicate as a social right, a prevailing standard of life to which all people, including the disabled, should have access. The influence of this legislation on society, however, is diminished by the inclusion of a qualifier. Unlike the ADA, which requires the establishment of a relay system, this legislation makes accessible telecommunications contingent on the changes being "readily achievable" for the communication industries. In this respect, the law misses the opportunity to more clearly mandate accessibility and ensure that cyberspace is a realm open to all.

CONCLUSION

The American disability community is a vast and multifaceted collection of persons who are in some way physically or mentally challenged. According to the ADA, over 43 million Americans have disabilities, and that number is expected to steadily increase. Many persons will someday— either suddenly or over the course of time—find themselves to be members of this group. By the age of fifty-five, 25 percent of Americans experience significant functional limitations, and at sixty-five years old, 50 percent of U.S. citizens are in some respect mentally or physically impaired (Kirkwood 1993). In the past, advancements in communication like TTYs and closed captioning have improved the daily lives of individuals with disabilities, and further advances could continue this trend. For instance, developments in cyberspace could allow deaf persons to sign to one another at great distances or individuals with mobility problems to be diagnosed by doctors without leaving home.

Fortunately, the accessibility of cyberspace continues to increase. On-screen keyboards with head pointers, voice command systems, and software providing graphic representations of concepts and multisensory interactions are among the innovations that continue to open doors to this realm. With greater access to the Internet and the expansion of computer networks with redundant inputs and outputs, many barriers to employment can potentially be circumvented. Computer-mediated communication could end the isolation experienced by many people with disabilities by allowing them to build online communities and to gain access to information, resources, and support (Schmetzke 1996), and to pursue their educational, professional, and personal goals through new avenues.

Without the electronic capabilities or economic resources, however, persons with disabilities may never experience these and other possibilities. They may find themselves in an electronic ghetto, disenfranchised because they are unable to gain access to the mechanisms of contemporary communication. Through careful policymaking, aspects of society that worsen circumstances for differently abled persons can be reduced and even eliminated, and the possibilities for their lives can be greatly enhanced. In society, the sum is often greater than its parts, and as persons with disabilities join the cultural conversation, the value of communication networks increases for everyone.

REFERENCES

Altschull, J. H. 1990. *From Milton to McLuhan: The Ideas Behind American Journalism.* New York: Longman.

Americans with Disabilities Act of 1990. 1991. Pub. L. No. 101–336, 104 Stat. 327–378.

Barbalet, J. M. 1988. *Citizenship: Rights, Struggle and Class Inequality.* Minneapolis: University of Minnesota Press.

Bebout, J. M. 1990. The Americans with Disabilities Act: American dream achieved for the hearing impaired? *The Hearing Journal* 43 (June):13–22.

Berlin, I. 1969. *Four Essays on Liberty.* New York: Oxford University Press.

Bowe, F. 1993. Access to the information age: Fundamental decisions in telecommunications policy. *Policy Studies Journal* 21 (4):765–74.

Browning, J. 1994. Universal service: An idea whose time is past. *Wired* (September):102–105, 152–54.

Calabrese, A. and M. Borchert. 1996. Prospects for electronic democracy in the United States: Rethinking communication and social policy. *Media, Culture & Society* 18 (2):249–68.

Congressional Quarterly Almanac, 101st Congress, 2nd Session, 1990, Vol. 66. 1991. Washington, D.C.: Congressional Quarterly Inc.

Dordick, H. S. 1990. The origins of universal service: History as a determinant of telecommunications policy. *Telecommunication Policy* (June):223–31.

Fiss, O. M. 1990. Why the state? In J. Lichtenberg, ed., *Democracy and the Mass Media: A Collection of Essays*. New York: Cambridge University Press, pp. 136–54.

Fowler, M. S. and D. L. Brenner. 1983. A marketplace approach to broadcast regulation. In E. Wartella, D. C. Whitney, and S. Windahl, eds., *Mass Communication Review Yearbook*, Vol. 4. Beverly Hills, Calif.: Sage, pp. 645–95.

Haller, B. 1996. *Balancing Acts: Government, Business, and Disability Sources in News Representations of the ADA*. Paper presented at the annual meeting of the Association for Education in Journalism and Mass Communication, Anaheim, Calif., August.

Holmes, S. 1990. Liberal constraints on private power? Reflections on the origins and rationale of access regulation. In J. Lichtenberg, ed., *Democracy and the Mass Media: A Collection of Essays*. New York: Cambridge University Press, pp. 21–65.

Horwitz, R. B. 1989. *The Irony Regulatory Reform: The Deregulation of American Telecommunications*. New York: Oxford University Press.

Jordan, I. K. 1993. Reflection on a new era. In L. O. Gostin and H. A. Beyer, eds., *Implementing the Americans with Disabilities Act: Rights and Responsibilities of All Americans*. Baltimore: Paul H. Brookes, pp. xxix–xxx.

Kirkwood, D. H. 1993. The ADA at one year. *The Hearing Journal* 46 (February): 13–14.

Marshall, T. H. 1950. *Citizenship and Social Class and Other Essays*. Cambridge, England: Cambridge University Press.

Marx, K. (1844/1972). Economic and philosophic manuscripts of 1844. In R. C. Tucker, ed., *The Marx-Engels Reader*. New York: W. W. Norton, pp. 52–103.

Mosco, V. 1990. The mythology of telecommunications deregulation. *Journal of Communication* 40 (Winter):36–54.

Mueller, M. 1993. Universal service in telephone history: A reconstruction. *Telecommunication Policy* 17 (July):352–69.

Pool, I. S. 1983. *Technologies of Freedom*. Cambridge, Mass.: Belknap Press.

President's Committee on Employment of People with Disabilities. 1990. President Bush: "Let the shameful wall of exclusion finally come tumbling down." *Worklife* 3 (Fall):2–7.

Rowland, W. D., Jr. 1983. The further process of reification: Continuing trends in communication legislation and policymaking. In E. Wartella, D. C. Whitney, and S. Windahl, eds., *Mass Communication Review Yearbook*, vol. 4. Beverly Hills, Calif.: Sage, pp. 621–44.

Schmetzke, A. 1996. Disability-related resources on the Internet: Electronic discussion groups make accessing the Internet worth the effort. *Intervention in School and Clinic* 32 (2):69–81.

Siebert, F. 1963. The libertarian theory of the press. In F. Siebert, T. Peterson, and W. Schramm, eds., *Four Theories of the Press*. Urbana, Ill.: University of Illinois Press, pp. 39–71.

Telecommunications Act of 1996, Pub. L. No. 104–104.

Wilson, K. G. 1992. Deregulating telecommunications and the problem of natural monopoly: A critique of economics in telecommunications policy. *Media, Culture & Society* 14(3):343–68.

5

Cyber-Soldiering: Race, Class, Gender, and New Media Use in the U.S. Army

Morten G. Ender and David R. Segal

The end of the Cold War, changing social trends, and diversity within the U.S. Army provide a new and unique context to study the burgeoning communication media revolution. This chapter describes the findings of a number of studies exploring the uses of two new communication media—e-mail and live interactive television—in a military context with a focus on the interaction of soldiers and their families. The stratified uses of new media in a military institutional context are explored in relation to gender, rank, race/ethnicity, military function, marital status, and location of residence during two U.S. military interventions in Somalia and Haiti. Some modest differences exist between the socio-demographic characteristics and uses of new media but stratification is not widespread. Overall, while significant gaps in new media use exist in the larger society, the people in the military only moderately reflect this trend. The findings are discussed relative to military interventions and predicting future new media uses in the military.

INTRODUCTION

"Humanitarian" aid in the culture of the simulated: While people are starving from Somalia to Bosnia, fans send "care" packages to actors who play impoverished characters on soap operas.
—Mark Taylor and Esa Saarineen

The communication media revolution and the end of the Cold War provide a new context to study the sociology of the military. A major characteristic of war has been the soldier's isolation from spouses, family, friends, and the larger society. New communication media can assist in overcoming the physical and social distance. Given the significant relationship between military family well-being and soldier functioning and a large married and parenting U.S. military force, an increasingly and especially important intervening and under-researched element in this relationship is the process between new communication media use and social stratification.

Background

Letter mail contributed significantly to the morale of soldiers during World War II (Litoff and Smith 1991; Shils and Janowitz 1948) and the Korean conflict (Little 1964). C. Moskos (1970) noted the popularity of tape recorders and cameras among Vietnam-era U.S. soldiers. Descriptive data on U.S. Army soldiers stationed around the world, excluding those in Vietnam, and mass communication use showed radio, television, and newspapers as the media of choice (Kroupa 1973). By the 1980s, the telephone became a pervasive medium in the desert environment of U.S. peacekeeping missions in the Sinai (Applewhite and Segal 1990) and for U.S. soldiers participating in the invasion of Panama (Ender 1995). The Persian Gulf war stimulated increased scholarly (Ebo 1995; Kellner 1992; Poster 1991; Wattendorf 1992), strategic (Powell 1995; Schwarzkopf 1992), and popular (Mathews 1990) attention to communication media in a forward military deployed context. The availability, adoption, and use of new communication media in a military context across this history has been evolutionary; new media do not supplant, but rather supplement the older media (Ender 1996).

Social science research addressing new communication media at the work-family intersection is sparse. Most studies focus on communities and networks (Wellman et al. 1996). A new area of research includes the examination of communication media during forward military deployments and offers new ways of thinking about soldiering and the military family (Schumm et al. 1995; Bell, Stevens, and Segal 1996). Mediated communication provides the impetus to upend some of the assumptions of military family conceptualizations and to develop, implement, and enforce new policies that would address the needs and interests of soldiers and their families.[1]

Information technologies are clearly considered a significant feature of the late twentieth century (Bell 1973; Mayer 1994; Williams 1983). The media technologies of television, cable television, video, telephones, cellular phones, pagers, facsimiles, and especially computer-mediated communication are reconfiguring social relationships, social institutions, and the political economy. Given the plethora of communication media in sectors of the larger society, we might expect soldiers and their family members to reflect this trend. Moreover, given that traditionally there have been disparities in technology access and use in the larger society as a function of one's social position, we might expect soldiers and their families to be stratified along certain social characteristics in their use of new communication media. Consequently, researchers studying the military would be remiss if they failed to consider the social impact of mediated communication on the experience of the military organization and its circle of significant others. The research questions remain: How do soldiers and their family members use specific communication media, and what are the social implications of using communication media in an organizational context? Overall, and similar to the larger society, we find that old and new communication media are available to soldiers and their families during a forward military deployment, yet the number of new media users is limited. Second, there is more homogeneity in new media use among these soldiers and families than in the larger society.

Social Stratification

Traditionally, any research attention paid a new communication medium quickly faded as the medium became commonplace; television viewing is the exception. The diffusion and proliferation of a communication medium in both the work and family domains can be best understood by examining the newest technological device available to workers and households before it becomes commonplace and a mainstay in society. A report from RAND's Center for Information Revolution Analyses provides a detailed investigation of home and work access to computers and communication networks among the U.S. population (Anderson et al. 1995). Using the Current Population Survey—a large-scale random sample survey of households—taken in October 1989 and October 1993, the researchers focus on the individual as the basic unit of analysis.[2] Overall, the study finds that there are more people in computer households than people using communication networks at home *and* at work and that use for both has approximately doubled in the past four years—confirming the themes of proliferation of media and low use despite availability. Results indicate that computer household and network use increase with increases in both income and education and that this gap has widened in the past four years. Asians and whites are almost three times more likely to live in computer households and use networks than are Hispanic, African, and Native Americans. Only gender shows no relationship in either category of use.

We have a basis for anticipating the direction of similarities and dissimilarities in the present study when communication media are first introduced to an organizational context such as the military. This chapter focuses on the use and implications of use of two modes of communication—electronic mail (e-mail) and live-interactive television teleconferencing—by soldiers and their families during two U.S. military interventions in Somalia and Haiti.

METHODS

What follows is a report of findings from a much larger study that compared old and new communication media (Ender 1996). The larger study research design triangulated three approaches to social research: qualitative, comparative, and quantitative. The methods included primary and secondary analysis of open and closed-ended surveys, in-depth group and individual interviews, and field observations. The data originated from eight sources focusing on four U.S. military interventions that occurred between 1989 and 1995. The overall sample size was quite large ($N = 2,787$).

The subjects for the data reported in this chapter participated in Operation Restore Hope (ORH), a U.S. humanitarian relief effort in Somalia in 1992, and/or Operation Uphold Democracy (OUD), a nation-building mission in Haiti in 1994. The U.S. Army established communication lines via a number of diverse communication media for soldiers, their family members, and friends, including e-mail and TV teleconferencing.

FINDINGS

This section discusses the uses and social implications of e-mail and TV teleconferencing during two military interventions across a number of social characteristics including military occupational function, gender,[3] race/ethnicity, rank, marital status, and location of residence.

Operation Restore Hope—Somalia

Soldier E-mail and TV Teleconferencing Use. A handful of soldiers, spouses and family members, and key personnel administering the program were surveyed about e-mail use after the soldiers returned home from the U.S. intervention in Somalia. Each group was asked to complete open-ended questions about the centralized community e-mail distribution program (Ender 1997). Online for 395 days, a total of 9,435 messages was processed. Soldiers reported they had learned about the e-mail programs through their leaders.[4] Many reported having sent fewer or about the same number of e-mail messages as they had written letters. A typical response was: "At times e-mail was impersonal, especially when I sent personal in-

Table 5.1
OUD Soldiers' Frequency and Percentage Distribution of E-Mail and TV Teleconferencing Use

Amount of Usage	E-mail		TV	
	f	%	f	%
Hardly Ever	166	82.1%	173	78.3%
Less Than 1 Per Month	13	6.4	18	8.1
About Once A Month	5	2.5	15	6.8
About 2-3 Times Month	6	3.0	4	1.8
About Once A Week	7	3.5	2	.9
About 2-3 Times A Week	2	1.0	4	1.8
Almost Every Day	3	1.5	5	2.3
Total	202	100%	221	100%

Totals are out of 366.

formation, like important personal stuff." Overall, soldiers would have preferred a more decentralized system.

Operation Uphold Democracy—Haiti

Soldier E-mail and TV Teleconferencing Use. Table 5.1 compares soldier e-mail and TV teleconferencing patronage during the U.S. intervention in Haiti ($N = 366$). About 12 percent of the soldiers reported using e-mail once a month or more. About 14 percent of the soldiers reported using TV teleconferencing at least once a month.

Use of e-mail and TV teleconferencing were analyzed against the social characteristics of the sample. Virtually no statistically significant relationships occurred. Married soldiers reported more e-mail (20%) and TV teleconferencing (25%) than did single soldiers (9% and 11%, respectively). This result reflects more communication media use by subgroups who potentially have a larger role set to communicate with or about or an organizational bias toward a large number of married soldiers.

Implications of Soldier E-mail and TV Teleconferencing Use. Soldiers were asked about their levels of satisfaction with both e-mail and TV teleconferencing. Table 5.2 provides a distribution of satisfaction levels of both communication media. About 20 percent reported being satisfied with e-mail, while 35 percent reported satisfaction with TV teleconferencing.

Table 5.2

OUD Soldiers' Frequency and Percentage Distribution of Satisfaction with E-mail and TV Teleconferencing Use

Levels of Satisfaction	E-mail		TV	
	f	%	f	%
Very Satisfied	5	3.3%	27	14.5%
Satisfied	26	17.2	39	21.0
Neutral	59	39.1	66	35.5
Dissatisfied	21	13.9	20	10.8
Very Dissatisfied	40	26.5	34	18.2
Total	151	100%	186	100%

Totals are out of 366.

The satisfaction levels of soldiers were compared. Two statistically significant relationships are noted in the analyses. More combat support (45%) and combat soldiers (41%) than combat service support soldiers (32%) were satisfied with e-mail. This statistic points to differences between forward and rear deployed soldiers and new communication media use, but not in the direction we would expect.

For TV teleconferencing, unmarried soldiers (40%) were more likely to report satisfaction than were married soldiers (32%). This result contravenes expectations and again may be the result of differences in use. Married soldiers communicate with immediate family and find the experience emotionally unsatisfying, while their single peers are more likely to communicate with less intimate extended family and friends and experience the use less emotionally and as more novel.

ORH–Somalia

Spouse E-mail and TV Teleconferencing Use. Table 5.3 shows ORH veterans' spouse responses to a questionnaire on TV teleconferencing and e-mail uses ($N = 665$). About one-quarter of the spouses used unit e-mail and 27 percent used the community e-mail program. The usage of the three communication media were cross-tabulated with specific social characteristics.[5] Officers' spouses were less likely (41 percent) than spouses of junior (65%) and senior (61%) enlisted soldiers to use community or unit e-mail. Unit e-mail use is not statistically associated with the race or ethnicity of the spouse. However, the difference in community e-mail use is associated with race and ethnicity, where lower-ranking soldiers' spouses of color

Table 5.3
ORH Spouses' TV Teleconferencing and E-mail Use

Amount of Use	TV	E-mail Modes	
		Unit	Community
Not at All	95%	76%	72%
Less than Once per Month	3	13	13
2-3 Times per Month	1	6	6
Once a Week	1	4	8
Daily	0	1	1
Total	100%	100%	100%
Number	579	577	587

Total is out of 665.

showed significantly less use of community e-mail and the white spouses of higher-ranking soldiers had more use.

Spouses of combat soldiers (55%) were more likely than spouses of combat support (70%) and combat service support (74%) soldiers to use either mode of e-mail. Given that resources and information for soldiers most forward during an intervention are traditionally sparse, these two statistics are not what we would expect.

White spouses (30%) were more likely to use the community e-mail than were spouses of color (19%). This statistic is not associated with the rank of the spouse. White spouses appear to have greater access to communication media not afforded spouses of color, who are either relegated to the older, less interactive, and less timely communication media or prefer it.

Last, spouses of combat soldiers (34%) reported the highest statistically significant relationship of any medium in the study by using community e-mail over combat support (18%) and combat service support (10%) spouses. Again, this last pattern suggests that spouses of the more front-line soldier used the system more. This finding suggests the most forward soldier is somewhat less deprived in terms of cutting-edge communication media relative to more rear-functioning soldiers. For some, military deployments are no longer the socially isolating and information-restricted experiences of previous generations of soldiers and families.

Implications of Spouse E-mail and TV Teleconferencing Use. Table 5.4 shows that TV teleconferencing had the most dissatisfied users (70.6%), although the numbers of users are small ($N = 17$). About 30% reported being dissatisfied or very dissatisfied with e-mail.

The satisfaction with e-mail was cross-tabulated with specific social characteristics. No cross-tabulations showed statistical relationships with the

Table 5.4
ORH Spouses' Satisfaction with the TV Teleconferencing and E-mail Use

Levels of Satisfaction	TV	E-mail
Very Satisfied	5.9%	21.9%
Satisfied	23.5	42.5
Dissatisfied	29.4	15.5
Very Dissatisfied	41.2	20.1
Total	100%	100%
Number	17	174

Total is out of 665.

exception of location of residence. Spouses of soldiers living on the military base were more likely to report satisfaction with the community sponsored e-mail program (78%) than were spouses living off-base (53%). This statistic reflects an access issue. Spouses living off-base had less immediate access and were obliged to drive on-base to ship and receive their messages from the centralized on-base community e-mail program office.

In a separate survey, family members reported that e-mail was too impersonal and strongly emphasized decentralizing the system to include such features as e-mail access from home computers. Many key personnel managing the program said a decentralized system would better meet the needs of families on the military base. Others reported that access should be improved for everyone. For example, one key worker commented, "Some units had greater access than others." Asked who used the system least or not at all, one key worker responded that the "young, inexperienced wives" and those whose first language was not English may not have used the system as frequently.

OUD–Haiti

Spouse E-mail and TV Teleconferencing Use. On another survey, spouses of soldiers were asked, "How often did you use each of the following methods to contact your spouse during your spouse's most recent deployment?" Table 5.5 provides a comparison between the two communication media. About 18 percent used e-mail and 14 percent used TV teleconferencing about once a month or more—a slight increase from ORH.

The social characteristics of the spouses using the two communication media were explored. The exceptional statistically significant difference was for military rank of the soldier. Spouses of officers reported more e-mail

Table 5.5
OUD Spouses' Frequency and Percentage Distribution of E-mail and TV Teleconferencing Use

Amount of Usage	E-mail		TV	
	f	%	f	%
Hardly Ever	52	73.2%	48	67.6%
Less Than 1 Per Month	6	8.5	13	18.3
About Once A Month	5	7.0	8	11.3
About 2-3 Times Month	4	5.6	1	1.4
About Once A Week	2	2.8	1	1.4
About 2-3 Times A Week	--	---	--	---
Almost Every Day	2	2.8	--	---
Total	71	100%	71	100%

Total is out of 89. Percent is due to rounding.

use (25%) than did those of enlisted soldiers (17%). This relationship remains when controlling for spouse race/ethnicity.

No spouses of army officers used TV teleconferencing, compared with 37 percent of spouses of enlisted soldiers. Officers' spouses appeared to adopt computer-mediated communication, telephones, and snail mail and deferred to spouses of enlisted soldiers the novelty of TV teleconferences. One explanation may have to do with the public versus private features of communication media. E-mail, telephones, and snail mail are potentially much less public than live TV teleconferencing hook-ups.

Implications of Spouse E-mail and TV Teleconferencing Use. Table 5.6 provides a distribution of satisfaction levels for the two communication media, including TV teleconferencing. While 26 percent of spouses of soldiers reported some satisfaction with e-mail, 66 percent did so for TV teleconferences during OUD. There were no statistically significant relationships between satisfaction and social characteristics. All in all, these results suggest no notable relationships existed between subgroups and their satisfaction with using newer media. Again, only enlisted soldiers' spouses used TV teleconferencing during ORH, and most were dissatisfied with it. However, whatever adjustments were made to the TV teleconferencing technology in the one year between ORH and OUD were significant enough to raise the satisfaction level among spouses overall.

Summary of TV Teleconferencing and E-mail Use and Implications. TV teleconferencing and e-mail are the most technologically advanced com-

Table 5.6
Frequency and Percentage Distribution of Satisfaction with E-mail and TV Teleconferencing Use (Including ORH Spouses)

| | | | TV Teleconferencing | | | |
| | E-mail | | ORH | | OUD | |
Levels of Satisfaction	f	%	f	%	f	%
Very Satisfied	5	11.9%	1	6%	12	27.3%
Satisfied	6	14.3	4	24	17	38.6
Not Satisfied or Dissatisfied	18	42.9	--	--	10	22.7
Dissatisfied	4	9.5	5	29	2	4.5
Very Dissatisfied	9	21.4	7	41	3	6.8
Total	42a	100%	17b	100%	44a	100%

ªTotals are out of 89; ᵇTotal is out of 665. Percent is due to rounding.

munication media available to soldiers and family members during a military imposed family separation and deployment. Live TV teleconferences involve a real-time, two-way satellite hook-up between a soldier or group of soldiers and family and/or other significant others. TV teleconferences were first featured during ORH in Somalia and spouses appeared very dissatisfied with their debut. However, one year later, during OUD in Haiti, use quadrupled and most of the patrons appeared to have been spouses of enlisted soldiers. TV teleconferencing received the highest overall mean satisfaction rating following OUD. Most soldiers were aware of its availability and few used it. Married soldiers patronized the system more and single soldiers found it the most satisfying.

Most noteworthy are the few officers using TV teleconferences. On the one hand, the public nature of the communication may have thwarted their using the system, and they had more privileges with other, more private communication media such as telephones or e-mail. However, perhaps some officers and their spouses, recognizing their higher status and privileged positions, allowed the enlisted soldiers and their spouses first access to the new and novel mode of live TV communication. Their motivations and restraint may be premised on contributing to higher morale for enlisted soldiers and peace of mind for their spouses.

Stratification in e-mail use appears modest at best as a dimension of the communication experiences of soldiers and spouses. While the differences in rank and uses of TV teleconferencing are clear (but the number of users is low), there are less clear differences in e-mail use and rank. White spouses or those living on the military base used e-mail slightly more than did spouses of color living off-base. Key personnel administering the program mentioned that certain groups found themselves structurally discriminated against relative to e-mail use—those living farthest off-base with no resources to access the base and spouses whose native language is other than English. A noteworthy finding is that a handful of spouses potentially needing communication media resources the most are marginalized with the least access to the higher-tech communication media. This finding is probably a function of military rank (socioeconomic class) rather than of race or ethnicity.

Soldiers showed even less stratification along social characteristics than did their spouses. The only groups using e-mail significantly more than their peers were married soldiers, reflecting a family need more than a personal one. Otherwise, soldiers' use of e-mail and TV teleconferences is relatively homogenous across most social categories.

DISCUSSION

In the last half of this century, soldiers and family members have adopted an array of new communication media while continuing to patronize the older media (Ender 1996; Ender and Segal 1996). However, before comparing across U.S. military deployments, the nature and location of the specific intervention that clearly influences soldier and spouse communication media uses and implications should be addressed.

The Missions: ORH–Somalia compared with OUD–Haiti

Operation Restore Hope, the humanitarian relief effort in Somalia, lasted approximately six months and was a barren telecommunication media environment—at least for soldiers. The U.S. military established limited personal communication resources for soldiers, including telephone, snail mail, and e-mail. The international press also established base camps early in the effort.

In contrast, Operation Uphold Democracy, a nation-rebuilding mission in Haiti, approximated the mission environment, social situation, and telecommunication infrastructure of the U.S. invasion of Panama in 1989. Although much lower in conflict intensity and deaths than in Panama, both were quick-strike, urban operations that took place in the U.S. time-zone, in countries with relatively established telecommunications infrastructures, and both were short in duration. However, some five years after the invasion of Panama, OUD had the new media of e-mail and TV teleconferencing available for soldiers and their family members to use.

Much like the initial situation in Saudi Arabia prior to the Persian Gulf war, active-duty U.S. soldiers responded to a crisis in Somalia. Both soldiers and their families suffered initially from low morale and limited peace of mind because of the ambiguity of the mission. In response, the U.S. Army again established centralized lines of communication via both old media and new media, including e-mail and live TV teleconferences. Yet soldier and spouse satisfaction levels were mixed relative to their media choices. The computer-mediated communication program made privacy, stratification, centralization, personal communication, and speed important new themes at the intersection of soldiers, leaders, units, families, and the larger society (Ender 1997).

One year later, U.S. soldiers were deployed to OUD in Haiti. Uses of traditional and newer media, such as e-mail and TV teleconferencing, matured and became somewhat more commonplace. The social outcomes of using such communication media appear mixed. Satisfaction levels with use increased markedly from ORH to OUD. For soldiers and their families and friends, OUD was a prolific and diffuse communication media experience.

Universal Access and Stratification

A report from RAND's Center for Information Revolution Analyses provides a detailed investigation of home and work access to computers and communication networks among the U.S. population and provides a basis for anticipating disparities when communication media are first introduced into an organizational context such as the military.

We can contribute to a growing body of literature by showing that new communication media are available but little used by soldiers and their family members. In terms of social characteristics, we found that some soldiers and their family members use certain communication media differently and the social implications of these differences are reflected in their levels of satisfactions with use. The outstanding disparities are within martial status and combat functions. However, the directions are not what one would expect. In some cases, married soldiers and spouses of lower-ranking soldiers in general used communication media more than their peers. And while some differences emerged relative to combat function, the results varied between functions, with the most forward-deployed combat soldiers and their spouses using communication media more in some cases than did combat support and combat service support soldiers and their spouses. These findings contravene expectations and the social stratification hypothesis.

Given the disparities in the larger society among groups and computer ownership and communicating electronically, some of these variables were explored in a military context. While gaps in information access appear stratified along lines of education, class, race/ethnicity, age, and location of residence in the larger society, the people in the military only moderately reflect this trend. In essence, the military and the military family continue to be influenced by communication media availability and use patterns in the larger society, but do not necessarily reflect communication media-use patterns in the larger society. However, these patterns should continue to be monitored in future military deployments as universal access is currently not the norm.

CONCLUSION

American soldiers stationed in Vietnam referred to the United States as the "Land of the Big PX." C. Moskos (1970) labeled their exorbitant purchasing of electronic devices such as tape recorders a new "materialistic ethic." U.S. military shopping centers around the world have traditionally provided some of the highest-quality electronic entertainment equipment, such as stereos and high-resolution televisions, at below civilian economy prices, to soldiers and their families. Many soldiers purchase these devices, perhaps to reflect status, and may eventually come to rely on them to communicate with family members during a deployment. We know soldiers and their families are communication media users—perhaps more so than their civilian peers. Our review of the findings across a number of surveys shows no outstanding differences in communication media use between soldiers. While a handful of differences exist, mostly in terms of combat function and marital status, we can conclude that there is more homogeneity among soldiers—at least during an extreme physical separation of a military forward deployment—than there is among their civilian peers. This finding, more than anything else, might well reflect the desire and need of soldiers to maintain high morale and a cohesive nature during a highly mobilized experience of a deployment and a need for the military to socially control information flow (Ender 1996; Ender and Segal 1996).

Spouses of soldiers provide slightly more support for the information stratification hypothesis. While spouses of deployed soldiers also have a need for peace of mind, they are less constrained by the norms of the military institution and are more likely to reflect their civilian peers in communication media use. For example, a noteworthy pattern of white spouses of officers using more communication media than others is evident in the results. This suggests spouses of soldiers are not as constrained by the social context of a forward military deployment as are soldiers and are willing to exert their information heterogeneity much like their civilian peers. However, this latter finding is probably not a function of race or ethnicity but some form of socioeconomic status. In this case, as in other studies (Shoemaker 1988), the best predictor of differences in new media use may be confounded by one's education, occupation, income, and attitude toward new technology. Highly educated spouses of officers with positive attitudes toward new technologies are more likely to adopt and use new communication media than are others spouses.

Much of the above discussion has focused on socio-structural characteristics and their relationship to communication media-use patterns. While research examining backgrounds as a demographic variable and communication media use is abundant, little research has examined the depth of the relationship between the two (Dobrow 1989). For example, L. N. Redd (1988) notes that the black families' economic lag behind whites is due to their telecommunication illiteracy as they do not keep pace with new information technologies. Moreover, the economic differences might be enhanced via mass-communication literacy among blacks. Others have argued that differences between racial/ethnic groups in uses of communication media might be better reflected in "taste publics," where media become a means of maintaining ethnic boundaries between self and others (Dobrow 1989). This is probably not the case among soldiers. Desegregation of the military began in 1948 and racial and ethnic tensions have been less tolerated in the military than in the larger society.

Socioeconomic class distinction may be the better predictor of communication media use in the military. The differences between officers and enlisted soldiers and their spouses reported here may reflect a social trend. The wedge between officers and enlisted ranks, traditionally a baccalaureate degree, and the gap in their communication media use may be widening. Officers are increasingly involved with knowledge work and high technology and in effect become information producers. They use computers with modems at home as well, helping them consolidate their status and position. Enlisted soldiers, if they work with technology at all, are merely the information processors. Enlisted soldiers and their families are likely to become more involved with gadgetry at home for entertainment purposes rather than knowledge consumption or production.

A variation and more critical view is lodged in communication media use in the larger society. Scholars have emphasized a diffusion and shift away from a society based on industrialization in the latter part of the twentieth century to one based on information (Bell 1973, 1983; Williams 1983). Rigorous debate has followed, casting the politicians and economists against the communication researchers and sociologists. The leading question is: Will the information revolution benefit everyone? While some would suggest the information superhighway might leave some people socio-politically disadvantaged, the information-challenged would eventually benefit from the trickle-down of jobs, the obsolete technology, and low-priced entertainment media. Others argue that the revolution in information technology does not benefit everyone—in particular minorities, the uneducated, and the poor (Anderson et al. 1995; Center for Media Education 1994; Johnson 1984; Redd 1988). These groups have traditionally had limited access to education, training, and gadgetry. Some social science researchers suggest a type of "information apartheid" is emerging in U.S. society (Anderson et al. 1995).

This chapter only moderately supports the increased stratification argument. However, more research is needed as social changes in the Age of

Information is rapid and diffuse. At this writing, Operation Joint Endeavor, the peacekeeping mission in Bosnia, can be monitored on the Internet. In some cases, efforts exist to censor incoming and outgoing soldier e-mail (Compart 1996). New media forms will continue to emerge. While these and other media modes are established and use increases, there should remain a constant study and evaluation of the social uses, implications of use, and the potential impact on the organization and culture via computer-mediated communication.

NOTES

This research was supported in part by the U.S. Army Research Institute for the Behavioral and Social Sciences under Contract No. DASW 01–95-K-0005. The views expressed in this chapter are not necessarily those of the Army Research Institute, the Department of Army, or the Department of Defense. An earlier version of this chapter was presented at the 1997 annual meeting of the American Sociological Association, Toronto, Canada.

1. For the most recent work and more elaborate reviews of the military family literature, see Bowen and Orthner (1989), Segal and Harris (1993), and Stanley, Segal, and Laughton (1990).

2. The sample consists of noninstitutionalized civilians in the United States living in households and thus omits soldiers and their families among other "institutionalized" populations.

3. No significant differences emerged between male and female soldiers. Too few male spouses of soldiers existed in the data sets to warrant any conclusions.

4. Two programs existed. Unit level e-mail is affiliated with the soldier's local military unit (approximately 60 to 200 soldiers) and a military agency-sponsored program that served the entire community in and around the base of which the soldier is a part, whereas a centralized Army Community Service Center serves approximately 10,000 soldiers, their spouses, and children. Personal computer use was possible but probably not widespread.

5. For TV teleconferencing, the sample cell sizes were too small for a statistical analysis.

REFERENCES

Anderson, R. H., T. K., Bikson, S. A. Law, and B. M. Mitchell. 1995. *Universal Access to E-Mail: Feasibility and Societal Implications*. Santa Monica, Calif.: RAND, Center for Information Revolution Analysis.

Applewhite, L. W. and D. R. Segal. 1990. Telephone use by peacekeeping troops in the Sinai. *Armed Forces and Society* 17:(1) 117–26.

Bell, D. 1973. *The Coming of Post-Industrial Society: A Venture in Social Forecasting*. New York: Basic Books.

———. 1983. Communication technology: For better or for worse? In J. L. Salvaggio, ed., *Telecommunications: Issues and Choices for Society*. New York: Longman, pp. 34–50.

Bell, D. B., M. L. Stevens, and M. W. Segal. 1996. *How to Support Families During Overseas Deployments: A Sourcebook for Service Providers.* Alexandria, Va.: U.S. Army Research Institute for the Behavioral and Social Sciences (Research Report 1687).

Bowen, G. L. and D. K. Orthner, eds. 1989. *The Organization Family: Work and Family Linkages in the U.S. Military.* New York: Praeger.

Center for Media Education. 1994. *Electronic Redlining.* Washington, D.C.: Center for Media Education.

Compart, A. 1996. E-mail: Not for your eyes only. *Army Times* June 10 p. 4.

Dobrow, J. R. 1989. Away from the mainstream? VCRs and ethnic identity. In M. R. Levy, ed., *The VCR Age: Home Video and Mass Communication.* Newbury Park, Calif.: Sage Publications, pp. 193–208.

Ebo, B. 1995. War as popular culture: The Gulf conflict and the technology of illusionary entertainment. *Journal of American Culture* 18(3):19–25.

Ender, M. G. 1995. G. I. phone home: The use of telecommunications by the soldiers of Operation Just Cause. *Armed Forces and Society* 21(3):435–53.

———. 1996. *Soldiering toward the Information Superhighway: Old and New Communication Media Use during Military Operations in the Post Cold War Era.* Unpublished doctoral dissertation, University of Maryland, College Park.

———. 1997. E-mail to Somalia: New communication media between home and war fronts. In Joseph E. Behar, ed., *Mapping Cyberspace: Social Research on the Electronic Frontier.* Oakdale, N.Y.: Dowling College Press, pp. 27–51.

Ender, M. G. and D. R. Segal. 1996. V(E)-mail to the foxhole: Isolation, (tele)communication, and forward deployed soldiers. *Journal of Political and Military Sociology* 24(1):83–104.

Johnson, R. C. 1984. Science, technology, and black community development. *The Black Scholar* 15(2):32–44.

Kellner, D. 1992. *The Persian Gulf TV War.* Boulder, Colo.: Westview Press.

Kroupa, E. A. 1973. Use of mass media by U.S. army personnel. *Journal of Broadcasting* 17:309–20.

Litoff, J. B. and D. C. Smith. 1991. *Since You Went Away: World War II Letters from American Women on the Home Front.* New York: Oxford University Press.

Little, R. W. 1964. Buddy relations and combat performance. In M. Janowitz ed., *The New Military: Changing Patterns of Organization.* New York: Russell Sage Foundation, pp. 195–224.

Mathews, T. November 19, 1990. Letters in the sand. *Newsweek,* pp. 26–32.

Mayer, W. G. 1994. The rise of the new media. *Public Opinion Quarterly* 58(1): 124–46.

Moskos, C. 1970. *The American Enlisted Man.* New York: Russell Sage Foundation.

Poster, M. 1991. War in the mode of information. *Cultural Critique* 19 (Fall):217–22.

Powell, C. L. 1995 *My American Journey.* New York: Random House.

Redd, L. N. 1988. Telecommunications, economics, and black families in America. *Journal of Black Studies* 19(1):111–23.

Schumm, W. R., D. B. Bell, B. Knott, and M. G. Ender. 1995. *The Desert FAX: Calling Home from Somalia.* Paper presented at the 65th annual meeting of the Eastern Sociological Society, Philadelphia, March.

Schwarzkopf, H. N. 1992. *It Doesn't Take a Hero: General H. Norman Schwarzkopf, the Autobiography.* New York: Bantam Books.

Segal, M. W. and J. J. Harris. 1993. *What We Know about Army Families.* Alexandria, Va.: U.S. Army Research Institute for the Behavioral and Social Sciences (Special Report 21).

Shils, E. A. and M. Janowitz. 1948. Cohesion and disintegration in the Wehrmacht in World War II. *Public Opinion Quarterly* 12 (Summer):280–92.

Shoemaker, P. J. 1988. Predicting media users. In F. Williams, ed., *Measuring the Information Society.* Newbury Park, Calif.: Sage, pp. 229–42.

Stanley, J., M. W. Segal, and C. J. Laughton, 1990. Grass roots family action and military policy responses. *Marriage and Family Review* 15(3–4):207–23.

Taylor, M. C. and E. Saarineen. 1994. *Imagologies: Media Philosophy.* New York: Routledge.

Wattendorf, J. M. 1992. The American soldier in a prewar desert environment: Observations from Desert Shield. *Social Science Quarterly* 73(2):226–95.

Wellman, B., J. Salaff, D. Dimitrova, L. Garton, M. Gulia, and C. Haythornthwaite. 1996. Computer networks as social networks: Collaborative work, telework and virtual community. *Annual Review of Sociology* 22 (September):213–38.

Williams, F. 1983. *The Communications Revolution.* New York: New American Library.

6

How the Web Was Won: The Commercialization of Cyberspace

James L. McQuivey

A theoretical explanation for the commercialization of the World Wide Web is explored and tested in this chapter. It is argued that commercialization of the Web is occurring not because plots are being made behind closed boardroom doors to dominate this new source of economic power, but because media users are too conditioned to expect less from the Web than it is technically able to provide. The theoretical discussion posits that users develop normative images, or sets of expectations, that they mentally employ when using the Web. The primary concern expressed is that these symbols might constrain users from taking full advantage of the World Wide Web's technological capacity for great diversity and engaging interactivity, not because users are not allowed to, but because they do not expect to. Thus, the habits of the mass audience are potentially a driver of Web commercialization.

INTRODUCTION

Welcome to the Future

It has been hailed as the great equalizer, a powerful innovation that has the potential to give voice and power to the entire citizenry. Speaker of the House Newt Gingrich (1995) has said that the new information revolution before us will allow individuals to wield economic power outside the bureaucratic and hierarchical organizations that currently dominate the economic realm. On the opposite side of the U.S. political spectrum, President Clinton and his Net-savvy vice president have declared that the future of our education system rests on the connection of every school in the country to the digital backbone called the Internet, adding that "it'll revolutionize education in America" (Presidential Campaign Press Materials 1996).

This kind of hyperbole is not restricted to political realms. Techno wizards and prophets have lined up along the side of the information superhighway to hand out road maps that clearly delineate a path to a glorious new future. Bill Gates, the venerated founder of the Microsoft empire, optimistically claims that the digital future will create a kind of perfect competition never before dreamed of by classical economists (1995). George Gilder, author of *Life after Television* (1992), enthusiastically explains that new communication technologies will give individuals the power to compete with large controllers of information and entertainment, such as commercial broadcasters. On the other side of the ideological spectrum, *Whole Earth Review* editor Howard Rheingold explains that the very nature of Internet technology holds promise for a more democratic society in which individuals create meaningful communities across cyberspace (1993).

The unbounded optimism of these thinkers is not entirely faulty. The growth of the Internet community does significantly alter the structure of our society and thus offers a great array of potential benefits. To be sure, this chapter rests on the assumption that inherent in Internet technology is the potential for significant social, economic, and cultural benefits. But the emphasis here should rest on the word "potential," and not on the word "benefit," as is often the case. After all the benefits are enumerated and explored, all our talking and writing about them will not have created significant growth toward their realization. That is why the focus of this chapter is on one of the major deterrents to the realization of these benefits: commercialization.

Commercialization of the Internet hangs over the entire discussion of future growth and diversity like a double-edged sword. Some wish to wield it as the engine that will drive the growth of the Internet; others wince as they see its blade cutting through the Internet's core essence, which embodies decentralized, distributed, nonhierarchical computing and communication power.

Commercialization's Inauspicious Roots

In a recent article in *Monthly Review*, Michael Dawson and John Bellamy Foster (1996) lay out what is essentially a neo-Marxist interpretation of how the information superhighway is and will continue to be dominated by the holders of economic power in the status quo. They end their discussion with a virtual "call to arms," a plea to all marginalized citizens to resist the domination of the Internet by such a small and powerful elite. Their argument, though lucid and insightful, rests on an essentially weak assumption, namely, that business interests have combined in a conscious effort to reduce the promise of this technology to a pale shadow of its real self.

If commercialization of the Internet is a threat, does that threat come from an organized effort by corporate board members to control all things powerful or does it come from a less sinister source? This chapter will seek to address that question by exploring the specific case of the World Wide Web, the Internet's most flamboyant offspring. It will be argued, based on data collected in in-depth interviews and through a nationally administered survey, that the real threat of commercialization of the Internet and all its constituent parts comes not from the shadowy world of corporate scheming, but from the innocent and rather unexciting behaviors and expectations of media users like you and me.

THEORY

Medium as Symbol

More than thirty years ago, Marshall McLuhan boldly stated that the "medium is the message" (1964). He argued that the media were not passive channels through which messages were passed, but rather contributed directly to the nature of the message by their form and structure. More recently, author and scholar Neil Postman (1985) has suggested that McLuhan may have overstated his case. Postman believes that a medium is powerful, not as a dictator of content, but as a metaphorical vessel into which only certain, metaphor-consistent messages are placed. Thus, Postman's corollary to McLuhan's maxim: The "medium is the metaphor." While Postman's modification of the original is useful in understanding how society constructs a medium and its uses, the present discussion would benefit from one further modification of the maxim: The medium is the symbol.

Similar to Postman's corollary, seeing the medium as a symbol itself allows us to focus not only on the properties of the medium itself, but on the way in which society constructs that medium. Much mass communications research has focused on the media as carriers of symbols; such a perspective was crucial to George Gerbner's original formulation of cultivation theory (Gerbner and Gross 1976). But little attention has been directed to the idea that a medium itself can become a symbol and it is this specific construction that lays the foundation for the argument put forth here.

The key to unlocking the power of this notion is understanding the role that the medium as symbol plays in shaping a user's interaction with the medium. A symbol not only embodies certain properties, it requires certain performances. To fully appreciate this, it is useful to borrow a notion first described by anthropologist Clifford Geertz (1973), who explained—when discussing the power of symbols in perpetuating a culture—that all true symbols carry a dual role. They are not only models *of* reality, they are also models *for* reality. That is, symbols are representative; they represent something beyond their literal selves. Yet they are also prescriptive; they prescribe specific attitudes or behaviors. Geertz uses this definition to separate true symbols from other signifying forms that are commonly called symbols but by his definition are not.

How does this relate to the World Wide Web? Reaching back to McLuhan, if it were true that the medium is the message, then the potential benefits of the Web for society would be almost certainly attainable. But if we look at the medium itself as a symbolic construction created by society or parts of it, then we can start to appreciate how fragile the potential of the Web is. The Web is not a technologically determined panacea. It is a bundle of technologies that will be socially constructed to fit whatever niche society needs it to. The real question is, what forces are determining how the Web is constructed?

The Construction of a Symbol

The origin of cultural symbols is not a topic that can be fully explicated in these few short pages. Anthropologists and other social scientists who have wrestled with this question for more than a century have bounced back and forth between different ideas. Emile Durkheim (1915) suggested early on in this debate that individual character and behavior are the result of social forces writ small. Later researchers like B. Malinowski (1948) reasserted the role of the individual, maintaining that social forces in fact first originate in the mind of the individual and then diffuse through the society until the social order reflects them.

This continuing debate is of use here because it provides the backdrop for a similar, though less developed argument in mass media research. With the uses and gratifications perspective, mass communication researchers have long suggested that individual users are the key creators of meaning in a media experience (Rubin 1994). Several studies have isolated "normative images," which are sets of expectations held by media users that shape how the user interacts with the medium, much as the "medium is the symbol" concept described above attempts to do (Lichtenstein and Rosenfeld 1984; Perse and Courtright 1993). One ambiguity in this body of research, however, is the dilemma faced by researchers trying to pin down the elusive origin of cultural symbols: Where do people receive their normative images from? Are they internally generated or determined socially?

The specific symbol at hand is the World Wide Web. If the Web is symbolically constructed in the minds of users, the expectations and images that constitute that symbol are more likely to be determined externally than internally. The Web can be viewed as either a new medium, which requires new symbolic construction, or as a variation on an old medium, which implies some adoption of a previously constructed symbol. In either case, it is likely that the eventual symbolic form—or normative image—constructed for the Web will be primarily externally defined. Three specific ways in which this construction can take place are explained below.

Socially Constructed Expectations. Jay Blumler (1985) dedicated a chapter of an edited volume to the social nature of media gratifications, arguing that media researchers had neglected to systematically observe the social context in which media gratification takes place. He argued that use of a medium is not driven solely by actual needs, but also by the socially constructed needs (expectations) that users have of a medium. An example he offered was that of women and sports: "Women (in general) not only do not follow sports reports; they are not supposed to" (p. 57). This is a social construction, a setting of expectations at the social level about the proper uses of a given medium.

A similar concept was explored by W. Russell Neuman (1991) in his book, *The Future of the Mass Audience*. Designed as an exploration of the potential demand for interactive television services, Neuman's study uncovered a major force that would inhibit the use of interactive television for diverse and provocative programming. This was the system of habits, expectations, and behaviors of the mass audience. He proposed that even though the technology holds the capacity for a more engaging and instructive media experience, such experiences would be few in number not only because it is not cost-effective to produce them, but because the media habits of the masses are so geared to passive, hierarchical, one-way communication.

It is this argument that the author applies to the World Wide Web. As discussed above, the Web has the potential to be used as a community-builder, a democracy-enhancing, diversity-enriching tool, but the expectations the mass audience brings to the table are such that this potential may go largely untapped.

A counter-argument to this proposition is the idea that the Web is different from interactive television, which was the topic of Neuman's study. Television is a passive medium, but computer interaction is not. How is it possible that such an interaction-rich medium could be constructed in predominantly passive, commercially dominated terms? Perhaps the next two types of expectation creation can help resolve this concern.

Borrowed Expectations. In the specific case of emerging media it has been argued that users will tend to apply their normative images of a more established medium to a new one (Williams, Phillips, and Lum 1985). When television was introduced, viewers expected a visual version of radio, or a small-screen version of the cinema. Precisely because the Web is such a unique medium, it is possible that users will be confused about how to engage it. They may turn to media-derived expectations by default. Exactly this kind of borrowed expectation was explored by the present author in the case of the World Wide Web (McQuivey 1996). Through in-depth interviews, it was discovered that many users did directly apply their understanding of other media to the Web when using it. The most common media images employed by users in that research were newspapers and magazines. The argument of the author at that time, which served as the basis for the present research, was that media-derived expectations would lead to media-derived use patterns. Thus, if a user believed the Web was a large entertainment magazine, he or she would expect to use it as such, browsing often, looking for short highlights on some topics and in-depth treatments of others. More relevant to this discussion is the idea that Web advertising could be more attractive to those who believed the Web was similar to an advertiser-supported medium like newspapers, magazines, or television, thus opening the door for further commercial influence.

Commercially Crafted Expectations. This special category of expectations that should technically fall under socially created expectations above is being drawn out here because of the topic of this chapter. This refers to those normative images created and/or reinforced by the commercial marketplace. This is especially relevant to the Web because many people's first exposure to the Web came from seeing URLs (universal resource locators, or Web addresses) so ubiquitous in magazine and television ads. As this activity became more common, many new users of the World Wide Web were provided with a plethora of creative and technically expert sites to visit. If one wants to cruise the Web, one needs simply to look up http://www.toyota.com or http://www.godiva.com in order to be entertained and amused.

Learning about Web sites through advertisements is particularly intriguing because it has the potential to carry the Web user's consumer mindset from the marketplace to the Web itself, thus shaping the user's expectations of the Web.

But commercial advertising is not the only means through which the consumer mindset can be applied to the Web. In a survey conducted by the Pew Research Center for the People and the Press (1995), 24 percent of Web users drawn from a national sample said they found out about Web sites they were interested in visiting from magazines and newspapers. Though many newspaper or magazine articles refer to the Web sites of nonprofit organizations and foundations, many more articles and reviews refer to the Web sites of corporations and other firms operating in the marketplace.

Symbolic Expectations of Web Users

If these social forces are successful in creating normative images that are commercial, it is logical that Web users would bring consumer expectations to the Web when using it. The question at this point is how to measure the expectations of Web users to see if the theory outlined above plays out in their minds.

As previously mentioned, the basis for this investigation was derived from previous in-depth interview work done by the author, which revealed that Web users do have elaborated symbolic expectations or normative images which they apply to the Web when using it (McQuivey 1996). The normative images employed by interviewees in that research were derived from newspapers, magazines, television, a library, and a shopping mall. The divisions among these five responses were such that there was an even split in emphasis between media-derived expectations and nonmedia-derived expectations. There was also a difference between more and less experienced Web users. Users with more experience tended to employ media-derived normative images less than did novice users.

This is a potentially significant finding because it could lend support to the theoretical discussion above. To understand this, consider diffusion of innovations theory. The basic premise of the theory is that a community or society can be divided into demographically or psychographically distinct groups with respect to their adoption of an innovation or a new technology. Early adopters are assumed to be different from late adopters in their willingness to try new things or make changes in their lifestyle (Rogers 1986). Previous research into the diffusion of new technologies shows that the early adopters are different from early and late majority adopters of a technology in their appreciation of the technical aspects of the innovation. For example, early adopters of home computers were much more informed about the different products and options available than are their late majority adopter counterparts (Zajas and Crowley 1995). This makes late adopters much more susceptible to the influence of brand-style marketing, in which advertisers attempt to create positive personalities or images with which consumers will associate their product. This marketing style is a classic example of how commercial enterprises seek to create symbols.

It is very possible that this same profile can be applied to later adopters of the World Wide Web. They are not as versed in the technological aspects of the Web. They do not know that the Web is a vastly different medium with potential for great diversity and interactivity. They only know what they've been told. And who has told them about it? Principally, the media, either directly through media content or advertisements that support them. These individuals are entering a more mature market and are looking for the "brands" on the Web—those sites that they can rely on for useful content. Some anecdotal evidence can be gathered for this argument by looking at the brand power that names such as Yahoo, Netscape, Microsoft, and America Online wield in the market.

Novice and Experienced Users

Based on the concepts elaborated above and the difference between novice and experienced Web users, the author developed two hypotheses:

H1: The less experienced a Web user is, the more likely that user is to employ media-derived normative images when using the Web.

H2: The less experienced a Web user is, the more likely that user is to be favorable toward Web advertising.

The first hypothesis directly tests the finding of the author's earlier research by measuring whether experienced users' normative images are different from those of novice users. Experience is operationally defined as a three-point, interval-level categorization in answer to the question: How long have you used the World Wide Web? Answers ranged from up to six months, six to twelve months, or more than twelve months. The user's normative images are elicited by asking the user to rate on a scale from 1 to 5 how much using the Web is like: 1) watching television; 2) searching through a library; 3) reading a newspaper; 4) walking through a shopping mall; or 5) reading a magazine.

The second hypothesis is the more socially significant of the two. It tests the proposition that newer users, due to their socially and commercially constructed expectations of the Web, are more likely to report that the Web is a commercial symbol. Thus, the acceptance of advertising is used to measure acceptance of commercialization of the Web. Operationally, this is defined through the following Likert-type questions: 1) I often enjoy advertisements on the Web; 2) I wish advertisers did not use the Web for advertising; and 3) I think advertising on the Web is an important part of the World Wide Web experience. Each item is measured along a 5-point scale from "strongly agree" to "strongly disagree." All items were coded so that a 5 on any of the three items indicates a favorable attitude toward Web advertising. The three items were also combined to produce a single measure of attitude toward Web advertising.

RESULTS

A self-administered, mail-in questionnaire was mailed in two waves to 750 computer-owning households across the nation during August 1996. The sample was selected systematically with a random start from a commercially obtained list of 250,000 names. The mailings produced 423 responses, for a response rate of 58 percent after factoring out surveys returned by the Postal Service unopened. Of respondents, 234 reported some use of the World Wide Web.

Table 6.1 shows frequencies for the interval level variables. It is interesting to note that of the five normative image questions, the most frequently employed is the library, with a 4.46 on a scale of 1 to 5. This is clearly the most used normative image and is directly contrary to the commercially dominated picture of the Web painted here.

Table 6.2 presents frequencies for nominative and ordinal data from the Web portion of the questionnaire. The demographic results are in line with research by the Pew Research Center for the People and the Press (1995), which also showed that higher-educated males tended to use the Web more than less educated segments of the population and females. Note that the breakdown of experience with the Web creates three roughly even groups.

Also note that the Web advertising attitudinal measures are combined into a scale ranging from 3 to 15 with a mean of approximately 9. This additive scale achieves a reliability score of alpha = 0.83.

To test the first hypothesis, that newer Web users would be more likely to choose media-derived normative images, correlation coefficients were calculated between the normative image items and the Web experience variable. Table 6.3 displays the correlation matrix. The Web experience variable correlated significantly with only two of the normative image measures, namely, the newspaper and the shopping mall. Both coefficients indicate the relationship is in the hypothesized direction. The newspaper coefficient is negative, meaning that more experienced users are less likely to choose the newspaper as a normative image, and the shopping mall coefficient is positive, meaning that more experienced users are more likely to choose the shopping mall as a normative image. While this provides some support for the hypothesis, it is confounding when one stops to consider that if a newspaper is an advertiser-supported medium that could create commercial expectations of the Web in the minds of users, the shopping mall is an even more blatant symbol of commercialization. Contrary to the theoretical discussion in this chapter, more experienced users are significantly more comfortable employing that commercial normative image when using the Web. This will be explored in more depth in the section below.

The second hypothesis was also tested in the correlation matrix presented in Table 6.3. It is apparent from this simple test that the positive relationship was not statistically significant. This will also be discussed below.

DISCUSSION

This chapter posits that users develop normative images, or sets of expectations, that they mentally employ when using the Web. The primary

Table 6.1

Means and Standard Deviations for Normative Image Ratings, Approval of Web Advertising and User Age Variables

Variables	Mean	Standard Deviation
Using the Web is like watching TV*	2.04	3.88
Using the Web is like searching through library*	4.46	0.97
Using the Web is like reading a newspaper*	3.37	1.02
Using the Web is like walking through a shopping mall*	2.35	1.31
Using the Web is like reading a magazine*	3.22	1.06
I often enjoy Web advertisements**	2.81	0.89
I think advertising is an important part of the Web experience**	3.04	1.06
I wish advertisers did not use the Web for advertising***	3.10	1.06
Favorability toward Web advertising index****	8.95	2.58
Age	40.93	14.13

*Rated on a scale from 1 to 5 where 5 is "most like" and 1 is "least like."
**On a scale from 1 to 5 where 5 is "strongly agree" and 1 is "strongly disagree."
***On a scale from 1 to 5 where 5 is "strongly disagree" and 1 is "strongly agree."
****Favorability toward Web advertising is a scale produced by adding the responses to the following items: 1) I often enjoy advertisements on the Web, coded from 1 to 5; 2) I wish advertisers did not use the Web for advertising, coded from 5 to 1; and 3) I think advertising on the Web is an important part of the World Wide Web experience, coded from 1 to 5, for a range from 3 to 15, where 15 signifies extreme favorability; alpha = 0.83.

Table 6.2
Percentages for Length of Web Use, Sex, Education, and Income

Variables	Percentages
How long have you used the Web?	
Up to.6 months	30.5
6 to 12 months	35.0
12 months or moer	34.5
	100.00 ($N = 226$)
Sex	
Male	62.0
Female	38.0
	100.00 ($N = 234$)
Education	
Below high school	4.7
High school graduate	5.7
Some college	39.2
College graduate	30.2
Graduate or professional degree	20.2
	100.00 ($N = 212$)
Income	
Less than $25,000	10.1
$25,000–$49,999	36.0
$50,000–$74,999	30.4
$75,000–$99,999	11.1
$100,000 or more	12.4
	99.9 ($N = 217$)

concern expressed is that these symbols might constrain users from taking full advantage of the World Wide Web's technological capacity for great diversity and engaging interactivity. Thus, the habits of the mass audience are potentially a driver of Web commercialization.

The hypotheses tested in this chapter focused on a particular part of the Web as symbol concept, namely, that Web novices would be more likely to bring commercial expectations to the Web when using it than would experienced users. The first hypothesis received moderate support, though the support must be qualified. As explained above, it appears that inexperienced users of the Web are more likely to think of the Web as a newspaper than are experienced Web users. While this supports the hypothesis, it does not support the theoretical discussion of Web commercialization.

Table 6.3
Pearson Correlation Coefficients for Independent and Dependent Variables (Normative Image Ratings, Length of Time as Web User, and Favorability Toward Web Advertising Variables)

Variables	2	3	4	5	6	7
1. Using the Web is like watching TV*	-.06 (206)	-.01 (204)	-.07 (204)	-.09 (205)	.01 (205)	.11 (170)
2. Using the Web is like searching through library*	-	.01 (206)	-.32[b] (204)	-.22[b] (208)	-.06 (220)	.00 (181)
3. Using the Web is like reading a newspaper*		-	-.37[b] (203)	.07 (206)	-.19[a] (206)	-.06 (170)
4. Using the Web is like walking through a shopping mall*			-	-.12 (205)	.21[a] (204)	.13 (169)
5. Using the Web is like reading a magazine*				-	-.11 (208)	.06 (172)
6. How long have you used the Web?**					-	.14 (186)
7. Favorability toward Web advertising scale***						-

* Rated on a scale from 1 to 5 where 5 is "most like" and 1 is "least like."

**Coded from 1 to 3 where 1 is up to six months; 2 is six to twelve months; 3 is twelve months and over.

***Favorability toward Web advertising is a scale produced by adding the responses to the following items: 1) I often enjoy advertisements on the Web, coded from 1 to 5; 2) I wish advertisers did not use the Web for advertising, coded from 5 to 1; and 3) I think advertising on the Web is an important part of the World Wide Web experience, coded from 1 to 5, for a range from 3 to 15, where 15 signifies extreme favorability; alpha = 0.83.

One potential reason that the differences sought between novice and experienced users didn't materialize may be the relative newness of the Web itself. The period covered by this study includes only two years. In the Pew Research Center's research from 1995, it was found that only 3% of the country's population was using the Web. In the past year, it is likely this number has doubled. Given the diffusion model, it is likely that in five years, all of those who currently use the Web will be considered innovators or early adopters. Only at that time will time-based comparisons yield fruitful results.

Coexistence of Commercial and Noncommercial Normative Images

The apparent contradiction in the results—that more experienced users seem to have less resistance to the mall normative image than do new users—raises an interesting question. Do experienced users have more commercial expectations of the Web than do new users? If so, what causes this disparity? It is possible that new users have yet to acclimate themselves to the Web environment. This could indicate that once users have experienced the Web for a time, they begin to use the entertainment aspects of the Web more. This would be similar to the consistent finding with personal computer uses and gratifications research that users almost always report utilitarian and information reasons for purchasing a computer, but invariably spend a large portion of their time with the computer playing games (Williams and Rice 1983; Dutton, Rogers, and Jun 1987).

Given this possibility and the conflicting results of this research, the original issue should be readdressed: What of the future of Web commercialization? Figure 6.1 provides some clue to that answer. It shows the relationships between Web experience and the five normative images tested in the questionnaire. Note that the most popular normative image, regardless of Web experience, is that of a library. This does inspire some hope. The public library as an institution has a very strong heritage in the United States. It has long been a place where communities build their citizens through free and open exchange of information. If a library were to sell advertising space on its shelves or tables, the community would probably demand a new librarian. If this is the principal expectation that people have of the Web, regardless of how long they've been on it, there is hope that the Web will be able to develop its full potential and avoid the domination of commercial interests. Yet when testing the second hypothesis, it became apparent that the users are still neutral toward Web advertising. There is no public revolt afoot. Figure 6.2 illustrates the strength of favorable attitudes toward Web advertising. There is a very gradual, but definite positive slope to the line. The more months users spend on the Web, the more favorable are their attitudes toward Web advertising. Though this relation-

Figure 6.1
Mean Rating of Different Web Normative Images by Length of Time as a Web User*

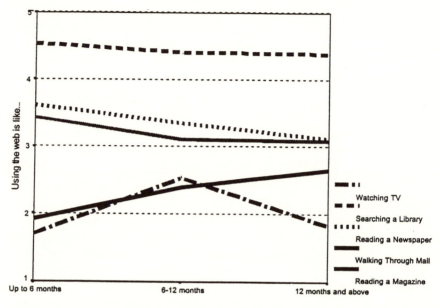

How long have you used the World Wide Web?

* Respondents were asked to rate the five activities on a scale from 1 to 5, where 5 indicated "most like" and 1 indicated "least like."

ship did not prove statistically significant, it does coincide with the apparent increase in use of the shopping mall normative image shown in Figure 6.1.

It only takes a few clicks on the Web to realize that the presence of commercial interests is pervasive. The Web page "banner" where most advertisements are placed is well recognized and expected by novice and expert Web users alike. Advertisements are everywhere, and there are few content sites that are not supported or underwritten by at least one advertiser. This points to an obvious but essential element of Web symbols. Though users claim that the Web is best compared to a library, they do not insist on only one symbolic image for the medium. Another look at Figure 6.1 will clarify this. Scores above 3 indicate acceptance of the symbol; scores below 3 indicate lack of acceptance. Of the five symbolic images proposed, three were simultaneously accepted by users as applicable to the Web: the library, a newspaper, and a magazine. One is entirely noncommercial, one is a daily information source that is driven by commercial advertising, and the last is a commercial medium that has the ability to adapt and fill various niches. In other words, users are flexible in their use

Figure 6.2
Graph of Favorability toward Web Advertising by Length of Time as a Web User*

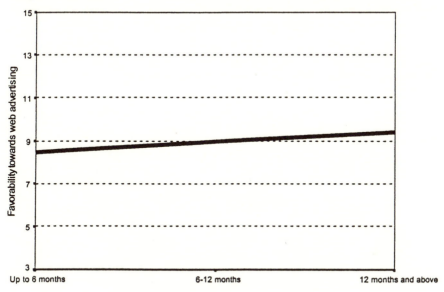

How long have you used the World Wide Web?

* Favorability toward Web advertising is a scale produced by adding the responses to the following items: 1) I often enjoy advertisements on the Web, coded from 1 to 5; 2) I wish advertisers did not use the Web for advertising, coded from 5 to 1; and 3) I think advertising on the Web is an important part of the World Wide Web experience, coded from 1 to 5, for a range from 3 to 15, where 15 signifies extreme favorability; alpha = 0.83.

of these symbols and do not feel as constrained by them as the literature would suggest.

CONCLUSION

Having shed light on the nature of Web commercialization, it is apparent that the future of the Web is not entirely held by the viselike jaws of private enterprise. Maybe the techno-prophets and the glorysayers will have their way and the Web will completely redefine the nature of community interaction and social discourse. The theoretical argument laid down here shows one potential way that such a glorious vision may not come to pass due to the socially constructed nature of Web user expectations. Tests of this idea at this time do not show conclusive evidence that normative images have a preponderant influence on the Web experience. As Web use continues to diffuse throughout the population, future researchers should keep an eye trained on the attitudes and behaviors of newer users.

As with any complex phenomenon, the commercialization of the Web—and all of cyberspace—is likely to be influenced by myriad factors, not just by the constrained expectations of its users. Commercial enterprises will attempt to exploit the value inherent in the World Wide Web. To expect them to do otherwise is foolish. But what the users will do is not as predictable. They have the opportunity to realize benefits that have traditionally escaped them. But for now, and in the shadow of Web commercialization, those benefits remain potentials, not realities.

REFERENCES

Blumler, J. G. 1985. The social character of media gratifications. In K. A. Rosengren, L. A. Wenner, and P. Palmgreen, eds. *Media Gratifications Research: Current Perspectives*. Beverly Hills, Calif.: Sage, pp. 41–59.

Dawson, M. and J. B. Foster. 1996. Virtual capitalism: The political economy of the information highway. *Monthly Review* 48(3):40.

Durkheim, E. 1915. *The Elementary Forms of the Religious Life*. New York: Macmillan.

Dutton, W. H., E. M. Rogers, and S-H. Jun. 1987. Diffusion and social impacts of personal computers. *Communication Research* 14(2):219–50.

Gates, B. 1995. *The Road Ahead*. New York: Viking.

Geertz, C. 1973. *The Interpretation of Cultures: Selected Essays by Clifford Geertz*. New York: HarperCollins.

Gerbner, G. and L. Gross. 1976. Living with television: The violence profile. *Journal of Communication* 26(2):172–99.

Gilder, G. 1992. *Life after Television*. New York: Norton.

Gingrich, N. 1995. *To Renew America*. New York: HarperCollins.

Lichtenstein, A. and L. Rosenfeld. 1984. Normative expectations and individual decision concerning media gratifications choices. *Communication Research* 11(3):393–413.

Malinowski, B. 1948. *Magic, Science, and Religion*. Garden City, N.Y.: Doubleday.

McLuhan, M. 1964. *Understanding Media: The Extensions of Man*. New York: McGraw-Hill.

McQuivey, J. L. 1996. *Uses of the World Wide Web: How Users Frame the Web*. Paper presented at the American Association of Public Opinion Researchers' annual meeting, Salt Lake City, Utah, May.

Neuman, W. R. 1991. *The Future of the Mass Audience*. Cambridge, England: Cambridge University Press.

Perse, E. M. and J. A. Courtright 1993. Normative images of communication media: Mass and interpersonal channels in the new media environment. *Human Communication Research* 19(4):485–503.

Pew Research Center for the People and the Press. 1995. *Technology in the American Household*. On line: http://www.people-press.org/tectop.htm (last searched, June 20, 1996).

Postman, N. 1985. *Amusing Ourselves to Death: Public Discourse in the Age of Show Business*. New York: Viking.

Presidential Campaign Press Materials. 1996. President Clinton's remarks in Las Vegas, Nevada, October 31.

Rheingold, H. 1993. *The Virtual Community: Homesteading on the Electronic Frontier*. Reading, Mass.: Addison-Wesley.

Rogers, E. M. 1986. *Communication Technology: The New Media in Society*. New York: Macmillan.

Rubin, A. M. 1994. Media uses and effects: A uses-and-gratifications perspective. In J. Bryant and D. Zillmann, eds., *Media Effects: Advances in Theory and Research*. Hillsdale, N.J.: Erlbaum Associates, pp. 417–36.

Williams, F. and R. E. Rice. 1983. Communication research and the new media technologies. *Communication Yearbook* 17:200–224.

Williams, F., A. F. Phillips, P. Lum. 1985. Gratifications associated with new communication technologies. In K. E. Rosengren, L. A. Wenner, and P. Palmgreen, eds., *Media Gratifications Research: Current Perspectives*. Beverly Hills, Calif.: Sage, pp. 241–52.

Zajas, J. and E. Crowley. 1995. Commentary: Brand emergence in the marketing of computers and high technology products. *Journal of Product & Brand Management* 4(1):56–63.

PART II

Race on the Net

7

Challenging the Mandarins: Comparing City Characteristics and Nationwide Newspaper Coverage of the Internet, 1993–95

John C. Pollock and Elvin Montero

A cursory inspection of a national cross-section of major city newspapers (at least fifteen each year) and articles (over 800) on the Internet printed from 1993 through 1995 suggests that the new technology has generated considerable excitement. A careful scholarly examination, however, of the association between city characteristics and a systematic content analysis of Internet coverage partially confirms the initial impression, but it also uncovers evidence of skepticism, even resistance regarding the new medium of communication. Curiously, the higher the percentage of college students in a city, the less likely a city's paper is to cover the Internet favorably. Possible reasons for this skepticism or resistance are discussed, including the reluctance of educational or political elite to witness rapid "democratization" or expanding access to the Internet, especially on the part of individuals or groups who have little respect for individual or corporate security or privacy. Far from portraying the new technology as relatively inaccessible or as "marginalizing" disadvantage citizens, the "community structure" approach to media coverage reveals that newspapers seem to be linked systematically to concerns about too much accessibility for too many too soon.

INTRODUCTION

Some have called it the "information superhighway," others the information infrastructure of the future, and some have been so bold as to call it the "prophet of the third millennium, th[e] technological John-the-Baptist" (Strangelove 1994: 11). The Internet has been available for years to researchers for government agencies and later by institutions of higher learning. Indeed, the government and higher learning institutions have been the leading promoters and developers of the Internet as we know it today.

The new interest from the public has aroused concern about the type of information available on the Internet. Issues of regulation, security concerns, and pornography flood the media today as Internet use becomes more widespread. In an articulated effort to protect the minds of children and unknowing citizens, legislators in Washington have launched debates about unregulated information available on the Internet. As public debate continues, a new area of interest emerges: How do newspapers report about this new technology, the Internet, and the various topics that surround it? The following research takes a closer look at nationwide reporting on the Internet by examining major city newspapers throughout the United States, analyzing both the amount of attention accorded the topic as well as content direction of newspaper coverage, ultimately testing the correspondence between article favorability and specific characteristics of cities.

A SURVEY OF COMMUNICATION LITERATURE: A RESEARCH GAP

How did the Internet grow so large? The information infrastructure began when the Department of Defense began the Advanced Research Projects Agency (ARPA) in 1957 (Zakon 1995). This agency was founded to research ways and possibilities to connect networks with each other. As the technology made internetworking possible and easier, more networks evolved. ARPANET came into existence in 1970 after years of development, and universities signed on in the 1970s and 1980s (Zakon 1995).

In the 1990s a monochrome style gave way to graphical interfaces and sound on the Internet with the introduction of systems like the Wide World of Web and Netscape (Cerf 1995: 23). Families with multimedia PCs in their homes have since taken the Internet from very few networks in 1989 to over 120,000 in 1995 (Zakon 1995), a growth spurring debates about safety, security, and various other topics, bringing the Internet to the front lines of news interest.

With such rapid growth, it is not surprising that the elite of the technical-computer world have much to say about the Internet. Scholars of communication, by contrast, have shown little concern with the Internet until recently. The *Journal of Communication*, for example, has had few articles dealing directly with the Internet. In the late 1980s, when the Internet was not yet clearly exposed to the public, there was some discussion among communication scholars about the use of the Internet as a ground for political change, giving the public (those who had access to a network of some type) the ability to obtain information to improve public discourse (Downing 1989), and Furlong (1989) wrote about a mediated community for senior adults. Little else was found, however in the *Journal of Communication* until a Winter 1996 special issue.

Exploring *Communication Abstracts* from the period of 1988 to the present produced only twenty-one relevant articles. In the late 1980s the scarcity of home PCs limited Internet access and its audience. Articles from this period focused on the wonders of e-mail (electronic mail) and its advantages (Shaefermeyer and Sewell 1988). The uncontrollable boundaries of intellects and ideas became an issue with R. J. Solomon (1988) in "Vanishing Intellectual Boundaries: Virtual Networking and the Loss of Sovereignty and Control." Realizing the lack of security in this information superhighway, *The Futurist* was among the first to look at "Tomorrow's Thieves" (Albanese 1988).

To be sure, the Internet is home to several communication online journals (*Journal of Electronic Publishing, Hour of Computer-Mediated Communication, Journal of Norwegian Media Research*, to name a few) that have been established to cover the topic of computer mediated communication. One journal in particular, *Interpersonal Computing and Technology: An Electronic Journal for the 21st Century*, presented many ideas regarding educational uses of the Internet (Cotlar and Shimabukuro 1993). And T. W. Loughlin (1993) in his "Virtual Relationships: The Solitary World of CMC" takes a personal approach in discussing how he is "connected to thousands, perhaps millions of people worldwide, while sitting in the solitary confines of . . . [his] own den" (online) via the Internet.

Yet communication scholars generally are missing a prime opportunity to examine the Internet and how the "virtual reality" it presents will affect the processes of interpersonal communication. Will children exposed to the Internet today be poor one-on-one "live" communicators, unable to express or relay a message to a person face-to-face in the future? Or will the comfortable confines of being at home and not having personal identities exposed allow people more freedom? These questions should be of interest to communication scholars.

The 1990s brought to the home a new vocabulary and new electronic equipment. Home PCs became more accessible and visible in middle-class households, increasing exposure to the Internet. M. E. Hepworth (1990) began to espouse the challenge of "Information City," asking what the future would bring. W. E. Halal proclaimed "The Information Technology Revolution" (1992).

The network that began in a defense lab had produced a worldwide Internet (Mills 1993). By 1994 the word "Internet" was a heading in the *Social Science Index*. Yet the Internet that now allows many civilized citizens to exchange thoughts also permits the ideas expressed by a John or Sally Doe to attack a cultural group, a gender, person, and so on. The multiplicity of access has yielded concerns about liability and the regulation of the Internet (Hecht 1994; Masood 1995; Trubow 1994), as well as whether to form an etiquette to govern interaction on the Internet—"netiquette."

Prominent issues like censorship and security (Mann 1995; McCrone 1995; "Regulating Cyberspace," *Science* 1995; Wallich 1995) became of special recent concern because of the increase of commerce on the Internet, in particular with sexually explicit materials becoming more accessible to children (Corbin 1995; "Censorship," *The Economist* 1995). Realizing the potential market of the Internet (Fodlen 1994; Kleiner 1995; "Net Profits," *The Economist* 1994) the business world has entered cyberspace by offering home shopping promotions online, some of which have led to regulatory interest on the part of the U.S. Senate ("Censorship," *The Economist* 1995). Futurists now examine the Internet's impact on the future generally (Woodward 1994), as well as on future consumption patterns (Hearn and Mandeville 1995). Growing concern by the public and government about the Internet's role in society (Davidson 1995), promotion of the Internet's use by education systems, and even President Clinton's concern in 1992 generate special urgency in scrutinizing the Internet.

A COMMUNITY STRUCTURE APPROACH

Whether one subscribes to diffusion theory, social marketing theory, or some other theory of new knowledge awareness and acquisition, the introduction of a new technology into society may be received differentially in different regions or cities. And those differences may be reflected in the way city newspapers cover the new medium of communication.

In general, newspapers are viewed by media scholars as closely linked to the communities they serve. In a structural-functionalist paradigm, long popular in the social sciences, "media may be viewed as prominent subsystems within the larger social systems of the community; thus they tend to reflect the values and concerns of *dominant groups* in the communities they serve." (Smith 1984: 260; emphasis added). Tichenor, Donohue, and Olien (1980: 102–103) have also documented the importance of newspapers as "mechanisms for community social control that maintain the norms, values and processes of a community, and . . . their functions necessarily fit into a pattern that varies predictably according to size and type of community."

A community or city structure perspective can help explain variations among newspapers concerning what several scholars call "critical events" (in this case, the introduction of the Internet), a perspective introduced in the 1970s by Steven Chaffee and others focusing on key coverage choices newspapers make (Chaffee 1975; see especially Kraus, Davis, Lang and

Lang, in Chaffee 1975: 196). In political reporting, for example, instead of focusing on the traditional routines of party politics and elections, a "critical event" perspective exploring significant committee hearings, civil disturbances, court cases or referenda can reveal a great deal about the ways newspapers function as gatekeepers and agenda-setters.

Adopting a "critical event" perspective, previous studies have found that certain city population characteristics measuring the proportion of relatively privileged (efficacious) groups in a city—typically high proportions of those with college degrees or professional or technical occupational status—can be linked to relatively favorable reporting on those making human rights claims, for example, regarding the 1973 U.S. Supreme Court decision on abortion (*Roe vs. Wade*), Cuban political refugees, and Anita Hill (Pollock, Robinson, and Murray 1978; Pollock, Shier, and Slattery 1995; Pollock and Killeen 1995). A related measure, city poverty level, is also linked to empathy for human rights in coverage of a 1971 prisoner uprising at Attica; reporting on a referendum to revoke homosexual rights regarding housing discrimination in Dade County, Florida; and coverage of a conflict between Caribbean-Americans and Orthodox Jews in Crown Heights, New York City (Pollock and Robinson 1977; Pollock and Whitney 1997).

In addition, the relative proportion of privilege in a city is also linked to relatively unfavorable coverage of events that strike too close to home for those who consider privilege to have purchased some "buffer" from life's vicissitudes. Thus, the higher the level of income in a city, the less favorable the likely coverage of Dr. Kevorkian's activities; while high proportions of professionals in a city are linked to unfavorable coverage of Magic Johnson's HIV announcement (Pollock, Coughlin, Thomas, and Connaughton 1996; Pollock, Awarachow, and Kuntz 1994). This prior research permits the formulation of several hypotheses connecting city characteristics with relatively favorable or unfavorable coverage of the Internet.

HYPOTHESES

The following hypotheses can be organized into four clusters: privilege, ethnic identity, PC use, and media size or saturation.

Privilege

Previous research connecting city characteristics with privilege suggests that, unless an issue is life-threatening (as with Magic Johnson or Dr. Kevorkian), the higher the proportion of privilege in a city, the greater the favorable newspaper coverage of human rights issues (such as Anita Hill or the "Open Door" policy toward Cuban refugees) and correspondingly unfavorable coverage of China's bid for the 2000 Olympics because of China's questionable record on human rights (Pollock and Killeen 1995;

Pollock, Shier, and Slattery 1995; and Pollock, Kreuer, and Ouano 1997). To the extent that the Internet is viewed as an extension of the quest for knowledge, cities with high levels of privileged citizens are predicted to be associated with relatively favorable coverage of the Internet. Specific rationales and hypotheses follow.

Education. The Internet and its many resources have been available to higher institutions of learning for decades. The National Science Foundation (NSF) still sponsors institutions of higher learning to allow them to give access to students, instructing them in the use of the Internet for research. Vice President Al Gore's big thrust during the 1992 campaign was to make the information superhighway a reality and to connect each classroom, aiming specifically at the grammar, middle, and secondary schools. This new opportunity allows more students to become familiar with the Internet and become avid users and fans of the Internet. Accordingly:

H_1: The higher the percentage of college students in a city, the more favorable the coverage of the Internet (The Lifestyle Market Analyst, 1995).

H_2: The higher the percentage of people with 16 or more years of education in a city, the more favorable the coverage of the Internet (The Lifestyle Market Analyst).

Occupation. Men and women in the professional world have considerable exposure to computers. Most companies today cannot function without the presence of computers and electronic mail in the office. Since they are more likely to use computers for office work, professionals are more likely to use the Internet and therefore know of the advantages of having access to it.

H_3: The higher the percentage of professionals and technicians in a city, the more favorable the coverage of the Internet (The Lifestyle Market Analyst).

Income. Getting online from home costs a great deal. While Internet use is free, several providers of access to the Internet charge monthly fees of $20 or more a month for limited amounts of time. Hardware is also expensive. Cities with relatively high median incomes contain more people who have entered the middle class and who therefore fit the profile of "primary users" of the Internet. Cities with relatively large proportions of families with incomes in six figures are also likely to contain an abundance of online users. Accordingly:

H_4: The higher the median income in a city, the more favorable the coverage of the Internet (The Lifestyle Market Analyst).

H_5: The higher the percentage of households in a city with an annual income over $100,000, the more favorable the coverage of the Internet (The Lifestyle Market Analyst).

Ethnic Identity

In most large cities several minorities may earn less then the posted median income. This lack of funds focuses resources on the necessities of life rather than big-ticket items such as computers. Though schools are beginning to offer the opportunity for all students to use the Internet while at school, the inability to have the same access at home may make some minorities uncomfortable.

H_6: The higher the percentage of minorities (nonwhites) in a city, the less favorable the coverage of the Internet (The Lifestyle Market Analyst).

PC Use

Most owners of computers are aware of the advantages of today's technologies. Most computers bought since 1993 have come with modems and trial subscriptions to online services offering access to the Internet. These people already have the hardware and software necessary to go online, affording them easy access to "surfing the Net."

H_7: The higher the percentage of computer users, the more favorable the coverage of the Internet (The Lifestyle Market Analyst).

City Size and Media Saturation

Size. In *Community Conflict and the Press*, Tichenor, Donohue, and Olien (1980) found that larger cities tend to display a wider range of group interests and perspectives than do smaller ones. This is due in part to the greater differences and complexities found in larger cities. Larger cities as well would be home to more technology driven companies, relying heavily on computers in running their corporations.

H_8: The larger the city, the more favorable the coverage of the Internet (The Lifestyle Market Analyst).

Media Saturation. Similarly, larger cities would have a relatively large total circulation for newspapers. The Internet is known as the "information superhighway," attracting those who want raw information or who want to stay ahead of the times.

H_9: The larger the total circulation size of newspapers (daily and weekly) in a city, the more favorable the coverage of the Internet (Gale Research 1994).

The greater the number of media outlets, the greater the opportunities for the public to express viewpoints or report on new technologies. The Internet has become a new way of advertising for television stations. Some networks, like Prodigy, offer online TV guides. Such guides could increase viewership for television shows, since people who use the Internet would have access to description of shows and times.

H_{10}: The greater the number of television stations in a city, the more favorable the coverage of the Internet (Gale Research 1994).

Continuing with the concept of larger cities having a wide range of groups expressing various views on issues, radio stations are another medium through which these views are expressed. Comparing city characteristics with coverage of AIDS patient Ryan White, a hemophiliac schoolboy, yielded significant correlations between the number of radio stations (particularly FM stations) and relatively tolerant or sympathetic coverage of the young boy (Pollock, McNeil, Pizzatello, and Hall 1996). Radio stations can also take advantage of the Internet by bringing pictures to their sounds. The possibilities of promotion on the Internet for radio or for any other media are limited only by imagination.

H_{11}: The greater the number of radio stations, the more favorable the coverage of the Internet (Gale Research 1994).

METHODOLOGY

The sample of newspapers was constructed by selecting for specific years, for geographic dispersion, and for availability on the DIALOG Computer Information Program. Although the Internet in 1993 was almost twenty-five years old, there was little knowledge of it in the public arena. The Internet was primarily a tool of the educated elite. This new technology gradually found its way into the public domain, due in part to two factors: the passing of the 1991 High-Performance Computing Act, which recognized the importance of U.S. leadership and set the group for expansion of national computer networks; and the publicity generated by the Clinton-Gore team during the election of 1992. Based on a search of the DIALOG newspaper database, few articles concerning the Internet or computer networks are seen in newspapers prior to 1993.

Several newspapers were selected from each of the nation's major regions, but the *New York Times* and *The Washington Post* were not included in the sample because their national status—politically and financially—may lead these papers to express views well beyond their city boundaries and demographics. Since the Internet was not a common topic of debate in 1993, some newspapers had few articles concerning it.

A total of forty-seven papers was examined over the course of Internet coverage: seventeen for 1993, fifteen for 1994, and fifteen for the last six months of 1995, for an average of 16 papers per sampling period. An average of seventeen of the longest articles in each time period was sampled. (Up to twenty of the longest articles in each paper were allowed, but in 1993 the Internet was relatively new, so all articles in all newspapers sampled were included, and few printed as many as twenty.) All articles were included that mentioned the Internet or any synonym (cyberspace, information superhighway, computer network, etc.) as the subject of discussion. Any article over 500 words that dealt with the Internet—by displaying the word or a synonym in the title or first two paragraphs—was included in the sample. In all, 815 articles were read and analyzed.

To compare differences in coverage, each of the newspapers was measured in terms of attention and direction of presentation. The first score was an "attention" or "display" score, ranging from 0–16 points. This sum represented the total scores for each of four factors: location of article placement, headline word count, article length word count, and inclusion of photographs. Newspapers with higher attention scores presented coverage of the Internet more prominently than did newspapers with lower attention scores. The second coding assigned a direction category representing the article's content "direction" on the Internet. Each article's content was evaluated as being "favorable," "unfavorable," or "balanced/neutral" toward issues about the Internet:

- Coverage "favorable" toward the Internet supported it by reporting on all the opportunities available online. These articles promoted the expansion of the new technology to all areas of life as the future information superhighway, showing how it would ease everyday life by allowing information to be retrieved almost instantaneously, students to finish their work faster, shopping and banking to be made easier, and even jobs on the online classifieds to be found more efficiently. These articles portrayed the Internet as the latest technology with limitless possibilities.

- Coverage "unfavorable" toward the Internet did not support its expansion. This new technology was seen as a threat to human interaction, and the growth of it was predicted to subordinate day-to-day interaction to online meetings, working from home, or talking to others via computer. While these issues may seem to epitomize the greatness of the Internet, reporters at times emphasized the negative side of working at home, going online, and so on. The convenience of the Internet was seen as a threat to interpersonal relationships. The problems and kinks in this new infrastructure were highlighted—lack of security, children meeting sexual offenders, pornography, and so on.

- Coverage "neutral" or "balanced" presented impartial coverage of the Internet. These articles gave basic information concerning the Internet, emphasizing neither positive nor negative attributes of the technology. The articles gave the reader

Table 7.1
Calculating the Janis-Fadner Coefficient of Imbalance

Definitions:

- f = sum of the attention scores coded "favorable"

- u = the sum of the attention scores coded "unfavorable"

- n = the sum of the attention scores coded "neutral/balanced"

- r = f + u + n

If f>u (or if the sum of the "favorable" attention scores is greater than the sum of the "unfavorable" attention scores), then use the following formula:

Coefficient of Favorable Imbalance

$$C(f) = \frac{f^2 - fu}{r^2}$$

Answer lies between 0 and +1

If f<u (or if the sum of the "unfavorable" attention scores is greater than the sum of the "favorable" attention scores), then use the following formula:

Coefficient of Unfavorable Imbalance

$$C(u) = \frac{fu - u^2}{r^2}$$

Answer lies between 0 and -1

tools and information to get online and presented a check-it-out-for-yourself attitude. *De gustibus non disputandum est* (of taste there is no dispute) was the tone of the coverage; whether you find the Internet helpful or unhelpful is for you to decide.

The assignment of direction scores by multiple researchers yielded an average Holsti's Intercoder Reliability of 0.89. Each article's attention and direction scores were combined into a single score for each newspaper by calculating a Janis-Fadner coefficient of imbalance, resulting in a single score for each newspaper between −1 and +1 (see Table 7.1). The scores

Table 7.2
Coefficient of Imbalance and Spearman Correlation

	1993	1994	1995 (July -Sept.)
Coefficient of Imbalance Range	+.053 - +1.00	+.024 - +.510	+.033 - +.710

	1993		1994		1995	
	Correlation	Probability	Correlation	Probability	Correlation	Probability
Percent of College Students in a City	-.58	<.008	-.52	<.01	-.56	<.025
Education (16 plus years)	-.19	<.25	-.3	<.25	-.43	<.05

above zero indicated relatively favorable coverage of the Internet and those below indicated relative unfavorability (see Janis and Fadner 1965: 153–60; Hurwitz, Green, and Segal 1976; Pollock and Guidette 1980).

RESULTS

Examining those coefficients, there are two main conclusions. First, there is considerable variation in the way newspapers cover the Internet. The ranges in Table 7.2 reveal that variation. Second, in addition to variation, newspaper coverage of the Internet is to some degree favorable, all of the newspapers in 1993, 1994, and 1995 are linked to relatively positive coefficients of imbalance.

Yet the variation in those coefficients was sufficient to confirm that different city newspapers reported on the Internet somewhat differently. The newspapers were ranked according to their coefficients of imbalance. Then Spearman-Rho rank-order correlation analysis was used to determine whether these reporting differences could be associated with differences in city characteristics, as suggested by the hypotheses. Hypotheses yielding significant results in correlations and probability levels are also listed in Table 7.2.

The Surprising Negative Link with Education

The two most striking findings are related to education. For one of the two sample periods, education (16-plus years) is significantly correlated with coverage of the Internet. And for all three periods, the percentage of college students in a city is linked significantly to coverage of the Internet. However, the correlations are not in the predicted positive direction. Rather, the higher the percentage of college students in a city (and in one case, the higher the education level in a city), the less favorable the coverage of the Internet.

This finding is so contrary to both conventional wisdom and prediction that it compels a reexamination of assumptions about the presumed link between admiration for education and a positive perspective on the advancement of knowledge through the powerful tool of the Internet. Perhaps the high negative correlations suggest that viewing the Internet as a symbol of a pathway to knowledge may be myopic and presumptuous. Perhaps the question to be asked is not whether or how much knowledge is advanced, but rather the classic political and economic question about the allocation of scarce resources: Whose interests does the Internet advance? That question deserves careful consideration because the answer may not be as obvious as may at first appear.

Missing Correlations

As curious as the surprising connection between presence of college students and unfavorable coverage of the Internet is the absence of a significant link between minority presence in a city and coverage of the Internet—suggesting that relative social marginalization is thus far unrelated to newspaper perspectives on the new medium. Another absence is remarkable: the lack of a significant relation between personal computer use and coverage of the Internet, suggesting that relative privilege in the form of easy access is also thus far unrelated to perspectives on the new medium. It is striking that two of the most obvious indicators of information access—the lack of it with minorities, and abundance of it with PC users—have little or nothing to do with newspaper coverage of one of the most exciting new frontiers to emerge in this century.

Beyond Excitement to Skepticism and Resistance

Perhaps these findings, when taken in combination, suggest that an older way of viewing privilege, associating it with years of schooling or PC use, may not be the most effective way to measure privilege as the United States enters the cyber age. Two explanations for the inverse relation between the percentage of college students and positive coverage of the Internet are plausible. One is the "skepticism" hypothesis, suggesting that cities with high proportions of students (and therefore educationally advanced professors likely to have experience with the Internet) and other well-educated citizens are somewhat skeptical about an online service that promises so much access to so much information for so many. It might be reasoned, accurately, that information is only as useful as the intelligent mind that chooses to do something constructive with it. There may be a modicum of biological hubris as well, a confidence or at least hope that no silicon-based unit can get the better of our human carbon-based systems.

But skepticism alone may not account for the possible concerns of well-educated citizens that younger and more computer-savvy new entrants into the job market will be able to retrieve more and better information faster and more efficiently than older, computer illiterate managers, technicians, and professionals. Although some indicators of privilege had no significant relationship to Internet coverage (various income levels, computer users), the striking and perhaps surprising negative association between the percentage of college students and newspaper Internet coverage suggests concerns about the way growing access to the Internet, and therefore to a wide spectrum of heretofore limited knowledge, may challenge the special claims to expertise and knowledge previously enjoyed only by the well educated. This sense of vulnerability might be considered a "resistance" hypothesis, in which well-educated communities might find their joy at access to information tempered by a preoccupation with questions about how to control or limit that access, seen most clearly in new issues about pornography, censorship, stalking, and the like.

All considered, a community-structure approach to newspaper coverage of the Internet finds it associated not simply with new opportunities, but even more pointedly with concern about access to what used to be a controlled technology. The older ways of learning and knowing that produced a social structure of well-educated people and markedly less well-educated people may be eroding under the influence of technological change, and the older knowledge "brahmins" or "mandarins" may be giving way to a far more varied and flexible social system and its association with knowledge.

Elite Resistance

Whatever the short-term socioeconomic consequences of the Internet, whether it initially widens the gap between those who know and those who don't, a clear theme in newspaper reporting on the Internet is a concern that the "cybernet" transformation has already been too revolutionary. The city-structure approach to reporting on the Internet suggests that the new medium ultimately seems unlikely to reinforce the educational class structure, but rather to shake up the distribution of educational advantages.

This kind of resistance among the privileged to the widespread dispersion of a new fountain of knowledge or communication has solid historical roots, whether in Plato's opposition to Sophists teaching "outside" his academy or the *Federalist Papers*, in which Hamilton, among others, challenged Jefferson's effort to extend political influence to non-elite, small farmers. The Internet's origins among defense experts and university researchers and the gradualism of its initial diffusion may have left educational and political leaders unprepared for the commercial gold rush that challenged previous boundaries and proprieties in the same fashion that the California forty-niners overturned accepted laws and customs at Sutter's Mill near Sacramento.

The "skeptics" might agree with John Scully, former chairman of Apple Computer Inc., who said, in referring to a new generation of privacy and security issues, that "the information superhighway has consumer potholes, too." (Jones 1994). But the "resisters" might go further, echoing the dark view of Neil Postman, who warned in his book *Technopoly: The Surrender of Culture to Technology*, that "there are losers as well as winners in a world tyrannized by this technological juggernaut." This jeremiad, noting that "people are talking—via the computer; communication IS direct, uncensored" (Kenaley, 1993: A1)—evokes the political and social concerns articulated in the 1840s by Alexis de Tocqueville, who remarked several of our new government's leaders were worried about a "tyranny of the majority." Whether they are best considered skeptics or resisters, there is some evidence that a substantial segment of educational and journalistic agenda-setters and gatekeepers are concerned that the information highway, previously the domain of high-end users, the equivalent of Mercedes and BMWs, is filling too rapidly with drivers of Fords and Chevrolets.

REFERENCES

Albanese, J. S. 1988. Tomorrow's thieves. *Futurist* 22 (September/October):24–28.

Bilodeau, A. 1994. Into the net: A reporter's transformation. *Computer-Mediated Communication Magazine* 1(3). Online: http://sunsite.unc.edu/cmc/mag/1994/jul/reporter.html

Censorship in cyberspace. 1995. *The Economist* 335 (April 8):16–17.

Cerf, V. G. 1995. *The Telecommunications* 23 (January):26.

Chaffee, Steven H., ed. 1975. *Political Communication: Issues and Strategies for Research*. Beverly Hills, Calif.: Sage Publications.

Corbin, L. 1995. Speeding up the data superhighway. *Government Executive* 27 (February):14–16.

Cotlar, M. and J. N. Shimabukuro. 1993. Stimulating learning with electronic guest lecturing. *Interpersonal Computing and Technology: An Electronic Journal for the 21st Century* 1. Online: http://www.helsinki.fi/science/optek/1993/n1/cotlar.txt.

Davidson, Keory. 1995. Liberté, egalité, interneté. *New Scientist* 146 (May 27):38–42.

Downing, J. D. H. 1989. Computers for political change: Peacenet and public data access. *Journal of Communication* 39:154–62.

Fodlen, A. 1994. Why is the Internet important for business information professionals? *Business Information Research* 10 (January):2–11.

Furlong, M. S. 1989. An electronic community for older adults: The seniornet network. *Journal of Communication* 39:175–53.

Gale Research. 1994. *Gale Directory of Publications and Media Sources*. Detroit: Gale Research.

Halal, W. E. 1992. The information technology revolution. *Futurists* 26 July/August):10–15.

Hearn, G. and T. Mandeville. 1995. The electronic superhighway: Increased commodification or democratization of leisure? *Media Information Australia* 75 (February):92–101.

Hecht, J. 1994. Lawyers ad challenges rules of 'netiquette.' *New Scientist* 143 (July 9): 19.

Hepworth, M. E. 1990. Planning for the information city: The challenge and response. *Urban Studies* 27:537–58.

Hurwitz, L., B. Green, and H. E. Segal. 1976. International press reactions to the resignation of Richard M. Nixon. *Comparative Politics* 9 (October):107–23.

Janis, I. L. and R. Fadner. 1965. The coefficients of imbalance. In H. E. Laswell, ed., *Language of Politics: Studies in Quantitative Semantics*. Cambridge, Mass.: Harvard University Press, pp. 153–60.

Jones, C. 1994. Information superhighway has a few consumer potholes, too. *Richmond-Times-Dispatch*, Metro Business (Feb. 7): E-29.

Journal of Communication. Winter 1996. Entire issue devoted to the Internet.

Kenaley, R. 1993. People are talking—via the computer communication IS direct, uncensored. *The Philadelphia Inquirer*, National (May 11): A-1.

Kiernan, V. 1994. Internet tricksters make a killing. *New Scientist* 143 (July 16):7.

Kleiner, K. 1995. Sweet sound of cash registers on the Internet. *New Scientist* 146 (June 3):7.

The Lifestyle Market Analyst 1995. 1995. Wilmette, Ill.: Standard Rate and Data Service.

Loube, R. 1991. The institutional conditions for technological change: Fiber to the home. *Journal of Economic Issues* 25 (December):1005–15.

Loughlin, T. W. 1993. Virtual relationships: The solitary world of CMC. *Interpersonal Computing and Technology: An Electronic Journal for the 21st Century* 1. Online: http://www.helsinki.fi/science/optek/1993/nl/loughlin.txt.

Mann, C. 1995. Regulating cyberspace. *Science* 268 (May):628–29.

Masood, E. 1995. Physicist will sue Internet providers over 'libelous' remarks. *Nature* 373 (June):525.

McCrone, J. 1995. Watching you, watching me. *New Scientist* 146 (May 20):36–39.

Mills, M. 1993. Networks from a defense lab . . . to a worldwide web of users. *Congressional Quarter Weekly Report* 57:830–31.

Net profits [electronic commerce on the Internet]. 1994. *The Economist* 332 (July 9):83–85.

Pollock, J. C. 1995. Comparing city characteristics and newspaper coverage of NAFTA. *Mass Communication Research* 22 (January):314.

Pollock, J., M. J. Awrachow, and W. Kuntz. 1994. *Comparing City Characteristics and Newspaper Coverage of the Magic Johnson HIV Announcement: A Community Structure Approach.* Paper accepted for presentation at the Health Communication Division of the annual meeting of the International Communication Association, Sydney, Australia, July.

Pollock, J. C., J. Coughlin, J. Thomas, and T. Connaughton. 1996. Comparing city characteristics and nationwide newspaper coverage of Dr. Jack Kevorkian: An archival approach. *Newspaper Research Journal* 17 (Summer/Fall):314.

Pollock, J. C. and C. L. Guidette. 1980. Mass media, crisis and political change: A cross-national approach. In Dan Nimmo, ed. *Communication Yearbook IV.* New Brunswick, N.J.: Transaction Books.

Pollock, J. C. and Karen Killeen. 1995. *Newspapers and the Clarence Thomas-Anita Hill Hearings: Comparing City Structures and Major City Coverage.* Paper accepted for presentation at the annual meeting of the Speech Communication Association, San Antonio, Texas, November.

Pollock, J. C., B. Kreuer, and E. Ouano. 1997. Comparing city characteristics and newspaper coverage of China's bid for the 2000 Olympics. *Newspaper Research Journal* 18 (Winter):3.

Pollock, J. C., K. McNeil, L. Pizzatello, and G. Hall. 1996. *Comparing City Characteristics and Newspaper Coverage of Ryan White: A Community Structure Approach.* Paper accepted for presentation at the annual meeting of the International Communication Association, Chicago, May.

Pollock, J. C. and J. L. Robinson. 1977. Reporting rights conflicts. *Society* 13:1, 44–47 (November/December):44–47.

Pollock, J. C., J. L. Robinson, and M. C. Murray. 1978. Media agendas and human rights: The Supreme Court decision on abortion. *Journalism Quarterly*, 53:3, 545–48, 561.

Pollock, J. C., L. Shier, and P. Slattery. 1995. Newspapers and the "Open door" policy toward Cuba in a sample of major cities: A community structure approach. *Journal of International Communication* 2(2) (December):67–86.

Pollock, J. C. and L. Whitney. 1997. Newspapers and ethnic conflict: Comparing city characteristics and news coverage of Crown Heights (Brooklyn) N.Y. *The New Jersey Journal of Communication* 5:2.

Regulating cyberspace. 1995. *Science* 268 (May 5):628–29.

Shaefermeyer, M. J. and E. H. Sewell, Jr. 1988. Communicating by electronic mail. *American Behavioral Scientist* 3 (November/December):112–23.

Smith, K. A. 1984. Perceived influence of media on what goes on in a community. *Journalism Quarterly* 6 (Summer):260–64.

Solomon, R. J. 1988. Vanishing intellectual boundaries, virtual networking and the loss of sovereignty and control. *Annals of the American Academy of Political and Social Sciences* 495:40–48. January

Strangelove, Michael. 1994. The Internet, electric gaia and the rise of the uncensored self. *Computer-Mediated Communication Magazine* 1(5). Online: http://sunsite.unc.edu/cmc/mag/1994/sep/self.html

Tichenor, P. J., G. Donohue, and C. Olien. 1973. Mass communication research: Evolution of a structural model. *Journalism Quarterly* 50 (Autumn):419–25.

———. 1980. *Community Conflict and the Press*. Beverly Hills: Sage Publications.

Trubow, George B. 1994. Traffic hazards on the superhighway. *IEEE Software* 11: 112–13.

Wallich, P. 1995. A rogue's routing [hackers may ignore individual PC's and undermine the net]. *Science America* 272 (May):31.

Woodward, E. H. IV. 1994. Interactive media communication technologies for the 21st century. *Media Development* 41(4):18–22.

Zakon, R. H. 1995. Hobbes' Internet. *Timeline* 2 (2) (August). Online: http://info.isoc.org./guest/zakon/Internet/HIT/html.

———. 1997. *Hobbes' Internet Timeline v2.5*. (March 13). Online: http://info.isoc.org/guest/zakon/Internet/History/HIT.html

8

Domination and Democracy in Cyberspace: Reports from the Majority Media and Ethnic/Gender Margins

Meta G. Carstarphen and Jacqueline Johnson Lambiase

Headlines in the majority press herald the emerging Information Age as a bonanza of publicly accessible information, as well as a new barrier-free terrain. However, the rhetoric of cyberspace instead may be emulating the power structures and hierarchies of the dominant discourse in the "outernet," making the Internet a domain far from free of built-in bias. In this chapter, the authors explore a rhetorical view of potential ethnic and gender barriers in cyberspace as posed by issues of access, experience, language/code, and canon.

How can we construct or conduct the public conversation of democracy so that we don't have permanent losers?
—Lani Guinier, professor of law,
University of Pennsylvania

Mapping the terrain in cyberspace is at once an ambiguous and contradictory idea. It is contradictory because the very nature of the Internet in all of its various permutations defies all typical and traditional spatial and categorical thinking. Entering the stage in cyberspace, to borrow from Kenneth Burke's conceptual ideal of situational language placement,[1] is not a fixed geography or even a fixed time period. In fact, entering the rhetorical moment can be in many ways totally unlike more traditional communication experiences in mediated or face-time connections. Is there a bridge between what we know and what we will know? When it comes to matters of "race" and gender in cyberspace, what we seek to learn should be more cautionary than exemplary.[2]

Headlines in the majority press herald the emerging Cyber Age as a bonanza of publicly accessible information, as well as a new barrier-free terrain. In 1993, a *New York Times* wire service article characterized the Internet as "an amorphous array of networks" where "millions of people communicate" (Andrews 1993: C3). Yet, that formlessness was both its appeal and albatross, for as the article continued to poll experts' views, a monolithic concern emerged that unless more convenient ways of navigating cyberspace were developed, the vast potential of this universe of text, image, and thought could be lost.

Significantly, it is from this issue of navigational ease within the Internet that concerns about giving people a sense of place has arisen, with all of its competitive and commercial significance. And as if to hone this particular aspect to its finest point, more recent coverage has targeted, with iconic and even mythic rhetoric, the financial titans who battle for dominance in cyberspace. A startling example of this pose shines through in one of the many *Time* magazine covers that have purported to educate its reading public on Internet happenings, featuring the visage of the most prominent poster boy of technology, Microsoft cofounder and the firm's current chief, Bill Gates. In a very literary-styled opening for this cover article, reporter Joshua Ramo deftly establishes the two central figures of his drama, Gates and competitor James Barksdale, the head of the Internet navigational product, Netscape, as dueling giants (Ramo 1996: 56). Readers receive details about each man's breakfast routine and his taste in cars. Ramo delineates an undeniable, militaristic framework in which each man is characterized as a general, each company as an army, and the Internet as the battlefield. From the idea of companies battling for financial control of navigational tools for cyberspace, it is not a far leap at all to characterize the Internet as real estate, with all of its accompanying ideas about value, place, and ownership.

POWERFUL OWNERS, POWERLESS PEOPLE

On the special fold-out, pin-up cover[3] of *Wired* magazine's June 1996 issue, Bill Gates floats on a raft. He wears a watch, a swimsuit covered with smiley faces, and no more. The photograph lives in virtual space, since Gates's body is not wet. Like so much Microsoft word-processed text, he has been copied and pasted into the scene, with only one drop of wetness near his navel.

Techno-culture is not alone in its embrace of Gates. *Time* magazine's September 16, 1996 cover features only Gates's face, surrounded by a neon green spiderweb.[4] He is at the web's center, beneath this sensational headline: "Whose Web Will It Be?" Smaller headlines tell readers that "He conquered the computer world. Now he wants the Internet. If Microsoft overwhelms Netscape, Bill Gates could rule the Information Age." Inside, an illustration shows a snarling Gates in full military dress (Ramo 1996: 57). *Wired* magazine's cover story heralds Gates with "Mr. Bill goes Hollywood: Microsoft morphs into a media company."

In *Triumph of the Nerds*, a 1996 PBS television series about the development of the American computer industry, the argument for techno-icons such as Bill Gates, Steve Jobs, and others is framed in its title. *Time* magazine's cover indicates that at least some Americans are not looking to Gates for friendship, but for leadership and domination. With the whole world listening, this minor god living on a West Coast mountaintop makes pronouncements, creates media events, and controls skittish financial markets. In many ways, the hype surrounding Gates, computer technology, and the Internet determines the kinds of discourse found in cyberspace, for much computer-mediated discourse relies on a rhetoric of domination and power.

OF LAND GRABS, HOMESTEADS, AND DISCOURSE

Real estate metaphors inevitably invite comparisons of value. Based on our real-time experience, where real estate is a finite and definable resource, elite estates necessarily coexist with deplorable ghettos. Both sensibilities work in opposition to each other. In a 1994 Web stream discussion on "mapping out communal cyberspace," just such a debate surfaced. When one participant argued eloquently about the need for a "world coordination system" with "positional addressability" (Layton 1994), many voices tackled that idea with serious questions. "If we create a world coordinate space, we create virtual real estate. Who owns virtual real estate?" answers one opponent (Goldsmith 1994). Another discussant, arguing for the continuation of an "unfixed" system, likens the Internet structure to a series of rooms, with defined entrances and exits that could give users sufficient sense of place, allowing them to identify localities based upon their own particular navigational paths (Wak 1994). Finally, another commentator argued for the possibility of having both fixed coordinates in cyberspace as well as the existence of "gates" which would allow nongeometric slippage between one place and another. Within this framework, issues of security and access as well as how to represent these realities, become inevitable questions: "If someone isn't supposed to see something, do they notice a gap where it should be, or is the gap filled by something else?" (Holt 1994).

But if the Internet is truly spatially limitless, then the battle for areas of value within cyberspace may not exist within the bordering of landscapes, but within the bracketing of ideas. Shifting the framework for viewing the Internet from real estate to discourse, from parcels of "land" to accumulations of "texts," may serve us better in anticipating how gender and ethnicity can be ghettoized.

Like so many advertisements touting the capacity of hard-drive memory, cyberphilosophers tout the Internet as the ultimate egalitarian gathering place, a nostalgic space where more direct democracy can be practiced. In *The Electronic Word: Democracy, Technology, and the Arts*, Richard Lanham (1993) begins his discussion of a technologized culture with the premise that electronic expression has created a newly democratized society. Along with Lanham's work, the texts of cyberphilosophers such as Nicholas Negroponte, Jay David Bolter, and George Landow have become a kind of canon,[5] formed after Marshall McLuhan's vision of a global village. They praise computer communication technology and hypertextual discourse as revolutionary forces that will affect humankind's modernist relationship with politics and culture, but none of these men investigates this revolution in terms of race, gender, or class. Charles Ess (1994), in one of Landow's texts, endorses the democratization claim made on behalf of hypertext and other computer-mediated discourse, but qualifies it by stating that discourse must be free from social coercion, including the "subtle but powerful cues of hierarchy, status, gender, and so on" (p. 252).

Ironically, the indefinite terrain of the Internet should serve as an ideal arena in which to absorb the equally variable markers of "race." Physical differences among people, history shows, have been used to mark status and caste, invariably to the pointed advantage of one group over another. Over time, far beyond their physical significance, racial characterizations have, as Henry Louis Gates identified it, "a trope of ultimate, irreducible difference between cultures, linguistic groups, or adherents of specific belief systems which—more often than not—also have fundamentally opposed economic interests" (1986: 5).

If "race" as a linguistic construction exists solely to signify difference, the accumulation of literature around this idea must support such a construction. Looking to our own ambivalent traditions in American literature, novelist Toni Morrison finds ample evidence that traditional canonical constructions of great works have built themselves around the invisible yet omnipresent character of the "other." Where one culture is dominant in discourse, others that may exist are silenced, functioning outside the main group for sound and stature. This imposed silence of the margins, of voices outside the dominant group, not only makes such groups invisible, but makes the issue of "difference" seem irrelevant in a potentially unresolved way. Thus, in criticizing the lack of critical discussions about how ethnicity has been suppressed in American literature, Morrison (1992: 5) makes an observation that could easily be applied to discourse structures as they might be established in cyberspace: "The situation is aggravated by the tremor that breaks into discourse on race. . . . It is further complicated by the fact that the habit of ignoring race is understood to be a graceful, even generous, liberal gesture." For adult discourse, she adds, full explorations of this difference is essential, for it breaks the tyranny of a canon of ideas that excludes other cultural participants.

But in cyberspace, where physical appearances are unseen (for the moment) and identities can be cloaked, are such considerations even necessary? Ostensibly, if all voices have comparable access to the Internet and the ability to "homestead" a place in cyberspace continues to be as easy as setting up a discussion group or putting up a Web site, the aggregate "space" of the Internet may indeed be an ideal site for what Mary Louise Pratt (1991) characterizes as a "contact zone."

CONTACT ZONE IN CYBERSPACE: ISSUES AND CHALLENGES

In her work with post-colonial literatures, Pratt describes the interaction between indigenous cultures and conquering ones as creating a space for a collision of ideas. Her view of these areas as "social spaces" where cultures "meet, clash, and grapple with each other" (1991: 33) allows a framework for her to describe the continuing and sometimes contentious exchanges in a classroom setting where students and teachers may differ on their views of the world.

However, extending this idea to cyberspace has some appeal, particularly if "fixed space" notions and characterizations of the Internet are rejected. Discussion groups, especially those with lively and dramatic exchanges, perhaps represent what it means to be in a discursive contact zone. And, although Pratt does not develop any stages of such an exchange, she does assert that along with the conflict, there are the "joys" of the contact zone possible, which emerge from "shared understandings, knowledges, claims on the world" (p. 40). Protecting this ideal, though, will be neither easy nor automatic in cyberspace, for it calls upon competing cultures to learn how to negotiate new power relationships through the collision of language and ideas. In the outer world, the dominant culture has the potential to supplant traditional outgroups through such strategies as fostering a deliberate disruption of narratives and forcing a "silence of the margins" through intimidation and lack of civility. Such strategies show up on the Internet also.

Opportunities for computer-mediated communication (CMC) that are free from social coercion are, of course, available on the Internet; it is this feature that makes the Web, at least in some ways, a serpentine, postmodern response to modernism's linear, hierarchical discourse. However, the Internet itself is established on a hierarchy of protocols and codes, with much of its communication overseen by webmasters, dungeon masters, listowners of electronic discussions, and hackers. Often, hierarchy in computer-mediated communication is established by those who control the topics available for discussion. Control in an electronic discussion "is gained by posting inflammatory and emotional messages, by 'misunderstanding' previous messages and construing them to conform to other topics, and by overloading the group with multiple postings about off-topic subjects" (Lambiase 1996: 2). Polemic language and "flaming," especially multiple postings containing this kind of discourse, discourage the presentation of other viewpoints. These tactics of a few powerful language users foil any chance for an egalitarian discussion of issues, because other members retreat in silence, withdraw from the group, or refrain from posting on unpopular or trivialized topics. In her studies of gender and computer-mediated communication, Susan Herring (1993, 1996) has found that a few male members often dominate electronic discussions "in terms of amount of talk, and rhetorically, through self-promotional and adversarial strategies" (1993: 10) and that women are censored when their contributions are ignored or belittled.

FROM DISCOURSE TO MEDIA REPRESENTATIONS

As a medium for mass communication, the Internet is unlike any other existing one, although media practitioners and visionaries have foreseen its evolution. McLuhan's admonition that "the medium is the message" rings with bold clarity today, as Internet purveyors experiment with ways to create, send, and receive messages in packaging compatible with the multimedia dimensions of this space. Theorist Walter Ong characterized all electronic media as forming the basis of a communication age of "secondary orality," maintaining that the "basic orality of language is permanent." He also held that orality was reflected through all other media, which in turn were "built upon the pre-literate oral days of early history" (as quoted in Gronbeck et al. 1991: 16).

Ong's vision of media and human communication was broad and evolutionary, combining a concept of culture that was more bound by time than space, and reflecting a social experience that was "simultaneously individualized, yet collectivized" (1981: 20–21). Breaking from traditional categories and patterns of definition presages a necessary transition from solely picturing the Internet as so much product to be partitioned out among its conquerors. Such a revolutionary view of reordering not only of what we know but of how we know is reminiscent of humanities scholar Michel Foucault's call for an archeology of knowledge that defines "discourses in their specificity instead of what precedes them, surrounds them, or follows them" (1971: 138). Much like the indeterminant, unfixed domain of the Internet, knowledge spaces can exist on the strength of their own self-determinant roles.

Such a flexible view of culture and media seems imminently transferable to the Internet, as long as its proponents and advocates are willing to reformulate the formula. QVC Chairman Barry Diller once chided media moguls for ascribing to limited visions and clinging to archaic models, stating that it was time "to do the tough conceptual work of coming up with a new discipline, a new vocabulary, a new paradigm for what is emerging" (1995: 83).

CASE STUDY: ONLINE IN THE CONTACT ZONE

An ethnographic study of a student electronic discussion at the University of North Texas was conducted to compare rhetorical strategies with these earlier studies of academic and public discussions. On the forty-three junior-, senior-, and graduate-level journalism students who participated in the discussion, only one had ever participated in an asynchronous electronic discussion, and only a few others had experience exploring the Web and/ or on-line chat rooms. The course itself, microcomputer applications for journalism, served as the discussion's designated topic; no other rules for participation were established. Although one of this chapter's authors, Lambiase, was the course instructor, she participated in the discussion by forwarding course-related materials and posting assignments but did not serve as moderator. Any message addressed to the group was immediately sent electronically to all members, with no screening.

Like the patterns charted for the academic and public electronic discussions, male students participated more than females did, even though thirty-three women and ten men were enrolled in the journalism course and the discussion. In the course were five African-American women, two Hispanic-American women, a Japanese-American man, and an Asian-American woman. Of the 216 messages posted by students to the discussion in eleven and a half weeks during the fall of 1996, 121 were posted by men and 95 by women. So while men made up only 23 percent of the class, they posted 56 percent of the messages.[6] Unlike broader studies in which it is sometimes difficult to track gender and exact numbers of participants, this ethnographic study provides more exact data. The high male participation rate cannot be explained by the usual reason that more men are online than women, because in this one part of cyberspace for one semester, women were in the majority.[7] Every student had access to a computer during required laboratory times, and all were required to scan their e-mail directories in order to collect assignments and other course information, ensuring that students participated minimally as "lurkers." At the end of the semester, however, students had vastly different perceptions of the discussion, depending on whether they felt comfortable with the topics discussed and with the tone of the discourse itself.

In the first few days, students posted short messages of trivial and social nature. One woman wrote, "Hey, this e:mail thing is pretty fun once you get the hang of it. Never mind that I'm neglecting my social life—I do that anyway."[8] Also included in her message was a suggestion for the group's name. Within two weeks of the beginning of the electronic discussion, a verbal skirmish erupted over what the group should be called. The act of naming, of course, is an act of power, of defining, of dividing, and many students—male and female—considered the task seriously, while others played with ideas. Several suggestions were made and considered, but when one woman offered "Queen Kitties" as a possibility, four of the 10 men enrolled in the course objected. "Okay, you finally moved me to act," wrote one male student. "I would like to go on record as opposing the name Queen Kitties. No offense. Now I'll go back to lurking." Another male student's post, with the subject line "Nate, preach on!!" first commends a student's long message about religion and computers, and then comments on the name controversy: "Amen brother!! Keep on preaching the gospel!! P.S. Queen Kitties does nothing for me. Back to the shadows . . ."

The third objection is the longest and most intense:

OH YES! "QUEEN KITTIES?" GIVE ME A BREAK! WHAT ABOUT THE MEN IN OUR GROUP? DON'T YOU THINK THERE IS A LITTLE BIT OF SEXISM OUT THERE? A NAME IS JUST A NAME! WE ARE ALL EQUAL & THERE SHOULD BE A NAME WE ALL CAN AGREE ON! If I have any suggestions, I will let you know.

The fourth male's objection is milder in tone, but similar in content: "Sorry to disappoint, and nobody out here probably even knows who I am, but Queen Kittles [sic] bites . . . [It] makes us sound like we're a bunch of panzies." This student posted another message that day, writing, "If this turns into Queen Kittles . . . I quit." A fifth male supported the idea, which turned out to be a joke between him and the woman who suggested it in the first place. She eventually sent a message to the group, once objections became heated, explaining that the suggestion had been intended as a joke.

During the name controversy, another woman forwarded a list of condom jokes. In response, the male who posted the most outraged objection during the name controversy quickly responded with his own condom jokes, which were much more sexually explicit and violent in nature. Several other students, women and men, objected to the content of the second message, with one writing, "Let us keep our sexual perversions out of the list serve." Another asked, "Jacque [Lambiase], are you here?" The instructor responded briefly, "I'm here, in this space,"[9] and made the following assignment a few days later for all students to consider: "Write at least five guidelines for an electronic discussion, in order to ensure that the group provides an egalitarian forum for the exchange of ideas."

Many of the guidelines recommended protocols that kept messages short, polite, and focused on journalism topics. Several women wrote, "No sexist messages" as a guideline, even though the only member of the discussion to bring up sexism had been a male. Some students wanted warnings if offensive material might be included in a message, and one student wrote, "We shouldn't allow these initial incidents to result in too much censorship." A few offered advice for students who could not determine whether content would be appropriate, such as: "A person might feel more willing to 'talk' via the computer, but the tone should be that of a discussion in the classroom," and "If you wouldn't blurt it out in a classroom setting, don't send it via bytes." Other students' guidelines included:

1. "As journalism majors, we of all people should know the power of the 'written' word, that it can take on a life of its own and come back to haunt you."

2. "Everyone on the discussion group is a human being and must be treated with respect" and "Try to be polite."

3. "Remember that you are speaking to a number of different people. What may not be offensive to you, may be offensive to someone else. While you do have a right to be heard, try to keep the potentially offensive stuff to a minimum. And then, if you do offend someone, be sensitive to their reaction."

4. "It's a good idea not to jump in on a discussion and immediately be the dominant presence."

Students discussed the guidelines among themselves, and some posted their suggestions online.

For a few weeks, there were no flame wars among discussion participants, until a male student posted a long message about Texans being poor drivers during icy weather. "Some stupid broad (I don't care if it's politically correct or not . . . I ain't) was STILL driving 25 mph . . . and we were a mile removed from the nearest bridge . . . or ice patch . . . or ice cube!" That message might have been attacked as offensive and sexist, if another message had not followed it, written by the same male who had most vehemently objected to "Queen Kitties" and who had shocked so many with his condom jokes. This message offended many students:

WARNING: The following message may be offensive for many WOMEN, PEOPLE OVER 60, ORIENTALS, and some OKLAHOMANS! . . . To ALL WOMEN out there . . . most of you have to learn to drive. . . . We men want you all to be safe & alive so that we can enjoy the essence of your beauty . . . Old people have no control over a sophisticated vehicle such as the car. . . . ORIENTALS, Welcome to the United States; not only do you have to learn English, but also the rules of the road. You are NOT above the law. . . . I want everyone above to know this is CONSTRUCTIVE criticism and not DESTRUCTIVE criticism.

After the above messages and others, this male student was flamed within the electronic discussion, but never confronted by others in class. He was a quiet student who participated minimally face to face, yet he posted more than two dozen messages online, a higher number than any other student.

In effect, the electronic discussion uncloaked his internal belief system and revealed that his ethos in each environment—virtual and real—was in conflict.

At the semester's end, students were asked to estimate the number of messages they had posted messages, among these choices: none, 1–5, 6–10, 11–20, more than twenty. Three of the ten men enrolled in the course said they posted 11–20 messages; only one women reported she had posted 11–20 messages (no one reported that he or she had posted more than twenty messages). Each male student participated at least once; sixteen of thirty-three female students never posted a message to the group, although several did write that they checked their messages and followed the discussion. Students also commented on their comfort level in the electronic environment and on limits to their participation. Both male and female students listed time and choice of topics as barriers to their participation; one woman mentioned that "fear of stalking" had limited her participation. Another female student wrote that she "realized it only created an opportunity for faceless people to judge and/or make fun of me." She also cited "inability to read body language of 'listener,' which made it difficult to set a 'tone,' " as a barrier to her participation. One female student, the only African-American woman out of five in the course to post any messages, determined that "the environment was hostile when it should be helpful. . . . I would not have felt comfortable posting an issue of concern of mine because I don't need the negativity nor does anyone." One woman claimed that she felt "relatively comfortable" as a participant and that she "liked controversy," but wrote "I'm cautious not to step on anyone's toes. I didn't want to start an argument."

Many women have been socially conditioned to avoid interpersonal conflict, while men have been conditioned to enjoy conflict as a game (Ong 1981), so some women may feel uncomfortable with the public discourse of an electronic discussion, much of which is predicated on conflict. All of the power moves—flaming, flooding the group with messages, and manipulating topics—by a few participants diminished the effectiveness of the forum, and for many, especially women, destroyed that forum. One female graduate student expressed her concerns about "nasty" discourse in cyberspace, asking, "Is it because we feel free in cyberspace to express aspects of ourselves that we feel need to be hidden in the everyday world?" She continued:

Normally, I would consider it good for people to express all aspects of themselves. However, why is so much expression in cyberspace sex related, often very demeaning to women? Ask any woman who has ever been in a chat room, and she'll tell you what kinds of propositions she gets from men. Never in real life have I, or anyone I've known, had men say the things to us that they say in cyberspace.

OF CLOAKING, CHAOS, AND LIBERATION

On a bulletin board dedicated to exchanging technical computer information, a lone voice illogically interjects a stream of vitriolic, racist text. On another bulletin board specifically designed to discuss remedies for discrimination, a cyberauthor posts an announcement about a peaceful march through several states to commemorate pathways of the Underground Railroad. To this, another voice angrily complains from a cybervoid about people who are "marching around everywhere" who should get jobs instead.

Informed observers and anecdotal evidence note an increasingly prominent display of racist and sexist talk inspired by the new electronic media. Warning of the Internet's "two faces," *The Christian Science Monitor* points out that joining an already alarming problem of sexual harassment towards women is a noticeable growth of bigoted language and ethnic slurs via the Net (1997: 20).

In a related but more personalized *Newsweek* account, Angela Bouwmsa shares her mother's startling experience on the Internet where one of her electronic friends revealed his deep-seated racism toward African-Americans. "The man, relying only on words as clues, assumed my mother was white, someone who would be sympathetic and to whom he could speak freely," she observed (1997: 14).

In her study of journalistic strategies employed in "race" reportage, Carstarphen identifies "cloaking" as a major approach used to mask the presence of diverse ethnic voices within the media. Two aspects, (1) the "absence" of the ethnic other in "significant news coverages," and (2) the concealment of certain behaviors under the cover of "race," particularly characterized this strategy (1993/1994: 202).

Absence of the ethnic other has been a traditional practice embraced by the media to marginalize what did not fit into its defined mainstream where, prior to the mid to late sixties, it was standard practice for majority news organizations to virtually ignore the activities of people of color. However, the rise of civil rights activities brought a new generation of articulate and bold spokespersons, as well as dramatic visual encounters between these passionate advocates and their opponents, creating news values that could not be ignored.

But while race since then has become more useful to overtly mark difference, that usage only heightened the concealment of ethnic identifiers for those subjects of Anglo or European descent. Only in stories purporting to examine trends or broad issues were "whites" uncloaked, but not by ethnic identifiers, such as German, Italian, Swedish, or other more specific markers. Instead, "white" became the blanket of concealment that linked varied Anglo and European ethnicities within a united front, in contradistinction to their darker others: how whites earn higher incomes than blacks or browns, or how children of color perform less well on standardized tests than white children. Without offering reasons that such inequities exist, current media unwittingly filter data through the lenses of social expectation and journalistic traditions, cloaking many of society's ills under the blanket of race.

However, in cyberspace, where subjects "self-report" through their participation in e-mail, bulletin boards, and list-serv forums, ostensibly everyone can be hidden under the equalizing influence of technology. Early signs are emerging, though, that cloaking and uncloaking strategies will parallel the social imperatives of the outernet.

Exchanges among the students in Lambiase's class case study further illustrate how these cloaking strategies become transferred to the Internet. On the one hand, voices from ethnic others are silenced in the face of a dominant voice. (Interestingly, such dominance does not have to be asserted by a clear physical majority; one shrill voice with the ability to shotgun multiple messages quickly and loudly into the discourse arena can usurp power.) Secondly, the individuality of the ethnic other can be hidden under the weight of blanket assertions that characterize all members of the group as holding some uncomplimentary trait. Extending such silencing techniques to women, too, also has its chilling effects.

However, just as an electronic discussion among students can reveal sexist and racist thoughts that would otherwise be hidden, so too can electronic discourse uncloak the suppressed narratives of marginalized groups and reveal dangerous rhetoric so that it may be attacked. Techno-culture cannot tell just one story filled with hype and dreams of egalitarianism, constructed through the looking glass of a computer screen in which pixels provide virtual reality and hyper-resolution. And while it may appear to match the hype in its promise of egalitarianism, computer-mediated communication reveals itself to be as arbitrary and hierarchical as what Alice found on the other side of her own looking glass.

CONCLUSION: PROMISES AND PITFALLS

The future of the Internet, and of its promise as a barrier-free medium, must rest on how we characterize its essential nature. Popular media offer little or no solace, with their continuing focus on ownership, economics, and battle. There is also little or no challenge to their presupposition that all experts have only one color and usually one gender. Media representations in the outer world should be challenged to show us non-Gatesian figures of authority on cyberspace, to allow for diversity of opinion, perspective, and discursive canon. But if, indeed, there are millions of voices now and more in the near future who will participate in the cyberspace life, the aggregate experiences of this mass must have weight. Clearly a crucial aspect of even this prospect is to provide—aggressively and without apology—access for diverse constituents within the outer world, into the amorphous new universe of cyberspace.

NOTES

1. Kenneth Burke's dramatistic pentad conceives of discourse as involving five key elements: act, scene, agent, agency, and purpose. He first offered this view in his 1945 text, *A Grammar of Motives*, as a way of analyzing how language describes motives.

2. In the tradition of Henry Louis Gates, Jr. (1986) and other scholars, "race" is used within quotation marks to indicate the use of this term as a socially constructed concept, as opposed to a factual representation.

3. Wired's cover may be viewed at: www.wired.com/wired/4.06/index.html

4. This cover may be viewed at *Time's* Web site at: pathfinder.com/@@SSFm@g YAOZCNUIq5/time/magazine/domestic/covers/960916.covbus.jpg

5. Lanham (1993), Negroponte (1995), Bolter (1991), and Landow (1992) all cite one another and build one another's reputations as authorities on electronic media. In effect, they have created a canon of their own work, much like Jane Tompkins's observations about Nathaniel Hawthorne's reputation being a product more of "political and social processes" than of "essential greatness" (1985: 4). She writes that the "literary works that now make up the canon do so because the groups that have an investment in them are culturally the most influential" (p. 5).

6. Males also participated more in a junior-level college writing class taught by Lambiase in fall 1995 at University of Texas-Arlington. Students were invited to join an electronic discussion, but it was not a requirement. Of the twenty-five students enrolled in the course, eighteen were women and seven were men; of those, five women and three men chose to subscribe to the group. Three female students posted sixteen messages and three males posted twenty-two.

7. Figures for those having Internet access vary; women are said to make up from 25 percent to 40 percent of Internet users, with gender equity expected some time in the next few years. A Nielsen Media Research survey, using males as the measure, reports that 67 percent of longtime Internet users are male (those users prior to August 1995), while 60 percent of new users are male. The same survey said that from 22 percent to 24 percent of people ages sixteen and older had Internet access (*PC Magazine*, Oct. 8 1996: 41).

8. Original spelling and punctuation for e-mail messages are retained.

9. The instructor, as ethnographer, tried to retain as much distance from the content of messages as possible, except in this instance when a student posted a message to the group seeking a response.

REFERENCES

Andrews, E. L. 1993. Will electronic highway be well traveled? *The Dallas Morning News* (October 17). C3.

Bolter, J. D. 1991. *Writing Space: The Computer, Hypertext, and the History of Writing*. Hillsdale, N.J.: Lawrence Erlbaum.

Bouwsma, A. 1997. Showing his true colors. *Newsweek* (February 24):14–15.

Carstarphen, M. G. 1993/1994. A discourse analysis of "race," rhetoric and media: Content and concepts in *The Dallas Morning News*. Doctoral dissertation, Texas Woman's University, 1993. *Dissertation Abstracts International, 54/10*, 3727.

Coupland, D. 1995. *Microserfs*. New York: Regan Books.

Diller, B. 1995. Don't repackage—redefine. *Wired* 3 (February):82–84.

Ess, C. 1994. The political computer: Hypertext, democracy, and Habermas. In G. Landow, ed. *Hyper/Text/Theory*. Baltimore: Johns Hopkins University Press, pp. 225–67.

Foucault, M. 1971. *The Archaeology of Knowledge and the Discourse on Language*. A. M. S. Smith, trans. New York: Pantheon.

Gates, H. L., Jr. 1986. *"Race," Writing and Difference*. Chicago: Chicago University Press.

Gau, J., and S. Segaller, producers. 1996. *The Triumph of the Nerds*. Washington, D.C.: Public Broadcasting Service and Oregon Public Broadcasting.

Goldsmith, K. June 13, 1994. Mapping out communal cyberspace. Electronic communication.

Gronbeck, B. E., T. J. Farrell, and P. A. Soukup, eds. 1991. *Media Consciousness, and Culture: Explorations of Walter Ong's Thought*. Newbury Park, Calif.: Sage.

Haraway, D. 1991. *Simians, Cyborgs, and Women: The Reinvention of Nature*. New York: Routledge.

Herring, S. 1993. Gender and democracy in computer-mediated communication. *Electronic Journal of Communication 3* (2).

———1996. *Who's Got the Floor in Computer-Mediated Conversation?* Paper presented at the International Pragmatic Association conference, Mexico City, July 8.

Holt, C. June 13, 1994. Mapping out communal cyberspace. Electronic communication.

Kellner, D. 1995. *Media Culture*. New York: Routledge.

Lambiase, J. J. 1996. *Hanging by a Thread: Topic Development and Death in an Electronic Discussion of the Oklahoma Bombing*. Paper presented at the International Pragmatics Association conference, Mexico City, July 8.

Landow, G. P. 1992. *Hypertext: The Convergence of Contemporary Critical Theory and Technology*. Baltimore: Johns Hopkins University Press.

Lanham, R. 1993. *The Electronic Word: Democracy, Technology, and the Arts*. Chicago: University of Chicago.

Layton, R. June 14, 1994. Mapping out Communal cyberspace. Electronic communication.

McLuhan, M. 1964. *Understanding Media: The Extensions of Man*. New York: Signet Books.

Morrison, T. 1992. *Playing in the Dark: Whiteness and the Literary Imagination*. Cambridge, Mass.: Harvard University Press.

Mr. Bill goes Hollywood. 1996. *Wired* 4 (6): cover.

Negroponte, N. 1995. *Being Digital*. New York: Knopf.

Ong, W. J. 1981. *Fighting for Life: Contest, Sexuality, and Consciousness*. Ithaca, N.Y.: Cornell University Press.

Pratt, M. L. 1991. Arts of the Contact Zone. *Profession 1991* 33–40.

Pryse, M. and H. Spillers. 1985. *Conjuring: Black Women, Fiction, and Literary Tradition.* Bloomington, Ind.: Indiana University Press.

Ramo, J. C. 1996. Winner take all. *Time 148* (13):56–64.

The net's two faces. 1997. *The Christian Science Monitor* (February 25):20.

Tompkins, J. 1985. *The Cultural Work of American Fiction, 1790–1860.* New York: Oxford University.

Wak, M. June 13, 1994. Mapping out communal cyberspace. Electronic communication.

9

Equity and Access to Computer Technology for Grades K–12

Paulette Robinson

Despite government efforts, access to computer technology in kindergarten through twelfth grade (K-12) continues to be unequal for minorities and the poor. This chapter discusses access in terms of three areas: 1) facilities, equipment and software; 2) teacher and student computer use; and 3) changes in social knowledge construction.

INTRODUCTION

The unequal access to quality K-12 education for minorities and the poor continues to surface in our country. Access becomes an even more pressing issue when the necessity for proficiency in the use of computers is thrown into the mix. M. S. Radlick has noted: "It is the responsibility of schools to prepare today's students for life in the 21st century. All students who graduate from our schools must be prepared to access, analyze, apply and communicate information effectively so that they can be successful, contributing members of the changing, information-based, global society in which we are now living" (Radlick 1993: 1).

The gap in access to technology for minorities and the poor, while improving in some areas, continues to widen overall. When the lack of minority participation in technology is examined, several access factors emerge: poverty and the overrepresentation of minorities in the ranks of the poor, lack of role models, the use of technology predominantly at the remedial drill-and-practice level, fear of technology by parents who see technology replacing them at work, de facto segregation, and an unconscious stereotyping of the abilities of minorities (Campbell 1984). These factors uncovered by P. B. Campbell in her 1984 investigation are still true today.

Equity and access to computer technology will be discussed from three perspectives: 1) facilities, equipment and software; 2) teacher and student computer use; and 3) changes in social knowledge construction. Each level is more difficult to measure because it is a more implicit access to computers. Children without sufficient access to all of these resources, regardless of their race or socioeconomic status, will find it impossible to play a role in our technological world.

FACILITIES, EQUIPMENT AND SOFTWARE

If schools cannot provide students with sufficient technological support or facilities for instruction and services, they may not be providing even roughly equal opportunity for all students to learn. This is particularly true in the central cities and in schools that serve high percentages of minority and poor students. (Government Accounting Office 1995: 15)

Most technology studies describe the facilities, the ratio of students to computers, the number of network or computer coordinators, the capabilities of the school buildings, and other relevant factors. These physical characteristics are easy to count and compare. However, it has only been within the last decade that national reports to establish baseline data have occurred.

The Government Accounting Office (GAO) commissioned a study to determine if the nation's schools were equipped for the educational needs of the twenty-first century. *School Facilities: America's Schools Not Designed or Equipped for the 21st Century* was released April 4, 1995. As the title implies, the GAO reported that schools in America are not able to meet the challenges of future education reform and technology. While inadequate facilities exist across the country, the worst conditions can be found for inner-city minority students, who make up more than one-half of the students in the inner-city schools (GAO 1996: 4).

Not all students have equal access to facilities that can support education into the 21st century, even those attending school in the same district. Overall, schools in central cities and schools with a 50 percent or more minority population were more likely to have more insufficient technology elements and a greater number of unsatisfactory environmental conditions—particularly lighting and physical security—than other schools. (GAO 1995: 3)

Table 9.1
Percentage of Minorities in K–12 Schools and Computer Access in New York State, 1993

Percentage Minority in School	Ratio of Students to Old Micros	Ratio of Students to New Micros	Ratio of Students to CD-ROMs	Percentage of Students Using Computers	Percentage of Teachers Using Computers
0-20	16.1 to 1	40.0 to 1	686 to 1	76.2	58.6
21-40	19.4 to 1	44.4 to 1	952 to 1	75.7	52.5
41-60	22.2 to 1	49.4 to 1	1052 to 1	68.3	43.1
61-80	25.8 to 1	43.1 to 1	959 to 1	68.8	42.3
81-100	30.3 to 1	70.2 to 1	1715 to 1	57.0	25.6

Source: Radlick, M. S. 1993. *Technology in New York State Public Schools: What Schools Have and How They Are Using It.* Albany, N.Y.: New York State Department of Education.

The funding picture to address inequalities in inner cities, in light of federal cutbacks, is bleak. The lack of a tax base to raise funds in low income areas leaves schools in inner cities unable to keep up (Kozol 1991; Wilson 1987).

It is not unusual for property-rich school districts to have much more diverse and much more advanced technology systems for learning, ranging from complete elementary school computer labs with the best software available to interactive foreign language labs. The property tax disparity alone will almost assure that the property-rich school district will have more and better in the way of learning technology for its students. (Swan 1995: 203)

In New York, the overall ratio of students to computers in 1993 was 24:1. The disparity in minority access was glaring (see Table 9.1).

The issue of access and inadequate computers is exacerbated by computers that do not work.

Escondito [an affluent section of the Palo Alto School District] has one computer for every 9 students; Menlo Oaks [in economically depressed East Palo Alto School District], one per 14 students. These numbers are impressive numbers compared with the national average of one computer in 18. But counting only usable computers—those in working order that faculty members can operate—Escondido holds at 9, but Menlo Oaks' ratio shoots up to one computer for every 60 students. (Piller 1992: 222)

The effective location for computers in the schools is an ongoing debate between a computer lab and the individual classroom. In a perfect world, all students would have a computer at their desks in the classroom. Unfortunately, we do not live in a perfect world. Exactly one-half of the computers used for instruction in schools are located in computer labs (Becker 1994: Table 1.4).

However, computer labs in economically depressed inner cities often face conditions where it is difficult to use the computers.

Magdalena Fittoria, director of bilingual education for the [East Palo Alto] district comments on her experience [with the computer lab], "Most of the lab's ten Macintoshes are broken. The working units are not used for any organized class activity, although a computer club sometimes meets after school for word processing and drawing. Budget cuts in East Palo Alto forced the school's computer teacher into a regular math-science job. The lab primarily serves as a detention center. (Piller 1992: 221)

Another location for computers is the classroom where the students spend the bulk of their instruction time. Most schools do not have the capability of connecting computers in their classrooms (GAO 1995). The percentages of classrooms with computers in elementary, middle and high schools were 41, 28, and 31, respectively (Becker 1994: Table 1.4). While some teachers have access to a few computers in their classroom, it does not appear to be sufficient for teachers to have students use them there (Becker 1994: 18).

Access to technology in school is particularly important in light of the increasing disparities in technology access outside of school. Families that can afford to purchase computers are giving their children an educational advantage, through supplementary learning activities and additional opportunities to do school work at home. (Office of Technology Assessment 1995: 10)

Table 9.2 displays the percentage of students with home computers based on family income and on ethnicity.

It is clear that family income and education are important factors in home computer access. The most telling disparity in home computer access is based on income. When race is considered in the statistics, white students have almost three times as much access to home computers as a group. The census figures in Table 9.2 do not show home computer access in terms of racial income groupings. Given the effects of income on home computer

Table 9.2
Percentage of Students with Access to and Use of Home Computers

Family Income	Total Access	Total Use	White Access	White Use	Black Access	Black Use	Hispanic Access	Hispanic Use
less than $20,000	9.2	5.6						
$20,000 - $29,999	18.5	11.3						
$30,000 - $39,999	26.5	16.9						
$40,000 - $49,999	35.2	22.9						
$50,000 - $74,999	47.3	31.6						
$75,000 0r more	62.8	42.4						
Education Level								
All students	36.1	26.5	43.3	32.2	16.1	10.8	15.2	10.3
Preprimary	29.6	15.3	35.8	19.0	12.3	4.1	11.7	5.6
First-Eighth	31.9	24.3	39.6	30.8	13.1	8.9	12.1	7.4
Ninth-Twelfth	37.2	28.1	46.2	35.1	14.6	10.3	14.4	9.6
Undergraduate	44.7	32.4	49.4	35.5	27.0	19.1	27.3	21.9
Graduate	60.4	51.8	61.4	52.8	56.7	47.6	56.3	52.2

Sources: Based on U.S. Department of Commerce, Bureau of Census, Current Population Survey, October 1993; NCES 1995 Digest of Educational Statistics.

access, the percentages for low-income blacks and Hispanics would no doubt reveal lower home computer access for these groups.

N. Fulford noted, "In order for schools to use technology appropriately and effectively to enhance the curriculum, they need to have access to telecommunications systems and information technologies through electronic networks" (Fulford 1994: 29). Networks require specialized equipment and connections that all add to a school's budget. Since networks provide an advanced method of connecting schools and enabling them to share information sources worldwide, they are becoming an important part of extending resources to schools. Because of the Internet's growing importance in the educational process, equity of access is a growing concern.

The Office of Education Research and Improvement in the U.S. Department of Education commissioned the *Advanced Telecommunications in U.S. Public Elementary and Secondary Schools E.D. TABS Report* in 1994 and 1995 (National Center for Education Statistics 1996). These two reports provide baseline data on the status of advanced telecommunications in public elementary and secondary schools. While the 1994 report did not include data with minority or poverty as variables, the 1995 report included data based on the percentage of minority enrollment and low socioeconomic status (SES) enrollments as measured by the percentage of students eligible for free or reduced-priced lunches.

The statistics reported from the *Advanced Telecommunications* report (1996) in this chapter will focus on minorities and students eligible for free lunch enrollment. These two categories are particularly revealing in terms of equity of access to computer technology. The report also provides statistics based on instructional level (elementary or secondary), size of enrollment, metropolitan size, and geographic region.

Table 9.3 shows gaps between schools with more minorities and SES enrollments. However, the data do not break down the computers as old, new, working, or inoperable. This information would provide a clearer picture of the number of computers capable of Internet access and would be more descriptive of any disparities.

Barriers continue to exist for schools that want to connect to the Internet. The major barriers to Internet access were funds not specifically allocated for telecommunications (60%), too few telecommunications access points in the building (56%), telecommunications equipment not easily accessible (44%), telecommunications links not easily accessible (43%), and lack of or poor equipment (42%) (NCES 1996). All of these barriers are common in schools with high minority and low-socioeconomic enrollments.

Equipment and the ability to connect via networks are only one part of the capital expenses for schools that need to enter the Computer Age. The choice of appropriate software is essential. The hardware available in schools often limits the software choices many schools can make. Software

Table 9.3
Internet Access

Enrollment	Students with Internet Access (percentage)	Instructional Rooms with Internet Access (percentage)	Mean Number of Computers	Percentage of Computers Connected to the Internet
< 6% minorities	50	10	60	15
50% or more minorities	40	5	80	8
< 11% SES	62	9	77	15
71% or more SES	31	5	65	10

Source: National Center for Education Statistics. 1996. *Advanced Telecommunications in U.S. Public Elementary and Secondary Schools, 1995.* Washington, D.C.: U.S. Department of Education.

choices form the boundaries of computer use for teachers and students. These choices will direct the type of thinking skills that can be developed. Since the cost of software has become astronomical, schoolwide planning that includes all teachers is critical for effective use of school resources.

Inner-city instruction is often plagued with the assumption that the poor and minorities lack the basics, and these basics must be mastered before moving on to higher-level thinking skills (Kozol 1991; Piller 1992). As a result of these assumptions, computers are most often used for drill-and-practice in the inner-city schools and to provide rich higher-order learning environments for more affluent schools (Kozol 1991; Piller 1992; Becker 1985, 1992, 1994).

Current educational software can provide rich learning environments for schools. It takes resources training, support, and clear instructional goals to effectively integrate software into the curriculum. Unfortunately, teachers often do not have the time or the skills to evaluate software. Software vendors often do not provide sample lesson plans or examples of how to use the software in their instructional goals. Without this basic support, the integration of computers into schools will be an uphill battle. "The critical questions about equality are about equal access to effective uses of technologies" (Becker 1992: 17).

TEACHER USE

Teachers are essential to effective implementation of computers or any change in the daily activities of students (Cuban 1986; Sarasan 1982). Data in Table 9.1 indicate the percentage of teachers using computers declined in New York as the percentage of minority enrollment increased. Only 25.6% of teachers in schools with 81% to 100% minority enrollments used computers. This is in comparison to 58.6% of teachers who used computers in schools with 20% or less minority enrollments.

National studies providing data on teacher computer use do not provide a very accurate picture of the extent of use. The 1992 International Association Evaluation of Education Attainment (IEA) survey, administered to principals and school-level computer coordinators, defined a "computer-using teacher" as a teacher who "has had a class use computers at least several times during the year" (Becker 1994: Table 4.6). The IEA study in 1992 also asked fifth grade elementary teachers and eighth and eleventh grade English teachers to complete questionnaires about their patterns of computer use. "The only teachers excluded from the definition of 'computer user' were those who never required computer work and for whom students never or rarely used computers during class" (Becker 1994: Table 4.7). Teachers were asked to report computer use based on three criteria: 1) 90% or more of their students used computers for their class; 2) each student used computers weekly; and 3) each student who used any of three types of software at least three times. Only 18 % of the fifth grade teachers, 15% of the eighth grade English teachers, and 12% of the eleventh grade English teachers reported using all three criteria (Becker 1994: Table 4.7). The frequency and sophistication of computer use by teachers appears to be low. The definition of computer user is generous and limits a more accurate conclusion about computer use.

In the IEA study, teachers reported the greatest software use for grades five and eight were keyboard skills (27% and 22%, respectively) and spelling checkers (26%) for grade eleven students. The second most prevalent use of software for computer-using teachers were word processing programs for grades five (21%) and eight (21%). Skills use of computer-using teachers were divided between skill practices and games, and word processing and writing. In grade five, 65% of the teachers used the computers for skill practice. For grades eight and eleven, 68% and 74% of the teachers, respectively, used word processing for writing (Becker 1994: Table 4.9).

The IEA study did not investigate teacher computer use with minority and low-SES student enrollments as factors. The questionnaire method is

Table 9.4
Percentage of Teachers and Students Who Have Access and Use the Internet in K–12 Schools

	Teachers' Internet Use			Students' Internet Use		
	Not at all	Small extent	Moderate or large extent	Not at all	Small extent	Moderate or large extent
All public schools	11	61	28	32	47	21
Percentage minority enrollment*						
Less than 6%	21	53	26	36	45	19
6 to 20 %	5	62	33	25	50	25
21 to 49 %	4	74	22	31	46	23
50% or more	12	57	31	36	49	16
Percentage students eligible for free or reduced-price lunches						
Less than 11%	10	57	33	24	47	30
11 to 30%	8	63	29	27	49	24
31 to 70%	16	60	24	41	45	14
71% or more	10	62	28	33	48	19

Source: NCES 1996. Advanced Telecommunications in U.S. Public Elementary and Secondary Schools, 1995.

*Note: Percentages in this table are based on the number of schools having access to Internet—50% of the public schools.

problematic because of self-selection. In the data collected from principal and computer administrator responses, school-wide averages were based on recollection and open to self-selection and inflation biases. Since the teacher survey is self-reporting, it may be biased to reflect a level of use that does not occur.

The Advanced Telecommunications survey measured teacher Internet use nationwide. Data reflected in Table 9.4 are based on the number of schools having Internet access (50% of all public schools). Internet use for the study was reported by either the head administrator or the computer coordinator for the school.

For those schools that have Internet access, teacher use of the Internet is fairly equitable in terms of the percentage of enrollments based on minority or low-SES student enrollments (see Table 9.4). As was discussed earlier, a disparity in Internet access exists in schools with a higher percentage of minority or low-SES student enrollments and therefore, an inequity exists in teacher use also.

Statistics on the use of computers by teachers alone do not indicate how teachers use the computer for instruction. In 1989, the Center for Social Organization of Schools surveyed school computer coordinators and found:

only half as many elementary teachers in poor-district/majority-black schools were judged to be "expert in using instructional software" as in other elementary schools. In addition, at the high school level, only half as many teachers were reported to be "competent at using software for their professional use." The greatest discrepancy in this survey data was that at the elementary level, a truly "exemplary" computer-using teacher [only 3% of all elementary school teachers were found to be "exemplary"] could be found among teachers in poor-district/majority-black schools only one-third as often as in other elementary schools. No data gathered since has refuted these findings. (Becker 1992: 17)

Teacher support throughout the implementation and integration of computers into the curriculum is critical.

Investment in the "people" costs of using technology—the formal training of teachers, the coordination and management of technology resources, the technical support for handling breakdowns and glitches, and the time required for informal and latent growth of professional competence and integration with other curricular goals—has simply not had the same priority as spending on hardware and software. (Becker 1994: 61)

Of the schools that have Internet access (50% of all schools), only 12% have a full-time network administrator. Only 6% of the schools with 50% or more enrollments of minority students and Internet access have a full-time network administrator compared to 15% of the schools with less than 6% minority enrollments. For those schools with access to the Internet with enrollments of 71% or more low-SES students, only 5% have a full-time network administrator as compared to less than 11% of the schools with an enrollment of 11% or less low-SES students (NCES 1996: 16).

According to the 1992 IEA study, school computer coordinators spent on average of 54% of their time in 1992 teaching and supervising students and only 9% of their time training and helping teachers use computers. Even in the schools that have computer coordinators as part of the staff, teachers get little of the coordinators' time or support.

Teachers are the key to the successful use of technology in the schools. Without the time to learn how to use the technology and adapt it to instructional goals, without the technological and peer support, and without adequate resources, teachers are condemned to struggle. They are caught between the social expectations for technology to be an integral part of education and the inadequate resources to meet these expectations. This dilemma is even more pressing in the inner cities, where the socioeconomic gap continues to widen.

STUDENT USE

The number of computers available best determines student use (Becker 1994). Access is available for students both at school and at home. Table 9.1 describes the student computer use in New York in 1993 based on minority enrollments. A significant disparity exists in student computer use as the percentage of minority enrollments increases.

The total amount of computer activity students reported in the IEA study was substantially less than estimates made by computer coordinators: "From the student data, the average [computer] experience works out to be just 24 minutes per week in grade 5, 38 minutes per week in grade 8 and 61 minutes in grade 11—at most one-third of the time estimated from computer coordination reports" (Becker 1994: 35). The data on student use does not describe use in terms of minority students. Given the disparity in computer access and the number of teachers using computers based on the New York study, a viable hypothesis could be made that the time a minority student uses a computer is less than the overall student use.

The use of computers at home reveals a greater difference in use between racial and socioeconomic groups (see Table 9.2). Only one-third as many black (10.8%) or Hispanic (10.3%) students use computers at home compared to white (32.2%) students. The census data didn't correlate race with income, but those minorities who are poor would have even less access to home computers.

How computers are used for instruction is also an important student-use issue. The 1992 IEA survey of fifth, eighth, and eleventh graders and the 1990 NELS88 survey of tenth graders are the only studies available with student-level national data on the use of technology. The information is fairly limited. For grades five and eight, games were the predominant software used ten times or more during the year by the students. Grade eleven students reported using word processors more than games. It is interesting to note that those students who were not taking a computer course used the computers significantly less. If the students do not have computer classes, they either have less access to use the computers and/or the teachers are not integrating computer use into the curriculum.

Becker calculated student computer-use percentages in higher-order and basic skill uses. He based higher-order uses on word processing, programming, spreadsheets, assignments to analyze data, and computers as part of laboratory experiments. Skill-based use included drill-and-practice, games, learning something new, and taking tests. The use of the computer for higher-order skills increased with grade level. While the skill-based skills decrease with grade level, the percentages betray a lack of sophistication and high-order computer use in the schools in general. Nothing is mentioned in the studies about the use of computers by minority children. Becker found in two earlier studies (1983, 1985) that students in lower SES schools were approximately three times as likely to be using drill-and-practice software as those in higher SES schools, while students at the higher socioeconomic level were three times as likely to be learning to program the computer.

COMPUTERS AND THE CONSTRUCTION OF KNOWLEDGE

Technology and computers are becoming the predominant mode of communication in our society. Access to computers is not simply the number of computers in the school, the time available for computer use, or even the extent to which teachers use and integrate computers into their classes. Access to the language of computing at the structural level of information processing or cognition has become increasingly important for social participation. Those who do not know the language of computing will find themselves struggling to communicate with the rest of society.

High-order thinking skills are the means by which children reconstruct and internalize new cognitive structures offered through their interaction with technology. Children from low-SES families are rarely exposed to higher-order thinking skills. As a result, they are less likely to internalize more sophisticated cognitive constructs. Since cognitive structures reflect the structure of information-processing in language, these children are being excluded from access to new forms of knowledge construction.

The low-SES children, who are disproportionately African American and Hispanic, were gaining most of their experience with a computer when it was in control, asking questions, expecting a response, and informing the student when he or she was correct. In contrast, the high-SES students, who are disproportionately White, were gaining considerable experience when they were in control, giving the computer a series of instructions, and observing the consequences of these instructions. (Sutton 1991)

In our society, access to technology in terms of the areas discussed in this chapter are critical. At present, access is dominated by white, educated, suburban males (Radlick 1993; Swan 1995; Becker 1985, 1994; NCES 1995, 1996). Minorities and the poor, the historical "have-nots," are less educated and have less resources with which to access technology. As a result, they are left out of the new technological forums for constructing social knowledge.

R. Muffoletto points out, "Access to information must also include equity in access to ways of 'thinking' about information. If information is to be used to empower people within democratic tradition, then educational experiences must provide a means for equal access to ways of thinking as well as valuing different ways of thinking" (1994: 53).

Understanding how to process information is a key to accessing technology. Without education, the meaning of the language of computing will fall on deaf ears. Without understanding the meaning of a language, participation in the construction of knowledge becomes impossible.

Discourse is shifting to a technological medium. "As a medium of experience (discourse), technology effects our consciousness, our visions, and expectations. The technological medium is more than a mind manager and a reality simulator, it is a consciousness generator—an ideological horizon line" (Muffoletto 1994: 52).

CONCLUSION

To have access to information, individuals will need computer skills that are not only technical, but also social and cognitive (Logan 1995 Vgotsky, 1962). "Our notion of technology should not be limited to hardware inventions, but rather, as the Greek word *tekhne*, meaning 'skill' or 'art,' indicates, should incorporate all human tools. These include physical tools used to organize the material world, the conceptual and cognitive tools used to organize information, and socioeconomic tools or institutions used to structure or organize society" (Logan 1995: 126).

Without these technological skills, individuals will be left standing outside of a crucial information stream for social economic opportunities as well as the opportunity to influence political decisions (Muffoletto 1994). Computers, instead of democratizing information, may serve to shut out whole segments of our society. Access to technology in this sense is not just having access physically to a computer in school or teachers who have the ability to integrate computers as a tool into the curriculum, it also exists on the level of information access and processing or cognition.

K-12 schools have not provided equitable access for all students. Minorities and the poor still lag behind suburban schools. While there are notable exceptions to the rule touted by the media, the overall conditions for these populations are dismal. These children often do not have the school facilities, computers that work, computer staff to provide support, or teachers trained to integrate high-order thinking skills into lesson plans. All of these conditions conspire to undermine learning the language of computing. Students leave inner-city schools without essential computing skills to participate in our society.

REFERENCES

Anderson, R. E. 1993. *Computers in American Schools, 1992: An Overview*. National Report from the 1992 International Association Evaluation of Education Attainment (IEA) Computers in Education Study. Minneapolis: Department of Sociology, University of Minnesota.

Becker, H. J. 1985. *How Schools Use Microcomputers: Summary of the First National Survey*. Baltimore, MD.: Center for Social Organization of Schools, Johns Hopkins University.

———. 1992. Equity the "Big Picture." *Technos* 1 (1):16–18.

———. 1994. *Analysis and Trends of School Use of New Information Technologies*. Washington, D.C.: Office of Technology Assessment (NTIS No. PB95-170981).

Campbell, P. B. 1984. The computer revolution: Guess who's left out? *Interracial Books for Children Bulletin* 15(3): 3–6.

Cuban, L. 1986. *Teachers and Machines: The Classroom Use of Technology Since 1920*. New York: Teachers College Press.

Fulford, N., ed. 1994. *Toward a Technology Infrastructure for Education: Policy Perspectives I*, Policy Briefs, Report 3. Washington, D.C. U.S. Department of Education, Office of Educational Research and Improvement.

Government Accounting Office. 1995. *School Facilities: America's Schools Not Designed or Equipped for 21st Century* (Report No. HEHS-95-95). Washington, D.C.: GAO.

Government Accounting Office. 1996. *School Facilities: America's Schools Report Differing Conditions* (Report No. HEHS-96-103). Washington, D.C. GAO (available to download from GAO Web site).

Kozol, J. 1991. *Savage Inequalities: Children in America's Schools*. New York: HarperCollins.

Logan, R. 1995. *The Fifth Language: Learning a Living in the Computer Age*. Toronto, Canada: Stoddart Publishing.

Muffoletto, R. 1994. Schools and technology in a democratic society: Equity and social justice. *Educational Technology* (February):52–54.

National Center for Education Statistics. 1995. *1995 Digest of Education Statistics*. Washington, D.C.: U.S. Department of Education, Table 414 (available to download at http://www.ed.gov/NCES/pubs/D95/dintro 7.html).

————. 1996. *Advanced Telecommunications in U.S. Public Elementary and Secondary Schools, 1995*. Washington, D.C.: U.S. Department of Education.

Office of Technology Assessment. 1995. *Education and Technology: Future Visions*. Washington, D.C.: U.S. Government Printing Office.

Piller, C. 1992. Separate realities: The creation of the technological underclass in America's public schools. *MacWorld* (September):218–30.

Radlick, M. S. 1993. *Technology in New York State Public Schools: What Schools Have and How They Are Using It*. Albany, N.Y.: New York State Department of Education.

Sarason, S. B. 1982. *The Culture of the School and the Problem of Change*. Boston: Allyn & Bacon.

Sutton, R. E. 1991. Equity and computers in the schools: A decade of research. In H. Levin eds., *Review of Educational Research*. Washington, D.C.: American Educational Research Association.

Swan, E. T. 1995. Equitable access to funding: The equal funding struggle. *Contemporary Education* 66 (4):202–204.

Vygotsky, L. S. 1962. *Thought and Language*. Cambridge, Mass.: MIT Press.

Wilson, W. J. 1987. *The Truly Disadvantaged: Inner City, the Underclass and Public Policy*. Chicago: University of Chicago Press.

10

On the Electronic Information Frontier: Training the Information-Poor in an Age of Unequal Access

Rebecca Carrier

Researchers agree that society is moving from the age of industrialization to an era that emphasizes information. As information takes an even greater role in determining social class, those who have the greatest abilities to retrieve and process the most important information will be separated from other members of society.

Scholars, policymakers, and educators are concerned about the distribution of communication resources and the widening gap between the information-rich and -poor. Public and private enterprises have attempted to equalize the uneven distribution of resources by supplying computers and other communication resources to public schools.

However, colleges have been responsible for finding their own funding for technology and information training. While well-endowed schools have met the challenge of the new Information Age reasonably successfully, schools that have fewer financial resources are unable to provide an information-rich education to their graduates. As a result, college graduates during the 1990s from poorer institutions risk becoming part of the information-poor.

This chapter explains why college graduates from poorer post-secondary institutions during the 1990s present the biggest risk for marginalization in the growing Information Age by examining: (1) the economic and social benefits of using advanced information technologies; (2) evidence of the emerging information society and the information gap; (3) the reasons the Internet threatens to exponentially widen this gap; and (4) the economic, institutional, and attitudinal barriers against Internet education and access in institutions of higher education. The chapter concludes with recommendations for improving the information skills of graduates during the 1990s by providing students with better Internet access and training.

During the last half of this century, scholars, policymakers, and educators have grown increasingly concerned about the distribution of communication resources and the widening gap between the information-rich and poor. Public and private enterprises have attempted to equalize the uneven distribution of resources by installing computers in primary and secondary schools, holding special in-house training sessions for teachers, and providing more advanced electronic resources for libraries. However, these efforts have been focused on public schools, while institutions of higher educations have struggled with the increased costs of providing training in an information environment that requires specialized faculty and expensive equipment.

Many well-endowed private and state institutions are able to meet the training demands of the new information society, but schools that receive less funding must cope with inadequate technology resources, unskilled faculty, and insufficient support staff. As a result, efforts to equalize the communication resources in the public schools have come too late to help those graduating from college, and these students will find it difficult to compete with those graduating from richer institutes of higher education who have received advanced technologies training.

College graduates from poorly funded institutions remain at risk for two main reasons. First, the programs that have attempted to equalize resources in primary and secondary education have come too late to benefit these graduates. Second, the information environment is changing so fast that colleges and universities are finding it difficult to supply the necessary instruction and resources to train students in the latest information skills. Conservative state and federal funding has forced universities to make cutbacks and has limited their abilities to invest in new technologies. The expense of computers, laboratory settings, and technical support staff is a substantial burden for institutions of higher education. The expense of equipment, laboratory space, trained faculty, and hardware maintenance is even more difficult for colleges and universities that receive the lowest level of funding.

In addition to the economic problems that universities face in providing information skills, institutions, faculty, and students face problems with keeping pace in the ever-changing information environment. Advances in computers, new methods of searching for information, and frequent changes in software make it difficult for institutions and faculty to provide the most up-to-date education in information technologies. These factors have contributed to the risk of marginalizing many college graduates during this decade. In fact, today's college students use computers at school less often than do younger generations of elementary and secondary school students (National Center for Education Statistics 1995). As a result, one of the most important challenges to educators is to ensure that college graduates of the 1990s have advanced information skills in preparation for the developing Information Age, and this challenge will be the most difficult to meet for universities that receive the least funding.

This chapter explains why college graduates from poorer post-secondary institutions during the 1990s present the biggest risk for marginalization in the growing Information Age by examining: (1) the economic and social benefits of using advanced information technologies; (2) evidence of the emerging information society and the information gap; (3) the reasons the Internet threatens to exponentially widen this gap; and (4) the economic, institutional, and attitudinal barriers against Internet education and access in institutions of higher education. The chapter concludes with recommendations for improving the information skills of graduates during the 1990s by providing students with better Internet access and training.

Although other information challenges exist, this chapter is concerned primarily with Internet access. Find/SVP, an Internet research organization, offers the following definition of the Internet:

The "Internet" is an umbrella term covering numerous electronic services provided via a super-network of networks, all of which employ the TCP/IP network protocol. Generally speaking, anyone who uses any services from e-mail to more complex applications such as the World Wide Web may be correctly termed an "Internet user." (Find/SVP 1996)

Of key importance in this definition is the large range of information services covered by the Internet. Providing access to this range of services will become increasingly important as information plays a larger role in casting social boundaries.

ECONOMIC AND SOCIAL BENEFITS FROM USING ADVANCED INFORMATION TECHNOLOGIES

What is unarguable is the role of computers in the information society. Today, computers provide access to libraries of information, a wealth of financial resources, and gateways to social and political exchanges. As access to information becomes more complicated and important, students' abilities to use new technologies for communication and information retrieval will have increasingly serious social and economic effects.

Bikson and Panis (1995) claim that access to computers and communication technologies are related to two major factors: individual income, and increased participation in communication activities. Studies indicate that individuals with computer access are generally better paid. Bikson and Panis (1995) found that workers who used computers on their jobs were paid 10 percent to 15 percent higher than non-computer users who held similar positions. Additionally, those who have Internet access tend to have higher than average incomes. A recent Internet survey found that the average household income for Internet users was $59,000 per year (Graphic, Visualization, & Usability Center 1996). Further, computer communication and information retrieval skills are associated with economic rewards. Krueger (1993) found that e-mail was the most highly rewarded task of all computer-based activities at work.

In addition to the economic benefits, Bikson and Panis (1995) found that information and communication technologies have increased individual participation in communication activities and reduced the effects of status-based social restrictions. Researchers have found that electronic-based communication networks have increased participation in decision-making and discussion at work (Sproull and Kiesler 1991). Further, Dubrovsky, Kiesler, and Sethna (1991) found that characteristics such as age, sex, race, and socioeconomic status were significantly less important in determining patterns of interactions when individuals were participating in electronic communication than when they were interacting face-to-face.

Bikson and Panis (1995) found several other benefits associated with Internet use. They claim that individuals with electronic communication knew more about the companies they worked for, were better informed about corporate decisions, and were better prepared to participate in the decision-making process. Additionally, Bikson and Panis found that electronic communication enhanced civic participation and gave citizens more access to government and political information. They claim that as civic organizations rely more on electronic communication, users of these technologies will reap greater economic benefits (Bikson and Panis 1995).

As a result of Bikson and Panis' findings, it is clear that college graduates during the 1990s need access to Internet technologies. However, access to technology is not enough; these students need advanced training in information skills to achieve economic and social advantages. As information technologies associated with Internet resources grow, those who have the highest level of skills and access will receive the greatest benefits. Providing these skills to graduates during the 1990s is critical as we move deeper into the Information Age.

THE INFORMATION AGE AND ITS INHERENT INFORMATION GAP

Most scholars agree that expansion of communication technologies coupled with the growing amount of information necessary to function in today's world mark the evolution from an industrial to an information society. For most of this century, telephones have made it possible to have immediate and direct contact with business professionals as well as friends. More recently, television and satellite technology have brought live coverage of international events directly to our living rooms. And most recently, computers and Internet access have facilitated access to libraries, government databases and documents, educational resources, as well as a host of commercial and personal information. All of these events have been used to document the growing importance of communication technologies in the rise of an information society.

Additionally, scholars point to the growth in communication and information industries as another milepost in the change from an industrial to an Information Age. In the last thirty years, the percentage of U.S. workers holding information jobs has doubled. Nearly 50 percent of the U.S. workforce is employed by some type of information industry such as accounting, banking, journalism, or engineering. While information jobs are increasing, service, industrial, and agricultural jobs are declining (Straubhaar and LaRose 1996). With the increase in communication technologies, expansion of available information, and the growth in information industries, there is little dispute that communication and information are essential to social welfare and play an increasingly important role in defining relationships between different levels of society.

However, the emergence of this Information Age has not served all members of society equally. Inequitable distribution of resources has generated an information gap that propels those with the greatest access to information and communication technologies far ahead of other members of society. The knowledge gap studied by mass media researchers Tichenor, Donohue, and Olien (1970), and Moore (1987) illustrates how the information elite is propelled far ahead of other members of society, thus generating an information gap between those with information resources and those without. Tichenor et al. (1970) and Moore (1987) found that people who have a large amount of knowledge about a particular topic are likely to learn more about related topics from current news. These media scholars claim that prior knowledge of a related topic significantly affects subjects' abilities to obtain more knowledge. Graber (1988) explains that the knowledge gap occurs because prior knowledge of a subject is evidence of interest in that topic. She claims that prior interest provides a schema that allows integration of old and new knowledge; thus, those with some knowledge are prepared to gain more, while those with little knowledge lack the interest and mental capability to process additional information. This creates a cycle that leaves some members of society well informed and others information-poor.

The emergence of Internet technology is expected to have an effect similar to that of the knowledge gap. The information elite consists of individuals who have the tools and knowledge to adapt to new communication technologies as they are developed. In turn, these new technologies increase access to information, and this additional information prepares elite members of society to incorporate the next generation of technology into their lives. The cycle spirals forth with some members of society riding the crest of the information tide, leaving others unable to catch up. Ultimately, the cycle produces a small group of information-rich members of society who are able to keep up with the constant changes in technology that enable them to fully function in an Information Age. Other members have neither the resources nor the abilities to access and control the main currency of this new age, information. The rapid development of communication technologies and the ever-increasing need for information has both increased the size of the chasm between the information-elite and the information-poor and accelerated the speed with which the gap widens. Those who are graduating from our institutions of higher education are not immune to this threat; many will not receive adequate resources and training to function among the information elite.

Of particular importance are the implications for economic class in this cycle that separates the information elite from others in society. Richer universities are better able to provide resources and training that ensure their college graduates are well prepared to function in the Information Age. However, poorer institutions that charge less for tuition, receive less state funding, or lack private endowments are unable to afford expensive new technologies. As a result, students who lack the economic or academic resources to enter richer schools are at greatest risk of marginalization because their educational institutions cannot afford to keep pace with the expensive technologies.

INTERNET'S POWER TO EXPONENTIALLY EXPAND THE INFORMATION GAP

Though every generation of communication technologies has contributed to the gap between the information-rich and -poor, Internet resources have exponentially increased the rift. The Internet has affected the information gap so significantly for three reasons. First, compared with all other communication technologies, the Internet makes a much greater amount of information available. The total amount of information available via the Internet is far beyond numbers we understand. Most Internet survey firms agree that the amount of traffic and information though the Internet makes it difficult to determine exactly how many users there are, or how much information is available.

However, there are two indicators of the expansiveness of the Internet: the number of computer hosts and domains, and the number of Internet servers and Web sites available. In a July 1996 study, Network Wizards estimated that 12,881,000 computers acted as hosts for Internet information. These computers were distributed over 488,000 domains, or institutions that supply links to the Internet. Together, these hosts and domains made available an estimated 275,600 servers that provided more than 30 million Web sites (Alta Vista 1996). And the number of hosts, domains, servers, and Web sites is expected to continue to dramatically increase over the next year (Find/SVP 1996). Given these statistics, it is clear that Internet technologies have increased the amount of information available to elite users in an unprecedented way. However, not everyone has access to this information.

The second reason Internet technology has played such an important role in broadening the information gap is that it requires extensive economic, technological, and knowledge-based resources. At a minimum, users must have access to a computer, communications software, connection line (such as a telephone and modem or ISDN line), and an account on an Internet service provider (ISP). The initial cost of hardware, software, and ISPs vary, but the resources required for access far exceed the reach of lower middle-class and impoverished citizens in the United States. A recent RAND study confirms that income and education are significant predictors of information access (Anderson, Bikson, Law, and Mitchell 1995). Anderson et al. explain that although information resources such as e-mail have expanded, they have not overcome the creation of an elite information society. These researchers claim that unless measures are taken to increase information access to non-elite members of society, the distance between the information-rich and -poor will continue to grow.

Internet user demographics also support the claim that Internet access is restricted to upwardly mobile sectors of the population. According to Nielsen Media Research (1996), less than half of U.S. homes have a computer. Nielsen reports that approximately 39.5 percent or 84 million U.S. citizens over the age of twelve have home computers, and 21.7 percent (or 46 million citizens) have Internet access. Only 8.7 percent claim to have access from home (Nielsen Media Research 1996). The Graphic, Visualization, & Usability Center (1996) found the estimated average household income for Internet users was $59,000 per year in 1995. Previous studies by the center also found that the income of most Internet users exceeds U.S. averages. In one study, the average income was reported at $63,000 and in a second study $69,000. These findings support the claim that Internet resources are not equally accessible to all members of society, and accessability is often related to economic factors. In general, surveys show that most U.S. homes do not have computers, most computer owners do not have Internet access, and most who do have access are from upper income levels.

In the near future, Internet access likely will become simpler and less expensive. For example, Apple Computer has teamed up with Bandai Digital Entertainment, and they have introduced a new service called @World, a Pippin based product that offers Internet access via the television (Apple press release 1996). Though not in extensive use, this product is expected to make Internet access cheaper and easier for mass audiences. Apple claims @World will sell for about $600, not including the television required for viewing. If the Pippin platform becomes popular, similar services will likely provide competition that should make Internet access even cheaper and possibly easier over time. Still, the unit price does not include the television or the monthly service fee for connection. Even with cheaper and easier technology, it is likely that lower-class and lower middle-class homes will be unable to afford Internet access soon.

Even if initial access is made affordable, rapid changes in the Internet environment will make it expensive for poor households to upgrade equipment, and the gap will continue to widen. Some argue that new software, increased access speed, and advances in computer hardware will make adapting to these changes easier and less frustrating. But these upgrades are expensive, and new browser software takes additional time to install and learn. As a result, the upgrades that are meant to make the Internet more accessible may do so only for the elite population that can afford them. These changes are doubly important because they affect both the way we retrieve information and the way we publish it.

The dual nature of the medium is the third reason the Internet threatens to widen the information gap even further. The same enhancements that have made Internet reception and searches easier have also made publishing more complicated. Internet publishing is becoming more complex because new Web-creating tools and programs are generated and modified to meet the frequent changes in HTML standards, HTML extensions, and third-party languages and protocols. Modifications in HTML standards include the addition of new text features, sizing options for pictures, and improvements in document formatting control. Changes in HTML extensions are similar to changes in HTML standards, except the extensions are generated by third parties who want to created unique Web browser features. The ability to create a frame that remains stationary while other frames are viewed and scrolled is one example of a Netscape extension that required modification of Web-creating tools. Additionally, advances in third-party languages and protocols (such as CGI scripts, Java, Hot Sauce, Cool Talk, Live 3d) have generated even more complex changes in Internet writing.

Frequent changes in all three of these levels of Web-creating require nearly continuous learning to keep pace with the ever-changing Internet environment. The rate at which new Web-creating tools are made available is evidence of the rate of publishing skill obsolescence. From December 1995 to December 1996, changes in Internet publishing programs occurred so rapidly that new Web-creating tools were produced on a weekly, and sometimes daily, basis. For the Windows95 platform alone, seventy-four new Web-creating tools were offered via one of the most popular software sites for the year (Windows95.com 1996). During the same twelve-month period, applications for Internet publishing introduced Java, frames, and hundreds of new CGI scripting programs. These new publishing tools enhanced Web publications with moving pictures, sounds, and scrolling capabilities and allowed database functions to be associated directly with Web sites.

Because the rate of change in Web-creating tools is so rapid, only the most sophisticated users can keep up with cutting-edge publication capabilities on the Internet. Thus, the very changes that are meant to make information access easier have complicated the ability to publish Internet information. Again, these changes have been to the advantage of elite users and have made it more difficult for others to remain equal in the Internet world.

The unprecedented amount of information made available, the cost of Internet access, and the volatility of the Internet environment threaten to widen the information gap far beyond the present breach. As the Information Age develops, more and more individuals are likely to find themselves on the other side of the rift. Not only is the gap widening, but the number of people caught on the information-poor side is increasing. Perhaps the most important implication is that those who lack the necessary information resources will be denied a voice that will be provided to those who are adept at using the new information technologies. Because economic factors weigh so heavily in determining who has training and access to the new information technologies, class implications must be considered.

The most important commodity in an information society is information. Those who have the most information and the best access to new information as it becomes available will be best suited to function in the coming age. As information industries grow, job placement and advancement will be closely associated with the skills in information access and processing. Internet technology will play an important role in aiding the most successful members of society because it will provide the greatest access to current information. If college students of the 1990s are to function to their fullest capacity, they will need the skills to obtain information and the ability to adapt to new modes of information as they become available. However, those students who graduate from poorer institutions are unlikely to receive adequate training to compete with graduates of richer colleges and universities. As a result, Internet technology is expected to generate even greater class divisions between the technological "haves" and the "have-nots."

ECONOMIC, INSTITUTIONAL, AND ATTITUDINAL BARRIERS

Internet technology has created important challenges to college educators. Will all colleges and universities be able to provide an education that will secure the futures of their graduates in the Information Age? Three barriers stand in the way of ensuring these graduates advanced information skills, and each of these barriers has important implications for class. First, conservative government spending has put pressure on institutions of higher education to reduce costs, and this pressure is at odds with expensive information technologies. Second, colleges and universities frequently fail to support faculty who attempt to implement innovative technology in the classrooms. Third, students have become more concerned with receiving the skills that will pay off immediately in finding good jobs, but they often avoid skills that may have more important long-term effects.

Funding for post-secondary education has become a matter of concern for nearly all public institutions. During a convocation address at Tennessee University, Robert Atwell, president of the American Council on Education, said that the most important problem institutions of higher education must face is the decrease in resources allocated to colleges and universities (Farrell 1994). Atwell claims there have been massive reductions in the amount of state and local support to universities and colleges. Further, he explains that programs in kindergarten through high school have received priority educational funding. As a result, Atwell claims, the federal government has been unable to meet the increasing needs of colleges and universities. A significant part of these increasing needs is caused by new demands for communication technologies and information skills.

Conservative economics have contributed to the barrier against providing comprehensive Internet access to college students because this access is expensive. Converting a traditional classroom to a laboratory that provides Internet access and enables faculty to teach information skills increases the cost of the classroom in at least three ways. First, the capital outlay required for new information technologies is significant. Laboratories of computers, software, broadband wiring connections to Internet resources, mainframes to serve accounts, and classroom space all contribute to the cost of providing information skills. In addition to the initial cost of building an Internet learning center, rapid changes in information technologies require frequent upgrades. Over time, computers will need larger hard drives, more RAM, and faster processors. Software upgrades are necessary every two to three years, and new software may dictate additional hardware improvements.

The initial cost of creating a computer classroom is significant, and the need for frequent upgrades requires additional expenses.

A second reason Internet classrooms increase educational expenses is that compared with lecture classrooms, computer laboratories serve a much smaller group of students for instructional time. As lecture class sizes increase to make colleges and universities more cost-effective, computer laboratories will become comparatively more expensive because they require a much greater amount of space. Both the equipment and the type of hands-on instruction necessary to learn advanced information skills are unadaptable to large classroom settings. Computers take large amounts of space; hence classrooms that might otherwise serve fifty or sixty students can only serve eighteen to twenty-five when they are converted to computer laboratories. It is unlikely that computer classrooms can be expanded to serve large numbers of students in a single instructional setting because teaching information skills requires hands-on instruction. Students or faculty would find it difficult to succeed in a classroom environment that prevented the instructor from making direct visual contact with all students; thus, computer laboratories remain limited to around twenty-five students per section.

A third explanation for the additional expense is that the cost of repairs and support staff to maintain computer labs increases the expense of computer-assisted education beyond that of traditional instruction. Special support staff are required to keep computers in working condition, to maintain servers, and to administer mainframe accounts. In a recent report on broadband networks for university research and instruction, an Educom task force recommended that additional support staff will be needed for client and server development, materials development for teaching, and scholarship support for faculty and student training (Educom Networking and Telecommunications Task Force 1995). Additionally, the report suggested that computer support staff have technical expertise, as well as knowledge of the content area served. In the humanities, this staffing will be particularly expensive because individuals with both technical expertise and a background in humanities research are rare. Although the cost of additional staff for computer labs is a problem, there are even greater problems for instructional faculty who attempt to educate students in the new information technologies.

Another barrier to providing advanced information skills is that most colleges and universities do not support faculty who implement these technologies in the classroom. Some educational policy analysts argue that the biggest deterrent to incorporating Internet skills into traditional education is the lack of institutional support. IBM academic consultant William Geoghegan (1994) claims that faculty members receive little support from their universities for incorporating innovative teaching techniques that rely on new technologies or for educating students in advanced information skills. According to Geoghegan, universities rarely consider software development, technical assistance, or the use of innovative technologies in classroom settings in the decision-making process for promotion and tenure.

Despite the time, education, and effort required, faculty who engage in providing students with Internet access and skills are seldom given economic or title benefits. Because the current system is designed to judge faculty by their publication records, teaching evaluations, and campus service duties, there is little incentive for faculty to write grants for new technologies, put their classes online, or do the research to keep abreast of the rapidly changing Internet environment. As a result, most faculty find it more profitable to spend additional time polishing their publication records, creating new course proposals, or increasing their university service duties.

Recent faculty forums in Wyoming and Wisconsin have attempted to address this issue. According to Rickly and Gardner (1996), members of the University of Wyoming English department who work with technology are not fairly rewarded by their institutions because the work they do does not count toward promotion, tenure, or release-time. Among other things, the Wyoming forum concluded that institutional support would improve if an accreditation and consulting program was created, if technology work was viewed as applied research, if a system to document work with technology was established, and if job descriptions included technology work (Rickly and Gardner 1996). These changes may improve the future of faculty in providing advanced technology skills, but currently the problem remains an important barrier to educating students in this decade.

In addition to staffing problems and the lack of institutional support, student attitudes present yet another barrier to educating 1990s graduates in advanced information skills. Nearly as soon as they enroll in college, students begin to fear underemployment, and projections indicate this fear may be justified. According to the Bureau of Labor Statistics, the supply of college graduates will exceed demand by an average of 330,000 jobs per year between now and 2005 (December Economic Trends 1995). As college graduates outstrip the market for available jobs, students begin to concentrate on the skills that will prepare them immediately for employment and shun those courses that concentrate on theories, methods, or philosophies. Universities concerned with enrollment rates and faculty concerned with teaching evaluations are trying to meet student demands for these immediate skills. A good example of this can be found in journalism and public relations programs that have shifted from concentrating on the principles of newspaper layout and design to teaching software applications such as QuarkXpress or PageMaker. Because many internships require students to have desktop publishing skills, college programs are trying to meet the demand so their students can receive valuable work experience. Often this focus on immediate skills interferes with more long range capabilities.

Because of the rapidly changing nature of the Internet environment, students who receive training that focuses on current information skills may lack the ability to adapt over time. To keep pace with the ever-changing information environment, students must learn not only the skills needed for available technology, they must also learn to adapt as the environment continues to change. As a result, a gestalt for information and communication technologies must accompany the practical skills provided. Theories of learning suggest that such a gestalt comes from both practical applications of a skill and deeper understanding of theories, methods, and philosophies about that skill. Although students may be reluctant to enroll in information theory courses, these courses are more likely to provide them with the long-term skills that will enable them to adapt to a changing environment.

Economic, institutional, and attitudinal barriers all present problems for providing advanced information skills to college graduates during the 1990s. However, these barriers are particularly acute for colleges and universities that have the lowest level of funding. As a result, those students who cannot afford more expensive and prestigious universities are at the greatest risk of marginalization in the information society because the institutions they attend are less likely to provide up-to-date equipment and faculty who are educated in providing advanced technologies skills. Moreover, course offerings may concentrate on applied skills in lieu of providing a gestalt to adapt in the ever-changing information environment.

CONCLUSION

As the Information Age progresses, access to communication technologies and resources will become increasingly important in determining social boundaries. Economic and social benefits are already associated with the ability to use advanced information technologies. Researchers have found that employees who use e-mail and other Internet resources are paid 10 percent to 15 percent more than comparable workers who do not use them. Additionally, electronic communication provides social benefits because it allows employees to be more involved in both corporate and civic decision-making. Researchers have found that those with access to information technologies are generally better informed. Electronic communication also prevents personal characteristics such as age, sex, and race from interfering with patterns of interaction, which in turn prevents discrimination on the basis of such characteristics.

However, these technologies are not equally distributed to all members of society. As the Information Age progresses, there is evidence that this distribution continues to become more unequal, resulting in a small information elite. Those who have access to current information technologies use that access to obtain information about developing changes. Those who wait to enter the information environment often find it difficult to do so because they lack the knowledge and resources to get started.

Internet technology plays an important role in perpetuating this information gap because it makes available much more information than any previous technology has allowed. Additionally, frequent changes in the software, equipment, and standards for receiving information from the Internet make it difficult for users to keep pace with the environment. Internet start-up costs and hardware upgrades are expensive, restricting access to those who can afford access. Further, changes in the Internet environment require frequent learning of new skills for receiving and sending information. The ability to publish information on the Internet is made more difficult by the programs that have been created to make receiving information easier. As a result, the interactive nature of the medium increases the Internet's ability to widen the information gap.

Most important, this gap will likely mark even greater distinctions between classes as those who attend poorer colleges and universities are not offered the same information resources that are available at richer institutions. Smaller, lower-funded universities and colleges are finding budgets harder to meet, and information technologies are expensive. Computer laboratories require additional maintenance and technical support that exceed the price of traditional lecture classes. For poorer institutions, the ability to attract and reward faculty for incorporating information technologies training into the classroom is more difficult because these institutions lack financial resources. Additionally, students do not have families who can support them through periods of unemployment. Thus, students demand courses that provide immediate skills, and they are less receptive to theory courses that would provide them with a gestalt to adapt to the new technologies of the future. These barriers lead to the question: Will all institutions of higher education be able to provide an education that will secure the futures of their graduates in the Information Age?

The answer to that question depends on four factors. First, colleges and universities must receive adequate funding for equipment, technologically skilled faculty, and support staff. Second, faculty have to incorporate information technologies into their content areas. Classes should be placed online with hypertext links to examples that enhance the teaching objectives. Course syllabi, electronic office hours, and instructor e-mail access will provide an incentive for students to practice advanced information skills. Third, faculty have to be rewarded for the extra time it takes to implement these advanced information technologies. One component of teaching effectiveness should be measured by how well the instructor incorporates information technologies into the content of the course. Faculty who administer department servers or help maintain computer labs should be given service credit, and those who spend time researching the latest changes in the information environment should be encouraged to share their findings publicly by receiving research recognition. Finally, core requirements that teach not only applied information skills, but also theoretical and critical approaches to information technologies should be added immediately to college curriculums.

If all college graduates of the 1990s are to share fully in the benefits of the developing Information Age, they will need both the immediate skills and the ability to adapt to the ever-changing information environment. Graduates of less well-endowed institutions are particularly at risk for marginalization because they come at a unique time when changes are occurring in information technologies so rapidly that few institutions can afford to keep pace with them. If we are to meet the challenge of the new Information Age in time for this decade's graduates, the current economic, institutional, and attitudinal barriers must be broken. Faculty have to incorporate advanced information skills into their course content, institutions need to support faculty for doing so, and students at all institutions must receive a deeper understanding of information and communication practices to ensure their success in a rapidly changing world.

REFERENCES

Alta Vista. 1996. Largest number of servers and web sites surveyed by November 1996. Online: http://altavista.digital.com/

Anderson, R., T. Bikson, S. Law, and B. Mitchell. 1995. *Universal Access to E-Mail: Feasibility and Social Implications*. Santa Monica, Calif.: RAND.

Apple press release. May 31, 1996. *First Products Based on Apple's Pippin Technology Unveiled in U.S.* Online: http://product.info.apple.com/pr/press.releases/1996/q3/960516.pr.rel.pippin.html

Bikson, T. and C. Panis. 1995. Computers and connectivity: Current trends. In R. Anderson, T. Bikson, S. Law, and B. Mitchell, eds., *Universal Access to E-Mail: Feasibility and Social Implications*. Santa Monica, Calif.: RAND, pp. 13–40.

December Economic Trends. 1995. *The Outlook for College Graduates*. Online: http://www.clev.frb.org/research/dec95et/labmar2.htm

Dubrovsky, V. J., S. Kiesler, and B. N. Sethna. 1991. The equalization phenomenon: Status effects in computer-mediated and face-to-face decision making groups. *Human-Computer Interaction* 6:119–146.

Educom Networking and Telecommunications Task Force. 1995. *Broadband Networks for University Research and Instruction: New Media Project Workshop Report*. Online: http://educom.edu/web/nttf/newmedia/newmedial.html#RTFToC9.

Farrell, J. 1994. American Council on Education president has harsh words, hope for higher education. *The Daily Beacon* (September 14), pp. 1, 2.

Find/SVP. 1996. *The American Internet User Survey: Internet User Trends, Profiles,*

Segments and Preferences. Online: http://etrg.findsvp.com/surveys/16page/ainetus.html#introduction

Geoghegan, W. 1994. *What Ever Happened to Instructional Technology?* Paper presented at the twenty-second Annual Conference of the International Business Schools Computing Association, Baltimore. Online: http://ike.engr.washington.edu/news/whitep/whg/wpi.htm

Graber, Doris A. 1988. *Processing the News: How People Tame the Information Tide.* 2nd ed. New York: Longman.

Graphic, Visualization, & Usability Center. 1996. *GVU's 5th WWW User Survey.* Online: http://www.cc.gatech.edu/gvu/user __surveys/survey-04–1996/

Krueger, A. 1993. Why computers have changed the wage structure: Evidence from microdata 1984–1989. *Quarterly Journal of Economics* 108 (1):33–61.

Moore, D. 1987. Political campaigns and the knowledge-gap hypothesis. *Public Opinion Quarterly* 51 (2):186–200.

National Center for Education Statistics. 1995. *Student Use of Computers at School, and Level of Instruction: October 1989 and 1993.* Online. http://www.ed.gov/NCES/pubs/D95/dfig032.gif

Network Wizards. 1996. *Domain Survey Notes July 1996.* Online: http://www.nw.com/zone/WWW/notes.html

Nielsen Media Research. 1996. *Home Technology Report.* Online: http://www.nielsenmedia.com/news/hotech-summary.html

Rickly, R. and T. Gardner. 1996. *ITC & CCCCCC Project to Establish Guidelines for Promotion, Tenure, and Academic Recognition of Those Working with Computer Technology.* Online: http://www.daedalus.com/promo/promo.html

Sproull, L. and S. Kiesler. 1991. *Connections: New Ways of Working in the Networked Organization.* Cambridge, Mass.: MIT Press.

Straubhaar, J. and R. LaRose. 1996. *Communications Media in the Information Society.* Belmont, Calif.: Wadsworth.

Tichenor, P., G. Donohue, and C. Olien. 1970. Mass media flow and differential growth in knowledge. *Public Opinion Quarterly* 34 (1):159–70.

Windows95.com. 1996. *Web Authoring Tools.* Online: http://www.windows95.com/apps/webauth.html

PART III

Cybergendering

Democratizing Internet Access in the Lesbian, Gay, and Bisexual Communities

Nadine S. Koch and H. Eric Schockman

This chapter is both a theoretical exploration and an empirical research analysis of the dimensions and forms of "political communication" expressed in a sampling of the lesbian, gay, and bisexual community in the creation of a research pilot project we called the Queer Cyber Center. Access, demographic, and user data were analyzed to ascertain some preliminary conclusions regarding this "marginalized community" and its own evolving "digital sexual identity," as well as its empowered collective potential to use new communication technologies to further democratize the established political order. Moreover, given the unique "rainbow diversity" of this marginalized subpopulation, our analysis also speaks to the intersection of racism, sexism, classism, and heterosexism and how "cyber-democracy" may advance community organizing, electronic advocacy, policy formation, and digital citizenship in the new millennium.

INTRODUCTION

Democratizing cyberspace for existing marginalized populations in the American political order is the intellectual charge of this study. We intentionally chose a subpopulation quantifiably understudied by researchers and social scientists and questioned how the diversity of the lesbian, gay and bisexual community might become transformed with access and usage of Internet technology; how this act might transform new "digital sexual identities"; and how this might advance new forms of "political communication," community organizing, electronic advocacy, policy formation, and digital citizenship in the advancement of "cyber-democracy."

Conceptualizing a more fully incorporated citizenship of a group of individuals whose socially constructive sexual identity has been labeled deviant is a complex task in and of itself. Demystifying stereotypes and emotional evaluations of those who "deserve" full democratic citizenship rights is a separate discourse beyond the realm of this study. Suffice to say here that insights of French philosopher Michel Foucault (1980, 1988, 1990) lay the intellectual groundwork, which explores the way relations of power and resistance to power continually construct our epistemic categories of sexual identity and their relationship to the state, as well as emphasizing both the historical contingency and the persuasiveness of these structuring relations.[1]

EVOLUTION OF GAY POLITICAL IDENTITY

So long as politics militates against homosexuals, homosexuality will remain inescapably political.[2] Gender nonconformity has been the nucleus of development for the lesbian, gay, bisexual community. Before we can discuss in more depth the impact that new communication technologies may have on "gay identity formation" and the subsequent manifestations of its unique forms of political communication, we begin by first positing the ubiquitous question: What constitutes identity formation in this subpopulation and how has this variable been transposed to the political arena?

In a nutshell, we see sexual minority identity formation as a dual reduction (along the lines of Gleason [1983] and Berger and Luckmann [1967]) compositing, first, what others have termed an "intrapsychic" variable denoting who someone really is; and second, an "acquired" definition of identity that is external and socially constructed.[3]

From the "intrapsychic" view of identity formation in this subpopulation, we know from the psychosociological literature that sexual orientation is established early in childhood, producing what Donald Webster Cory (1951) terms "inverts"—those who are attracted to their own sex. Note here the essence of true feelings being fomented into the partial development of one's identity. The early dissonance between one's true feelings and societal/parental judgments soon interjects the external, socially constructive perspective within the fragile evolution of full identity formation.

Identity is a socialized sense of individuality (in Habermas's sense), an internal organization of self-perceptions concerning one's relationship to the social order, as well as the introspective analysis that views the self through a prism of external views held by others. Development of a theory of sexual identity formation is a critical component in the research into the lives of homosexuals, and to the similarities and differences they exhibit compared with the heterosexual majoritarian population.

With this duality of sexual identity formation, lesbian, gays, and bisexuals have grown up in a homophobic world in which part of their socially constructive identity formation has encrusted them to the surreal realities of "passing for heterosexual" or living a more liberated life by "coming out." A community, culture, and lifestyle have been restructured from the prevailing external threats of heterosexism and homophobia, binding lesbians, gays, and bisexuals together. "Gay America" has become a parallel structure in the evolution of the civil order, complete with its hidden meeting places, its linguistic passwords, its underground literature, even its own gay "vacation ghettos," from Palm Springs to Fire Island.

In light of this discussion, how may we next advance the treatment of a distinctively gay political identity formation? How does sexual identity collectivize into potent political forces, exerting a more-or-less generalized policy agenda and a priority of political demands? In the reduction to the individual, can we hypothesize that there is really a "gay vote"—a unified bloc of voters who have prioritized their sexual identity over myriad overlapping "identities" (e.g., gender, religion, occupation, income status)? While there is much anecdotal literature on this inquiry, only a few serious scholarly empirical studies, like Bailey (1997) and Schockman and Koch (1995, 1996) have made intellectual headway into this phenomenon.

John D'Emilio (1983), for example, has argued a counter-tack (although without much empirical validation) that homosexuals are moving both in lifestyle and politics closer to heterosexuals. D'Emilio essentially endorses a "desexualized" lesbian, gay, and bisexual identity by claiming that "homosexuality and lesbianism have become less of a sexual category and more of a human identity" (p. 248).

We tend to place little credence in D'Emilio's analysis, especially in this "convergence hypothesis" between straight and gay politics. If anything, there perhaps has been a "resexualized" gay (especially male) political identity in the wake of the AIDS pandemic and governmental inaction. Another factor is the rise of the politicized religious right over the past two decades, and its ability to elevate constitutional homophobia to new heights. The American pluralist mythology that all interest groups compete equally in the eyes of governmental leaders has lost all credibility.

We think a more compelling analysis of gay political identity is a derivation of the analogous "ethnic minority model" of political identity.[4] Ethnic minority political patterns have been well documented and researched. Scholars have studied the surprising generational longevity and profound impact ethnic voting blocs have had on the American political process. While racial, cultural, linguistic, and other manifestations conspire to formulate this initial ethnic model, the underlining compelling force tends to be (initially) the intentional exclusion and discriminatory patterns exhibited by the mainstream status quo. This sense of collective persecution and the resources minorities pull together to overcome this dilemma lead us to conclude that the lesbian, gay, and bisexual community is a "neo-ethnic" political model following in the steps of more traditional minority political incorporation. Perhaps this model may be unraveling even as we describe it as lesbians, gays, and bisexuals move away from a victimization mentality, and as homophobia gets chipped away by local domestic partnership ordinances and as openly gay and lesbian elected officials become visible.

To sum up, we have hypothesized that there is indeed a distinct and (for the purposes of this study) measurable entity we label as "gay political identity" that has manifested itself within the margins of the American democratic process. We argue that sexual identity for lesbians, gays, and bisexuals does become collectivized for common political gains and follows in some analogous patterns the rise of ethnic minority blocs. What we don't know at this point is how lesbians, gays, and bisexuals communicate politically. Are there unique forms of political communication this subpopulation has undertaken to position itself as a viable political force for elites to hear and respond to? Will new communication technologies such as the Internet produce a profound difference in the political communication power balance between the status quo and marginalized communities such as this one? To address these questions, we turn to a brief literature analysis of the traditional theoretical forms of political communication and attempt to draw some preliminary conclusions as to their relevancy for the lesbian, gay, and bisexual community.

POLITICS AS COMMUNICATION

The centrality of scholarship in this area links the various forms of political communication in any society as an adaptation of some variation of social control or social order. The study of political communication is essential to the understanding of overt and covert power relations within political systems, the distribution and allocation of resources, and to a large extent the maintenance of the social order.

Robert Meadow (1980) offers a cogent typology of the leading theoretical approaches in political communication research. Adapting Meadow's classifications that are the most relevant to this current study, we chose three research approaches for investigation: the systems approach, linguistic approach, and symbolic approach.

The systems approach, pioneered by Karl Deutsch (1963) and David Easton (1964, 1965), expounds a cybernetic-systems conceptualization in the study of the flow of political communication. At the core of this theoretical work is the understanding that political power sets up a pattern of system responsiveness and that political communication is the maintenance function of the control of information and direction of policy outcomes.

The linguistic approach, similar to the systems approach, is also concerned with social control. According to C. Muller (1975), language is the vehicle through which social control is exercised. Muller and other language based theorists argue that elites who speak the same language understand one another and hence have access and power and get results. Non-elites, having a diminished political voice (or language), remain outside the delivery system. Thus, language is determined by political contexts and institutions and favors the status quo.

Finally, the symbolic approach starts with the premise that politics, like communication, is largely a symbolic interchange. Symbolic processes in politics are manipulated by leaders for their own ends. In Murray Edelman's (1964) analysis, the process by which these symbols are created and disseminated should serve as the focus of analyzing what truly stands for political communication.

Blending these three theoretical approaches produces a more useful analysis on how political regimes support themselves through the manipulation of the channels of political communications. Using power, language, and symbols to booster "heteronormality" is one of the political means to stifle favorable public policies and the further political incorporation of lesbian, gays, and bisexuals. In essence, through, we are still viewing only one theoretical side of the equation: the view of political communication "from above." We offer the next short analytical section as a theoretical enhancement to the existing literature, especially the view of political communication "from below," within the homosexual political community.

TALK AS POLITICS

Political theorists have long acknowledged the importance of participation by members of the polity, especially in democratic political regimes. In reality, participation levels are relatively low overall, and abysmally low within specific subpopulations. The traditional measures of political participation employed by political scientists have focused on electoral related behaviors.[5] Voting in elections is believed to be one of the easiest and therefore the most prevalent form of participation. Other measures of participation are thought to be more demanding on the individual's resources. Belonging to a political club, contributing financially to a candidate's campaign, or attending a political rally or dinner all require the expenditure of money and time. McCain and Koch (1985) have argued that the traditional measures of political participation may be economically, socially, and culturally biased. They have put forth less biased measure of political involvement: the simple act of talking with others about politics in the course of one's everyday life. Engaging in political discussions with others is less demanding of valuable resources; one does not have to join any formal organizations, travel to organized activities, or contribute money.

As described below, the Queer Cyber Center (QCC) provides lesbians, gays, and bisexuals the opportunity to connect with others in order to discuss issues salient to their community. Talking with others about politics in general, and sexual minority life experiences in particular, is political participation. As members of a diaspora, a splintered community numbering somewhere between 3 percent and 10 percent of the general population, it is critically important that there exist a vehicle for communication. The QCC is such a vehicle. In tracking QCC user-access patterns, there is at least three-to-one ratio between use of "chat" rooms and use of the other QCC non-talk, non-interactive resources. Lesbian, gay, and bisexual users are using the Internet to talk, and one would have to assume that a subset of the overall talk is political in nature.

CASE RESEARCH MODEL: THE QUEER CYBER CENTER IN HOLLYWOOD AND IN CYBERSPACE

Richard Davis (1996) identifies four political functions of the Internet: (1) access to political information and news; (2) linkage between the governed and those who govern (government Web sites); (3) a forum for political discourse (news groups); and (4) public opinion measurement providing reaction to events and decisions. The Internet has become a tool for political discourse as well as serving other needs. Media scholars have found that individuals will utilize a medium if it serves some basic utility, such as providing information, guidance, and reinforcement (Katz, Blumler, and Gurevitch 1974). Other scholars have argued that accessibility and availability of the medium have an impact on the individual's proclivity to use that medium (Phillips, Boylan, and Yu 1976). Realizing the need in the lesbian, gay, and bisexual community for the types of information and resources found on the Internet and the lack of resources among many in this community to access the Internet, it was believed that if "we built it they would come" (to quote from a popular film, "Field of Dreams"). To this end, a cyber center was established with a grant from the University of Southern California's Annenberg Center for Communication. The Queer Cyber Center is a computer-equipped facility providing free public access to the Internet. The pilot research project QCC is at the Los Angeles Gay and Lesbian Community Services Center in Hollywood, California. The purpose of this community cyber center is to bring free Internet access to lesbians, gays, bisexuals, transgendered, and straight individuals who would not otherwise have access to computers and the Internet. The Los Angeles Gay and Lesbian Community Services Center's clientele is very diverse in terms of economic background, race, ethnicity, needs, and demands. To provide equal opportunity for members of this sexual minority subpopulation to avail themselves of this new technological forum and repository of information, it was imperative that low-income, low-status individuals have access to computers and assistance in utilizing them. Otherwise, the dire predictions of scholars such as Anderson et al. (1995) will be realized and only those with ample resources will be able to participate in this new, virtual construct of the "village square." The economically and technologically disadvantaged will be denied access to this public forum, violating one of the cornerstones of democracy: access to the "free marketplace of ideas."

In addition to the physical QCC, a Web site <http://www.qcc.org> was created to disseminate information about the QCC. The Web site highlighted community events and available resources, as well as numerous links to other political Web sites.[6] The QCC Web site went online in March 1996. By the beginning of 1997, there had been over 7,500 visits to the QCC Web site. All those who visited the QCC Web site were required to register. A series of closed-ended demographic questions constituted the online registration. The analysis described in the following section relies on the results of this data collection through user registration. Of the over 7,500 registered visitors, we have collected data on 7,210 users. This large sample provides us with a detailed profile of those who are availing themselves of this new technology and addressing some other intellectual and theoretical propositions raised in this chapter.

USER PROFILES

For almost 20 percent of the users, their visit to the QCC Web site was the first time they had used the Internet. Over half of the first-time QCC users were accessing the QCC Web site from the computers at the Gay and Lesbian Center. Nearly 5 percent of the users indicated that their primary access to the Internet was through the center's facilities. The data suggest the center and the QCC Web site catered almost exclusively to lesbians, gays, and bisexuals. Fewer than 3 percent of the users, from within and outside the center, indicated their sexual identity as "straight."

It is important to note that the Internet as a tool of political communication transcends geographic borders. Nearly 20 percent of the users were from outside the United States. The Internet allows for marginalized groups to engage in community building and group consciousness-raising on an international scale. For many living in sexually repressive cultural regimes or oppressive political regimes, the Internet provides the opportunity to connect with other members of their group. Bimber (1996) describes this communitarian view of the Internet, "the most valuable function of the Net is neither connecting citizens with government nor citizens with political organizers, but rather connecting citizens with one another. The effects of the Net occur in the domain of culture, socialization, and norm-and belief-building" (p. 5).

Some scholars have criticized the Internet's anonymity: "One major problem . . . is participants can hide behind a veil of relative anonymity" (Davis 1996: 15). Yet it is for this very reason that this medium is attractive to members of marginalized groups. For the sexual minority community, being "out" may have serious consequences, even in societies exhibiting relatively tolerant attitudes toward homosexuals. Many have experienced isolation, social distancing, physical brutality, economic hardship, and familial estrangement. The anonymous nature of this communication medium allows for frank and open dialogue without fear of retribution. It may very well be the case that for many, this is the only communication vehicle they have to discuss issues, gain a sense of identity, retrieve information, identify important resources, and—we suspect—become further politically socialized.

GENERAL DEMOGRAPHIC PROFILE

Sexual Identity

Of the over 7,000 users, nearly 55 percent identified themselves as gay, 7 percent as lesbian, almost 19.5 percent as bisexual, and 2 percent as "queer." Nearly 3 percent answered they were straight and 14 percent didn't know their sexual identity or refused to answer. Females were very much under-represented as users. Overall, 13 percent of the users were female and 87 percent were male.

Age

The average age of the QCC Web site user was 34. Well over a third (38%) of the users were between the ages of twenty-six and thirty-five. Nearly equal percentages of the users fell into the age ranges of eighteen to twenty-five and thirty-six to forty-five years (27% and 23%, respectively). Fewer than 15 percent of the users were forty-six years or older.

Ethnicity

The QCC Web site survey data indicate that the Internet is used predominantly by whites. Of those QCC users indicating membership in a race or ethnic group, only 16.3 percent were members of minority ethnic groups. Blacks represented 4.7 percent of the minority group users.

Educational Level

Over half of the QCC users had a college or post-graduate degree (29% and 24%, respectively). One-third indicated having completed some college course work, and over 13 percent had an educational level of high school or less.

Occupation

Students and the unemployed, retired, or disabled were almost equally represented among QCC users (22% students; 19% unemployed, retired, and disabled). This group constitutes over two-fifths of the visitors to the QCC Web site. White-collar workers account for 24 percent of the users and, not surprisingly, the largest occupational group of users is composed of professionals (35%).

In summary, it appears that college-educated, white, gay men under the age of forty-six constitute the largest group to visit the QCC Web site. However, it is also evident that students, the retired, unemployed, or disabled, members of minority groups, and the less educated are also utilizing the Internet and visiting the QCC Web site.

POLITICAL PROFILE

Ideology

The dominant political ideology of visitors to the QCC Web site was liberal (over 50%), with moderates constituting the second largest category. Few indicated they were conservative or radical.

Political Party Affiliation

Slightly less than half (46%) of the users indicated affiliation with the Democratic Party. Republicans and Independents were close in numbers (12% and 14%, respectively). A surprisingly large percentage (28%) indicated they have no political party affiliation.

Registered to Vote

Visitors to the QCC Web site are among the more politically active, with nearly 80 percent registered to vote.

In summary, the typical QCC Web site visitor is politically liberal or moderate, and a Democrat or a non-party identifier (possibly indicating disaffection with the two established political parties) who probably votes.

It is interesting to note that QCC Web site users are in many ways similar to other Internet users. A recent online Web survey of users was conducted by Georgia Institute of Technology.[7] Table 11.1 compares the user profiles of those responding to the Georgia Tech online survey with those registering at the QCC Web site.

QCC Web site users are less conservative, more aligned with the Democratic Party, and more likely to not identify with any political party. Both groups of users have very high voter registration rates. QCC users have

Table 11.1
Comparison of Surveys of Internet User

	Georgia Tech Online Survey (n=11,700)	QCC Online Survey (n=7,210)
AVG. AGE	33 years	34 years
GENDER	31.5%	13.3%
UNITED STATES	73.4%	80.3%
HOME ACCESS	55.4%	70.6%
POLITICAL IDEOLOGY: MODERATE	30.1%	40.4%
DEMOCRAT	25.4%	46.3%
REPUBLICAN	21.1%	11.8%
INDEP. (LEANERS)	26.7%	*
INDEP. (PURE)	7.4%	13.8%
NO PARTY	*	28.1%
REGISTERED TO VOTE	92%	79.5%

* = Data not available.

higher rates of home access to computers, possible due to high use by students (22%). Both groups are similar in age but dissimilar in terms of gender representation. Females are under-represented in the group of QCC users.

LIMITATIONS OF RESULTS

Readers must be reminded that online methods of data collection are a recent phenomenon. We wholeheartedly agree with the researchers at the Georgia Institute of Technology (1996: 11) "WWW based surveying techniques are pioneering and as such, require conservative interpretation of collected data due to the absence of time-tested validation and correction metrics." Because the sampling method was nonrandom and self-selecting, one must use caution in generalizing from the data presented to the general population of lesbian, gay, and bisexual Internet users.

CONCLUSION

The creation of a pilot research project—a public-access, community Internet facility located within the largest nonprofit, social service agency in the country catering to the myriad sub-sexual minority communities (the Los Angeles Gay and Lesbian Center [LAGLC])—enabled collection of a significant body of information about the political communication patterns and Internet use by a marginalized population.

The Queer Cyber Center has been a tremendous success. Usage has been very high and available by both novices and experienced Internet users. The naming of this cyber center as "queer" was expected initially to provoke use by a more self-identifying, radicalized element of this subpopulation. The data have suggested, however, a different pattern of self-labeling (and perhaps identify formation)—individuals overwhelmingly prefer to self-identify as lesbian, gay or bisexual, instead of queer.

A significant number of the public users at the cyber center could be described as the "marginalized-of-the-marginalized"—homeless individuals, the unemployed, youths living in several nearby shelters, and the borderline mentally ill who came to the LAGLC seeking psychological services and ventured into the QCC. These are not the "archetypal" users one generally associates with the population on the Internet, and it has been fascinating to study the ease of their engagement, high level of interest, and repeated, regular use of this previously unavailable technology. We later added free e-mail accounts for these public users, which proved not only popular, but in some cases were the first "virtual home-address" many ever had. Many of these individuals had few other "positive" environments available to them. The QCC provides a social space that allows for interaction between this population and the more "conventional" Internet user. The overwhelming success of the QCC as a pilot project gave USC and LAGLC the impetus to permanently establish the cyber center as a prototype of democratizing access that could occur at other community-based service centers.

Moving from the research case model to the theoretical ground covered in this chapter, what tentative conclusions can we offer regarding the politicization, identity formation, forms of political communication, and socialization of the lesbian, gay and bisexual community in a newly developing cyber democracy?

We see the Internet as a useful self-empowering tool for the political advancement and self-identity enhancement of this subpopulation. As with other comparative ethnic subgroups in search of "a rooted community" (e.g., Armenians, Jews), we consider lesbians, gays, and bisexuals as diasporic peoples who have been scattered around the globe. The Internet has the potential to bring "an imagined community" or a "virtual homeland" to this population once the access and availability issues have been overcome. This is a powerful concept for a marginalized subpopulation. Perhaps at first people will gravitate to comfortable "cyberghettos" to find strength in numbers and a collective political will. At least within the ghetto there is a reduction of homophobia and the potential to overcome the victimization so many marginalized populations begin to own.

The potential to find a new "digital gay (or queer) identity" and to de-emphasize negative socially constructed paradigms is within the realm of this new technology. We may also find the advancement of the modality aiding in what we term the "leveling of gender," and thus the reduction of prejudice and discrimination based on gender nonconformity. We see evidence today—from AOL's chat rooms to the recently overturned "Internet Indecency Law"—that sexual speech and gender-blending are preoccupations with the current majority Internet users (mostly white heterosexual males). Will the Internet relax strict male and female societal-based gender categories? Only time will tell.

Last, the Internet can be a democratizing tool for the marginalized and disenfranchised. New forms of political communication are being adopted to redistribute power relations. The sexual minority community seems well positioned to make significant political gains if it is able to empower itself for collective action, electronic advocacy, engagement in policy formation, and demanding that digital citizenship entails full civil and human rights.

NOTES

1. In the first introductory volume (titled *La volonté de savior*, the will to know) Foucault argues that "discursive practices" would locate the truth for homosexuals, enabling them to escape the false dichotomy between repression and liberation. Thus he begins to set up a new paradigm for analysis: the opportunity to do more than just resist, or what he terms the dawning of the idea of a modern gay *askesis*.

2. For the purpose of this treatise we will use interchangeably the terms homosexuality with gay, lesbian, and bisexual although there are greater definitional distinctions mixing sex, sexual orientation behavior, and gender categories. See for more clarity the definitional offerings of human sexuality in LeVay and Nonas

(1995). Furthermore, we shall use the term "queer" in referring to the more politically radicalized, nonassimilationist segment of the lesbian, gay, and bisexual community.

3. We find helpful Steven Epstein's (1992) use of the terms "essentialist" to define the core intrapsychic identity formation and "constructionist" to denote the socially imposed adoption of identity.

4. For example, see Glazer and Moynihan (1963), Jackson and Preston (1991), Browning, Marshall, and Tabb (1984).

5. See University of Michigan's National Election Studies scale of political participation in W. Miller, D. Kinder, and S. Rosenstone (1992). *American National Election Study*. ICPSR#6067. ICPSR University of Michigan.

6. The Web site was also designed as a gathering point for additional groundbreaking social science data on the political attitudes, behaviors, and voting patterns of the lesbian, gay and bisexual community. A series of survey instruments were employed to query myriad political dimensions. Results of these online surveys and further cross tabulations and analysis will appear in a forthcoming Sage Publications book by Schockman and Koch, titled *Rainbow Politics: The Making of Gay and Lesbian Political Behavior*.

7. The Georgia Institute of Technology's online survey was conducted April–May 1996, coinciding with the QCC online survey, conducted from March 1996 through January 1977.

REFERENCES

Anderson, R., T. Bikson, S. Law, and B. Mitchell. 1995. *Universal Access to E-Mail: Feasibility and Societal Implication* [MR-650-MF]. Santa Monica, Calif.: RAND.

Bailey, Robert W. 1997. *Sexual Identity and Growth Control Politics: Conflicting Themes in Lesbian and Gay Involvement in San Francisco Politics*. Paper presented at the annual meeting of the Western Political Science Association, Tucson, March 13.

Berger, Peter L. and Thomas Luckmann. 1967. *The Social Construction of Reality*. New York: Anchor Books.

Bimber, Bruce. 1996. *The Internet and Political Transformation*. Unpublished paper. Online: http://alishaw.sscf.ucsb.edu

Browning, Rufus, Dale Rogers Marshall, and David Tabb. 1984. *Protest Is Not Enough: The Struggle of Blacks and Hispanics*. Berkeley, Calif.: University of California Press.

Cory, Donald Webster. 1951. *The Homosexual in America: A Subjective Approach*. New York: Greenberg.

Davis, Richard. 1996. *Political Communication and the Internet*. Paper presented at the annual meeting of the American Political Science Association, September 1, San Francisco.

D'Emilio, John. 1983. *Sexual Politics, Sexual Communities: The Making of a Homosexual Minority in the United States, 1940–1970*. Chicago: University of Chicago Press.

Deutsch, Karl. 1963. *The Nerves of Government*. New York: Free Press.

Easton, David. 1964. *A Framework for Political Analysis*. Englewood Cliffs, N.J.: Prentice-Hall.

———. 1965. *A Systems Analysis of Political Life*. New York: John Wiley.

Edelman, Murray. 1964. *Symbolic Uses of Politics*. Urbana, Ill.: University of Illinois Press.

Epstein, Steven. 1992. "Gay politics, ethnic identity: The limits of social constructionism." In Wayne R. Dynes and Stephen Donaldson, eds., *Homosexuality and Government, Politics and Prisons*, Vol. 10. New York: Garland Publishing, pp. 117–62.

Foucault, Michel. 1980. *The History of Sexuality: An Introduction*, trans. Robert Hurley. New York: Random House.

———. 1988. *The Case of the Self*, trans. Robert Hurley. New York: Random House.

———. 1990. *The Use of Pleasure*, trans. Robert Hurley. New York: Random House.

Georgia Institute of Technology. 1996. *GVU's 5th WWW User Survey*. Online: http://www.cc.gatech.edu/gbu/user-surveys/survey-04-1996

Glazer, Nathan and Daniel P. Moynihan. 1963. *Beyond the Melting Pot: The Negroes, Puerto Ricans, Jews, Italians and Irish of New York City*. Cambridge, Mass.: MIT Press.

Gleason, Philip. 1983. "Identifying identity: A semantic history." *Journal of American History* 69 (4):910–31.

Jackson, Byran and Michael B. Preston, eds. 1991. *Racial and Ethnic Politics in California*. Berkeley: University of California IGS Press.

Katz, Elihu, Jay G. Blumler, and Michael Gurevitch. 1974. "Uses and gratifications research." In W. Phillips Davidson and Frederick T. C. Yu, eds., *Mass Communication Research*. New York: Praeger.

LeVay, Simon and Elizabeth Nonas. 1995. *City of Friends: A Portrait of the Gay and Lesbian Community in America*. Cambridge, Mass.: MIT Press.

McCain, T. and Nadine Koch. 1985. "Gender differences in political communication: A look at the 1980 presidential election." In Keith Sanders, Linda Kaid, and Dan Nimmo, eds., *Political Communication Yearbook*. Carbondale, Ill.: Southern Illinois University Press.

Meadow, Robert. 1980. *Politics as Communication*. Norwood, N.J.: ABLEX Publishing.

Muller, C. 1975. *The Politics of Communication*. New York: Oxford University Press.

Phillips, W. Davison, James Boylan, and T. C. Frederick Yu. 1976. *Mass Media: Systems and Effects*. New York: Praeger.

Schockman, H. Eric and Nadine Koch. 1995. *The Continuing Political Incorporation of Gays and Lesbians in California: Attitudes, Motivations and Political Development*. Paper presented at the annual meeting of the Western Political Science Association, Portland, March 15.

———. 1996. *Political Behavior of the Gay, Lesbian and Bisexual Community: A California Case Study*. Paper presented at the annual meeting of the American Political Science Association, San Francisco, September 1.

12

Communicative Style and Gender Differences in Computer-Mediated Communications

Kevin Crowston and Ericka Kammerer

This chapter reports on an experiment that explored how gender interacts with communicative style to affect decisions to participate in computer-mediated communications (e.g., Usenet newsgroups). Although some field studies indicate that style has a differential effect on men and women, the data fail to confirm this hypothesis. However, significant differences were found in interest in topics, as well as effects of style across all subjects, which have implications for the design of future studies on this topic.

INTRODUCTION

In the familiar world of face-to-face communication, gender is one of the most obvious factors that affect perceptions of what people say and do. Unfortunately, it is believed that these perceptions often work to the detriment of women, reducing their influence in many situations. In the world of text-based computer-mediated communication (CMC), such as electronic mail or computer conferencing, there are no visual or auditory cues to indicate a speaker's gender (or indeed, most other personal characteristics). Previous CMC research has suggested that by diminishing the salience of social cues in electronic discourse, the use of CMC should eliminate or at least lessen gender-influenced inequalities (Rice 1984; Culnan and Markus 1987; Huber 1990; Kahn and Brookshire 1991; Sproull and Kiesler 1991). In fact, in some situations it is possible for contributors to be anonymous or deliberately ungendered (Bruckman 1993), which again might be expected to make gender-based discrimination all but impossible.

Unfortunately, other field research suggests that the reduced social cues afforded by computer mediation do not seem to be a panacea for gender inequalities (e.g., Kramarae and Taylor 1993; Shade 1993). S. Herring found two electronic-mail discussion lists she studied to be male-dominated (Herring 1992a; Herring et al. 1992); We (1994) reported that of 595 messages posted to two Usenet newsgroups (alt.feminism and soc.women), 480 were from men and only seventy-one from women (the gender of the sender could not be determined for the remaining forty-four messages). The imbalance in these figures (87% male, 13% female) is striking, even given the under-representation of women in the overall population of Internet users (one estimate suggests women are 36% of Internet users [Quarterman and Carl-Mitchell 1995]).

It is possible that women are simply not interested in the topics being discussed, although it seems odd that men would be so much more interested in feminism. Evidence suggests, however, that many women (and some men) simply do not feel comfortable participating in these discussions (Herring 1994). An explanation for such discomfort is that other cues—communicative style, in particular—effectively convey gender information and potential posters respond to these embedded cues (Herring 1992).

The purpose of this study was to understand how gender interacts with communicative style to affect participation and thus contribution and influence in CMC settings. Communicative style is defined generally as gender-related differences in the use of language. Understanding the role of gender and antecedents of gender-based inequalities in CMC participation is crucial. CMC is increasingly used in corporate environments; it provides the necessary communications infrastructure for the emerging "virtual corporation." In the future, CMC may also be widespread in public discourse in general, for example, in the form of online "electronic town meetings." It is therefore important to understand how or if communicative style differentially affects women's and men's desire to participate in such conversations. As an initial approach, these effects were studied in an experiment, using Usenet newsgroups as a context.

THEORETICAL BACKGROUND

This research is at the intersection of research on gender differences in communicative style and on computer-mediated communications. This section reviews prior research on both topics and on their intersection, deferring detailed discussions of methods and measures to the next section.

Research on Gender and Communicative Style

In the linguistics literature, there have been numerous studies of language differences between men and women (e.g., Lakoff 1975; Thorne and Hen-

Table 12.1
Characteristics of Adversarial and Supportive/Attenuated Communicative Styles

Adversarial	Supportive/attenuated
strong assertions	attenuated assertions
self-promotion	apologies
presuppositions	explicit justifications
rhetorical questions	true questions
authoritative tone	personal tone
challenges others	supports others
humor/irony	

Source: Herring, Susan C. 1992. Gender and participation in computer-mediated linguistic discourse. Paper presented at the Annual Meeting of the Linguistic Society of America, Philidelphia, Jan. 9–12. Also available as ERIC document ED345552.

ley 1975; Tannen 1990). In her review of this literature, J. Coates (1993) identified eight characteristics that figure prominently: verbosity, importance of topics (which she includes in her discussion of verbosity), minimal responses, hedges, tag questions, commands, swearing and taboo language, and compliments. For each of these phenomena, prior research has proposed differences between men's and women's communicative styles. Herring (1992a) used a somewhat different set of features, shown in Table 12.1. It should be noted that these characteristics are tendencies, not absolutes; women do use men's speech and vice versa, but less commonly.

As well as preferring different styles in speaking, some evidence suggests that men and women are more comfortable participating in different types of conversations. Production of and comfort with a style seems not to have been separately studied in face-to-face conversations, perhaps because talking and listening are so interwoven. However, in a survey of mailing list participants, Herring (1992a) found that while both women and men were intimidated or annoyed by the adversarial tone of the debate (women somewhat more so than men), women produced less adversarial discourse and avoided participating in discussions dominated by an adversarial style, despite the fact that the women claimed to be very interested in the topic being discussed and to have the required time and computer skills necessary to participate.

To summarize, this literature suggests that women and men produce and prefer different communicative styles, both in verbal and in computer-mediated communications.

Research on CMC and Equality of Participation

As mentioned above, the CMC literature suggests that the use of CMC promotes more equal exchanges by de-emphasizing social context cues or by permitting anonymity. As well, Hiltz and Turoff (1993) hypothesized that in CMC it will be less likely that a single dominant individual will emerge and that there are more likely to be multiple leaders because one person's response, however quickly offered, does not preclude the responses of others. In a pilot study, they found that equality of participation overall was higher in CMC groups than in face-to-face discourse.

Selfe and Meyer (1991) report on "Megabyte University," an electronic group for English composition teachers to discuss the use of computer technology in the classroom. They found that men and higher-status individuals contributed significantly more messages and words, introduced more topics, and disagreed with others more often. No significant differences in politeness of messages were reported. Interestingly, these differences did not disappear when subjects could post pseudonymously, although there was some evidence that the option of pseudonyms prompted some individuals to start posting.

Berdahl and Craig (1996) report on a study of three- to four-person groups meeting face-to-face (FTF) or using a synchronous CMC system. Groups were either all male or female or had one "solo" of a different gender. In comparing self-reported levels of participation, they found that CMC groups initially were less equal than FTF groups, but the conditions converged by the end of seven weeks. This finding highlights the danger of studying initial uses of CMC systems. Contrary to their expectations, solo males in computer groups had more influence on an essay task than non-solos did, and this ratio was significantly greater than the ratio for solo females. Although some differences were found in levels of task participation in different conditions, these did not translate into significant differences in task influence.

To summarize, the CMC literature and studies are equivocal. Some suggest that the use of CMC allows more equal levels of participation and influence; others find that the use of CMC can leave differences in perceived contribution and influence.

Research on Communicative Style and CMC

Finally, there are several studies on the use of CMC that address communicative style differences. Sproull and Kiesler (1986) studied the use of electronic mail in a large corporation. They report that electronic mail messages exhibited uninhibited behavior, such as "flaming" or flouting of social conventions, which they attributed to lessened social context cues (p. 1508). Sproull and Kiesler also reported that women posted significantly fewer messages (955 vs. 293) which were significantly shorter in length (p. 1504), although they did not attempt to explain this difference.

Herring has investigated gender and communicative style on several electronic mailing lists: the Linguist discussion list (Herring 1992b), Megabyte University (Herring et al. 1992), and in nine discussion groups (Herring, in press-a). In all three studies, she and her colleagues found two distinct styles of postings, which she called "adversarial" and "supportive/attenuated." She notes that men and women use both styles, but that men tend toward adversarial and women toward supportive/attenuated. The extremes of each are used "almost exclusively by one gender and not the other" (Herring, in press-a). In the remainder of this chapter, these will be referred to as M- and F-styles, respectively. Since the characteristics of flaming and M-style speech overlap to some extent, Sproull and Kiesler's finding suggests that electronic communications may be more likely to be M-style.

To summarize, this literature suggests that gender difference in communicative style and level of participation and contribution are found in CMC as well as in face-to-face communication.

HYPOTHESES AND VARIABLES

Based on the prior work summarized above, and especially Herring (1992a; 1992b), it was hypothesized that in the context of text-based computer conferencing, gender will affect level of participation through the intervention of gender-specific communicative style. The rest of this section discusses the choice of theoretical concepts and presents specific hypotheses.

Prior research has used various outcome measures for gender equality, such as contribution or influence. This study will focus on participation. Simple participation is important because women may be systematically deciding not to participate in CMC. For example, Truong (1993) reports cases of women feeling harassed to the point of dropping out of online discussions. In other words, participation is a necessary precondition for contributing to or influencing a group.

It is hypothesized that there will be a link between communicative style and participation: Women will be less likely to participate in a heavily M-style discussion and, conversely, men will be less likely to participate in a heavily F-style discussion. If this pattern is seen, it can be inferred that communicative style does indeed differentially affect individuals' choices on whether to participate in a particular conference above and beyond the influence of topic.

Usenet News

Usenet News was chosen as the context for our study. Usenet News is a distributed worldwide computer conferencing system organized into a hierarchy of newsgroups on a diversity of topics, including computer systems, social issues, hobbies, and current events. Users create messages and post them to a particular newsgroup or newsgroups, where they can be read and replied to by anyone who chooses to read that newsgroup. (In this respect, Usenet News acts somewhat like an electronic-mail mailing list to which anyone can subscribe.) For example, a user might ask a question of the list or state a position in an argument. In response, other users might post public answers, statements of support, or rebuttals.

Usenet newsgroups are a particularly appropriate context for this experiment (and for more in-depth follow-on studies) for several reasons:

- Data are easily and inexpensively accessible. Popular newsgroups have hundreds of postings a week, making it feasible to collect large volumes of data. It is estimated that a total of 127,000 messages are posted each day.

- There are newsgroups on a wide range of topics (recent listings included 1,720 official newsgroups and 3,516 on "alternative" topics). It should therefore be possible to find newsgroups with a range of theoretically interesting characteristics.

- Usenet News is available to many users, from many organizations. It is estimated that Usenet News is read by on the order of 10 million people on approximately 330,000 host computers. This diversity has several advantages. First, contributors are unlikely to communicate in other settings, so the public messages provide a nearly complete record of a newsgroup's discussion. Second, possible effects of corporate cultures are effectively randomized, giving the study wider applicability. Finally, the absence of a corporate framework reduces possible confounds from interpersonal power differences.

- The exchange of messages more closely parallels a conversation, as opposed to the publishing model of the World Wide Web.

In a sense, Usenet News is a model for a community-wide public discourse system. However, these findings should also be applicable to corporations, which are increasingly using CMC systems to assemble teams composed of individuals from different divisions, regions, or even companies, who may not otherwise interact.

EXPERIMENTAL DESIGN

This study attempts to answer the question: Does communicative style differentially affect men's and women's interest in participating in a newsgroup? This question was addressed experimentally by administering questionnaires asking subjects to rate their interest in participating in newsgroups with messages of different communicative styles. Because individual and gender differences in interest in the topic of newsgroups could confound our results, our design controlled for interest in topic.

Instruments

The experiment was run twice (as explained below), both times administering two questionnaires. The first questionnaire measured interest in participation in forty-eight newsgroups to be able to control for differences in initial interest. For each message, subjects were simply asked to report on a 7-point scale how interested they would be in participating in a newsgroup on the topic, where 1 meant "Not at all interested in reading a newsgroup on this topic" and 7 meant "Certain to read a newsgroup on this topic." Unfortunately, space considerations restricted the measure to this single question. Subjects were also asked to report their gender, as well as other demographic data, including age, school, school year, and level of use of Usenet.

To determine subjects' reactions to messages of different communicative styles, a second questionnaire was administered approximately two weeks after the first questionnaire. This questionnaire presented sample Usenet messages with different communicative styles. For each message, subjects were asked to report on the same 7-point scale how interested they would be in participating in a newsgroup with messages like the one presented. As well, they were asked to say why they responded as they did.

To develop the second questionnaire, newsgroups of high interest were identified from the first questionnaire. From each, representative messages of F- and M-style were selected. Messages were edited to remove cues to the gender or affiliation of the poster, the name of the newsgroup, and in some cases, for length or to make the style more extreme. Responses to the two questionnaires were linked by having subjects write an identifying word or two on both questionnaires.

Subjects

The questionnaires were administered to undergraduate students in an introductory information systems class. For the first questionnaire, a total of 126 responses were received, seventy-three from men and fifty-three from women. For the second, forty-nine usable responses were received for the first pass, twenty-eight from men and twenty-one from women, and thirty-five for the second, twenty from women and fifteen from men. Because this was an exploratory study, the effect sizes were not known in advance, making it impossible to calculate the necessary sample size. As it turns out, the size of the effect is small and so the power of some tests is low.

RESULTS

First Questionnaire

The results of the first questionnaire from both passes combined are shown in Table 12.2. The average rating for all topics was approximately the same for men and women, 3.26 and 3.22 out of 7, respectively. However, women and men differed in their evaluations of numerous topics, mostly in stereotypical ways. Men's and women's responses were compared using the Mann-Whitney U—Wilcoxon Rank Sum W test.

The interests of business undergraduates were also compared with those of other students. These interests differed significantly for only four topics. In other words, men's and women's interests differed more than did those of students in different degree programs.

Second Questionnaire, First Pass

Based on these results, ten of the most popular groups were selected (indicated by the in Table 12.2), taking care to select the most popular groups for each gender. A second questionnaire was created (as described above) by selecting one message of each style from each group.

To determine how communicative style affected subjects' interests in participating, the difference between the initial reported interest in each topic and the interest after seeing a message of each style was calculated, giving two new variables for each of the ten newsgroups; the average change for men and women for each style is plotted in Figure 12.1. These variables indicate how much reported interest changed after seeing a message of each style. Using SPSS, a repeated measures analysis of variance was performed on these twenty variables, representing ten levels of TOPIC and two levels of STYLE within subjects, with GENDER as a between-subjects variable. Table 12.3 shows the significance of the factors and the reported power of the tests at an alpha level of 0.05.

It had been hypothesized that women and men would react differently to messages of different styles, that is, that the interaction between GENDER and STYLE would be significant. As Table 12.3 shows, every variable and interaction was significant or nearly significant with reasonable power, except for this interaction. In other words, for these ten groups, subjects' changes in reported interest were significantly different:

- for different topics (TOPIC)
- for message of different styles (STYLE)—on average, interest dropped by 0.82 after seeing M-style messages and by 0.44 after seeing F-style messages.

These differences differed (TOPIC by STYLE).

Table 12.2

Comparison of Interest in Newsgroups Topics by Men (N = 73) and Women (N = 53) and by Business (N = 65) and Non-business (N = 61) Students on a 7-point Scale, and Significance of Difference from Mann-Whitney U—Wilcoxon Rank Sum W Test

Topic	Overall	Male	Female		Business	Non-	
✓Travel in Europe.	4.88	4.34	5.60	**	4.83	4.93	
Postings of resumes and "situations wanted"	4.80	4.24	5.57	**	4.57	5.05	
✓NBC's comedy Friends.	4.78	4.48	5.19	*	5.20	4.33	*
✓College, college activities, campus life	4.63	4.25	5.15	**	4.77	4.48	
✗The TV show Seinfeld.	4.54	4.73	4.27		4.77	4.28	
✓Airline travel around the world.	4.53	4.04	5.21	**	4.48	4.59	
✓Jokes and the like.	4.47	4.38	4.58		4.42	4.52	
✓Basketball on the collegiate level.	4.38	4.70	3.94	*	4.37	4.39	
✗Laptop (portable) computers.	4.27	4.26	4.28		4.05	4.51	
✓US-style college football.	4.22	4.71	3.55	**	4.40	4.03	
Forum for sharing information about stocks	4.18	4.47	3.77		3.95	4.41	
✗Interactive multimedia technologies of all kinds	4.10	4.07	4.13		3.85	4.37	
✓Food, cooking, cookbooks, and recipes.	3.87	3.36	4.57	**	3.82	3.92	
✓Backpacking and activities in the great outdoors	3.85	3.90	3.79		3.59	4.13	
Beer.	3.80	3.97	3.57		3.92	3.67	

Table 12.2 (continued)

Topic	Overall	Male	Female		Business	Non-
✔Q & A for users new to the Usenet.	3.59	3.32	3.98		3.25	3.95 *
Books of all genres, and the publishing	3.55	3.36	3.81		3.51	3.60
Driving automobiles.	3.48	3.49	3.47		3.48	3.48
MS Windows issues in general.	3.47	3.39	3.58		3.29	3.66
The TV show The Simpsons.	3.43	3.73	3.02		3.31	3.56
Arcade-style games on PCs.	3.23	3.41	2.98		3.00	3.48
Ice hockey.	3.21	3.58	2.70	*	3.40	3.00
All aspects of golfing.	3.11	3.67	2.34	**	3.43	2.77 *
Pets, pet care, and household animals in general	3.09	2.83	3.44		3.17	3.00
The TV show Melrose Place.	3.09	2.48	3.92	**	3.37	2.79
Macintosh applications.	3.02	3.16	2.81		2.31	3.75 **
Classical music.	2.99	2.93	3.07		2.95	3.02
Children, their behavior and activities.	2.87	2.44	3.45	**	2.78	2.95
The band REM.	2.87	2.60	3.23		3.08	2.64
Baseball.	2.86	3.25	2.34	*	2.88	2.85
Collectors of many things.	2.81	2.93	2.64		2.92	2.69
Writing in all of its forms.	2.70	2.36	3.17	**	2.55	2.85
Movies with a cult following.	2.70	2.97	2.32		2.58	2.82
Soccer (association football).	2.63	2.90	2.26		2.80	2.45

Discussion and hints on board games.	2.60	2.66	2.53		2.49	2.72
Hobbyists interested in scuba diving.	2.53	2.68	2.32		2.49	2.57
Written science fiction and fantasy.	2.53	2.81	2.15	*	2.45	2.62
For the posting of poems.	2.53	2.33	2.81		2.34	2.73
All Sega video game systems and software	2.47	2.85	1.94	*	2.26	2.69
The TV show X-Files.	2.42	2.62	2.13		2.27	2.57
Rotisserie (fantasy) baseball play.	2.36	2.92	1.58	**	2.43	2.28
Japanese animation.	2.31	2.36	2.25		2.23	2.39
The band Phish.	2.25	2.23	2.26		2.18	2.31
A group for (Grateful) Dead-heads.	2.16	2.38	1.85		2.15	2.16
Buying, selling & reviewing items for cycling	2.04	2.22	1.79		2.11	1.97
Motorcycles and related products and law	2.02	2.19	1.79		1.92	2.13
The singer Tori Amos.	1.96	1.89	2.06		2.05	1.87
The sport of cricket.	1.62	1.79	1.38		1.77	1.46

Notes: * ratings significantly different, $p < 5\%$; ** ratings significantly different, $p < 1\%$; ✔ included on survey 1; ✘ included on survey 2.

Figure 12.1
Average Change in Reported Interest in Participating in a Newsgroup after Seeing Messages of Different Styles, by Gender of Subject, for Pass 1

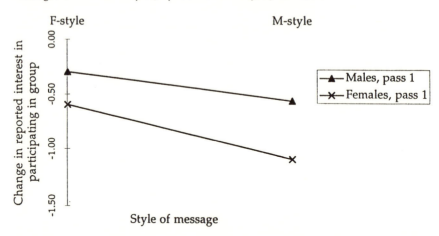

As well, men's and women's changes in reported interest were significantly different: On average (GENDER)—men's interest dropped by 0.43 on average while women's dropped by 0.84—but not for messages of different style (GENDER by STYLE was not significant). However, note the low power for the nonsignificant results, meaning that we cannot be confident of our decision not to reject the null hypothesis.

Second Questionnaire, Second Trial

While these results are interesting, and confirm that men and women react differently to different topics, they offer no support for our main hypothesis. It was thought that these results might have been due to the difference in interest in topic overwhelming differences in reactions to messages of different styles. Therefore, the experiment was rerun with a new pool of subjects. On this trial, the second questionnaire included messages from three newsgroups (indicated by the ✖ in Table 12.2) for which the difference between women and men's interests was nonsignificant. Two messages of each style were selected for each newsgroup, for a total of twelve messages.

The results of the analysis of these two questionnaires is shown in Table 12.4 and plotted in Figure 12.2. Again, the difference between the initial reported interest in each topic and the interest after seeing a message of each style was calculated. A repeated measures analysis of variance was performed on these twelve variables, representing three levels of TOPIC, two levels of STYLE, and two levels of a dummy variable TRIAL within subjects with GENDER as a between-subjects variables. Assignment of the

Table 12.3
Results of a Repeated Measures Analysis of Variance Showing Effects of TOPIC, GENDER, and STYLE on Difference in Reported Interest Initially and after Seeing Messages, on First Pass ($N = 42$)

Variable	Multivariate F	Significance	Power at .05
GENDER	5.32	2.6%	0.614
TOPIC	19.376	0.0%	1.00
GENDER by TOPIC	2.09	5.7%	0.78
STYLE	14.36	0.0%	0.959
GENDER by STYLE	0.33	57%	0.053
TOPIC by STYLE	5.733	0.0%	1.00
GENDER by TOPIC by STYLE	2.105	5.6%	0.78

pairs of messages of the same style from the same newsgroup to a TRIAL condition was arbitrary, and the variable and its interaction terms were expected to be nonsignificant.

For these newsgroups, subjects' change in reported interest was significantly different:

- for different messages (TOPIC by TRIAL) even within the same topic
- for message of different styles (STYLE)—on average, interest dropped by 0.40 after seeing M-style messages but remained about the same after seeing F-style messages (while the levels are different than in the first pass, the difference between them is about the same).

These differences differed (TOPIC by STYLE and TOPIC by TRIAL by STYLE).

In this case, however, GENDER and most of the interaction terms including GENDER were not significant, reflecting our choice of groups with nonsignificant gender differences. The exception is GENDER by TOPIC by TRIAL by STYLE; again, women and men differed in their reactions to messages of different styles differently for different topics. Unfortunately, GENDER by STYLE was again nonsignificant, indicating that women and men again did not differ significantly in their reactions to messages of different styles overall.

Analysis of Qualitative Data

As well as the quantitative data, the open-ended responses (in which subjects described why they rated their interest in participating) were qual-

Table 12.4

Results of a Repeated Measures Analysis of Variance Showing Effects of GENDER, TOPIC, STYLE, and TRIAL on Difference in Reported Interest Initially and after Seeing Messages, on Second Pass ($N = 33$)

Variable	Multivariate F	Significance	Power at .05
GENDER	2.12	15.5%	0.292
TOPIC	2.00	15.2%	0.38
GENDER by TOPIC	2.03	14.9%	0.39
STYLE	10.08	0.3%	0.867
GENDER by STYLE	2.19	14.9%	0.300
TRIAL	0.35	56.1%	0.061
GENDER by TRIAL	0.25	61.9%	0.055
TOPIC by STYLE	4.05	2.7%	0.68
GENDER by TOPIC by STYLE	1.35	27.4%	0.27
TOPIC by TRIAL	3.48	4.3%	0.61
GENDER by TOPIC by TRIAL	0.133	87.6%	0.07
TRIAL by STYLE	0.18	67.5%	0.055
GENDER by TRIAL by STYLE	0.07	79.1%	0.049
TOPIC by TRIAL by STYLE	5.53	0.9%	0.82
GENDER by TOPIC by TRIAL by STYLE	3.47	4.4%	0.61

Figure 12.2
Average Change in Reported Interest in Participating in a Newsgroup After Seeing Messages of Different Styles, by Gender of Subject, for Pass 2

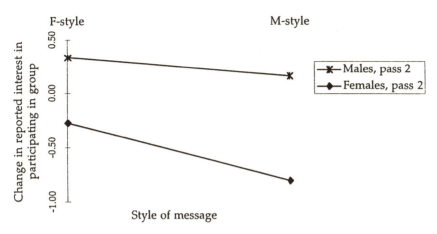

itatively analyzed. For this purpose, the responses to both sets of questionnaires were pooled. Responses were transcribed into Q.S.R.'s NUD·IST package for analysis and coded for the sex of the respondent, style of the message, newsgroup, and explanation for rating (interest in topic, utility of information, understandability, and message style). Some example responses are given in Table 12.5; 196 responses were coded, eighty-four from eight men and 112 from thirteen women.

There was considerable variation in explanations from subject to subject. Some subjects appeared to rate newsgroups primarily on their interest in the topic (e.g., they said they would read if they found the general or specific topic interesting), others appeared to rely primarily on utility (e.g., they would read if they needed that type of information at the moment and not otherwise), and still others seemed to take a wider variety of factors into account, preferring to read groups that were pleasurable to read as well as informative or interesting. Women were twice as likely to complain that a group was too technical or that they did not understand the message as men (23 percent of women's explanations vs. 10 percent of men's explanations), regardless of the style of the message.

Table 12.6 shows the number of responses that commented on the style of the message. Negative comments are more common for M-style messages than for F-style messages, although both are relatively rare. In these cases, when the men commented negatively on the style of these M-style messages, they did not comment on how mean people were or how strong their opinions. Instead, they picked out features traditionally associated with *women's speech* to criticize (gossip, too personal, irrelevant).

Table 12.5
Examples of Explanations for Ratings of Interest in a Newsgroup from Men and Women

---

Examples by women:

"People are not very nice."

"Although I like the topic, I don't like the writing style."

"I'm not interested in reading about other's strong opinions."

Examples by men:

"Too much gossip."

"Like the idea but comments are too personal and irrelevant."

DISCUSSION

The first result is that men and women differ in their reported interest in many topics. Therefore, differences in the number of women and men participating in a particular forum might be due to *a priori* differences in interest in the topic(s) being discussed. Any study of participation differences must therefore take this possibility into account.

The second result is that the communicative style of a message does have an effect on interest in participation. Both women and men were significantly less interested in participating after reading messages of M-style than after F-style, as shown in Figure 12.3. However, contrary to expectations and to the findings of past field studies, these men and women did not differ significantly in their reactions to these styles. However, the qualitative data show women are more likely to comment negatively on the style of M-style messages, although these comments are still rare.

CONCLUSION

In conclusion, this study makes a modest contribution to knowledge about the antecedents of gender inequalities in participation in systems like Usenet news. No studies seem to have experimentally tested the assumption that women and men respond differently to the communicative style of

Table 12.6
Count of Positive (+) and Negative (−) Responses to M- and F-style Messages by Women and Men

		M- style (7)	F- style (7)
men (8)	−	7% (3/41)	2% (1/43)
	+	2% (1/41)	0
women (13)	−	17% (9/54)	3% (2/58)
	+	2% (1/54)	2% (1/58)

Negative comments on style of M-style messages are more common than negative comments on the style of F-style messages.

messages in CMC and we found no support for this hypothesis with these data.

Of course, this simple experiment is hardly the last word on this subject. The reliability of the initial topic measure might be improved by asking subjects to commit to reading groups on certain topics, rather than simply stating interest. The effects of differences in interest in specific message subjects can be averaged out by having subjects react to many messages rather than one or two.

Future studies should move beyond participation to examine other measures, such as influence (e.g., Berdahl and Craig 1996). For example, it would be interesting to observe the response to messages that contrast with the dominant style of a newsgroup (it is expected that F-style messages will be less influential in primarily M-style newsgroups) and the strategies of posters in opposite gender newsgroups. Herring (in press-b) suggested that "members of the minority gender on each list shift their style in the direction of majority gender norms." This question could even be approached through an intervention in a CMC system, for example, by posting messages of a particular style and observing the reaction or by setting norms for participation in a newsgroup in an attempt to promote more equal interaction. Such a test would provide the most concrete advice for those introducing and managing communications systems on maintaining gender equality.

NOTE

The authors gratefully acknowledge Rachel Barish for assistance in the literature review, Tom Finholt and Stephanie Teasley for advice on the design of this study, George Widmeyer, Scott Moore, and David Murray for allowing us to experiment in their classes, and the subjects for taking the time to respond to our questionnaires.

Figure 12.3
Average Change in Reported Interest in Participating in a Newsgroup after Seeing Messages of Different Styles, by Gender of Subject, for Both Passes Combined

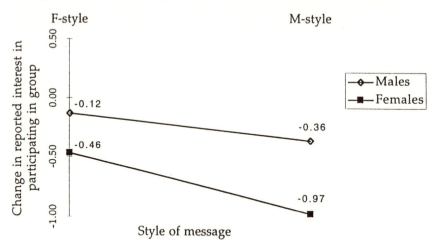

REFERENCES

Berdahl, J. L. and K. M. Craig. 1996. Equality of participation and influence in groups: The effects of communications medium and sex composition. *Computer Supported Cooperative Work* 4:179–201.

Bruckman, A. S. 1993. Gender swapping on the Internet. In *Proceedings of INET '93*. San Francisco.

Coates, J. 1993. *Women, Men and Language*, 2nd edn. London: Longman.

Culnan, M. and M. L. Markus. 1987. Information technologies. In F. M. Jablin, K. H. Roberts, L. L. Putnam and L. W. Porter, eds., *The Handbook of Organizational Communications: An Interdisciplinary Perspective*. Newbury Park, Calif.: Sage Publications, pp. 73–90.

Herring, Susan C. 1992a. Gender and participation in computer-mediated linguistic discourse. Paper presented at the Annual Meeting of the Linguistic Society of America, Philadelphia, Jan. 9–12. Also available as ERIC document ED345552.

———. 1992b. *Men's Language: A Study of the Discourse of the LINGUIST List*. In Crochetiere, Boulanger, and Ouillet, eds., *Proceedings of the XVth International Congress of Linguists*. Quebec: Université Laval.

———. In press-a. Posting in a different voice: Gender and ethics in computer-mediated communication. In C. Ess, ed., *Philosophical Perspectives on Computer-Mediated Communication*. Albany, N.Y.: SUNY Press.

———. In press-b. Two variants of an electronic message schema. In S. Herring, ed., *Computer-Mediated Communication: Linguistic, Social and Cross-Cultural Perspectives*. Amsterdam: John Benjamins.

Herring, S., D. Johnson, and T. DiBenedetto. 1992. Participation in electronic discourse in a "feminist" field. In *Locating Power: Proceedings of the Second*

Berkeley Women and Language Conference, April 4 and 5. Berkeley, Calif.: Berkeley Women and Language Group, University of California, Berkeley.

Hiltz, S. R. and M. Turoff. 1993. *The Network Nation.* Cambridge, Mass.: MIT Press.

Huber, G. P. (1990). A theory of the effect of advanced information technologies on organizational design, intelligence, and decision making. *Academy of Management Review* 15:47–71.

Kahn, A. and R. Brookshire. 1991. Using a computer bulletin board in a social psychology course. *Teaching of Psychology* 18(4):245–49.

Kramerae, C., and H. J. Taylor. 1993. Women and men on electronic networks: A conversation or a monologue? In H. J. Taylor, C. Kramerae, and M. Ebben (eds.), *Women, Information Technology, Scholarship.* Urbana Champaign: University of Illinois Press.

Lakoff, R. 1975. *Language and Woman's Place.* New York: Harper and Row.

Quarterman, John S. and Smoot Carl-Mitchell. 1995. Is the internet all male? *Matrix News* 5(5), May. Online: http://www3.mids.org/ids2/gender.505.

Rice, R. E. 1984. Mediated group communication. In R. E. Rice, ed., *The New Media.* Beverly Hills, Calif.: Sage.

Selfe, C. and P. R. Meyer. 1991. Testing claims for on-line conferences. *Written Communications* 8(2):162–92.

Shade, L. R. 1993. *Gender Issues in Computer Networking.* Web page http://www.inform.umd.edu:8080/Educational_Resources/AcademicResources ByTopic/WomensStudies/Computing/Articles+ResearchPapers

Sproull, L. and S. Kiesler. 1986. Reducing social context cues: Electronic mail in organizational communication. *Management Science* 32:1492–1512.

———. 1991. *Connections.* Cambridge, Mass.: MIT Press.

Tannen, D. 1990. *You Just Don't Understand: Women and Men in Conversation.* New York: William Morrow.

Thorne, B. and N. Henley. 1975. Difference and cominance: An overview of language, gender, and society. In B. Thorne and N. Henley, eds., *Language and Sex: Difference and Dominance.* Rowley, Mass.: Newbury House, pp. 5–41.

Truong, H.-A. 1993. *Gender Issues in On-line Communications.* Web document http://www.inform.umd.edu:8080/Educational_Resources/Academic ResourcesByTopic/WomensStudies/Computing/Articles+ResearchPapers

We, G. 1994. Cross-gender communication in cyberspace. *The Arachnet Electronic Journal on Virtual Culture* 2(3).

13

Netsex: Empowerment Through Discourse

Charlene Blair

The Internet has become an increasingly popular medium of exchange for many people in the United States. Users are able with the aid of a computer and modem to log on to different areas of the Internet, "pull up a chair and chat" with virtual strangers all over the world. This largely unregulated forum provides individuals with opportunities to create and share erotic encounters. Because Internet encounters are primarily exchanged dialogue, the idea of discourse and its power implications become an important area of discussion. Types of dialogue, developments in computer interactivity, and questions of empowerment and self-awareness are examined in this chapter.

INTRODUCTION

This chapter is an examination of the phenomenon of Internet sex and the implications it has for female power roles. The power role examined in this chapter is the ideal expressed in *The Female Gaze* (Gamman and Marshment 1989: 182), which explains Michel Foucault's idea of power as rooted in discourse. On the information superhighway or the Internet, women enter into an ongoing discourse in which they are "leveled" with men and others. The Internet offers a unique place for the exercise of power by women because the system is based on discourse. Discourse is the vehicle to power because its strengths are enhanced by the anonymity of cyberspace. If a person has access to the superhighway he or she can exercise personal power through cyber-discourse. According to Douglas Rushkoff, "[C]omputers and networks provide unprecedented expressive capabilities to anyone who can get access to a terminal and modem. A tiny laptop in Montana can be as high a leverage point as a system of mainframes in Washington, D.C.; no text message sent out onto the net has any more intrinsic power to affect the whole system than any other" (*Media Virus!* 1994:235). The ultimate expression of power a woman can display on the net is manifest in cyber-discoursed sexual relations with men or others. It is within this relationship that the concept of leveling becomes paramount, enhanced by a woman's power and its expression. The woman who can master the discourse and can achieve satisfaction from it controls the direction of her sexuality in this medium.

Sex and power relationships have been traditionally repressive for women who have had to acquiesce to male dominance because in most instances, they have not been on a level playing field in the society. Women have not found many outlets for their repressed sexuality; neither have they been allowed to explore channels to power through their sexuality. In recent studies of romance readers (Radway 1984; 1989), it was found that women enjoy romance erotica because it provides a vicarious sense of power and satisfaction. But in most cases this type of expression has not been reciprocal. Net sex offers women a chance to give and receive pleasure in a way superior to romance erotica. This forum allows for the woman to have an interactive experience both in the creation of the text and control of the story. The reader, creator, and text are linked in an unending erotic exchange that is finally consummated by mutual orgasm.

"PULL UP A CHAIR AND CHAT"

Internet sex has evolved from a process of interactive discourse between consenting partners via computer modem linking, usually in an Inter-Relay Chat (IRC) format. By connecting via a modem to other computers linked similarly, the operator is participating in a worldwide network made up of interconnected "servers" (interfaces) and millions of computers. According to researcher Gunnar Liestol, "Ever since its emergence in electronic-digital form, the computer has been a meeting place of some kind. Like an agora, computer technology and environments have, in their different stages of development, constituted a *place* where persons, disciplines, media and information have converged and interacted" (Andersen, Holmqvist, and Jensen 1993: 265). Computer-mediated networks such as the Internet have created a space of "virtual" or "global" communities in which participants work, play, and communicate with one another (Dery 1994:225).

In the Internet format, a person logs into an electronic "chat" network in which the individual can be linked with others who are logged into the same address. In the language of cyberspace, the address is call a channel or "room" and individuals who log into the space are invited to "pull up a chair and chat." According to Gareth Branwyn:

Users are able to view a list of rooms that have been created by other users. The conversational theme of each room, embodied in its name, runs the gamut of possible interests from politics ("Boomers in the White House" and "Women in Politics"), to teen concerns ("Beverly Hills 90210," "Alternative Music," "Teen Club"), to religion and ethics ("Mormons On-Line," "Sanctuary," "Pro-Choice Forum"). By far the single largest theme represented in the room titles, however, is sex. On a given night, the list might include "Naughty Negligees," "Men for Men," "Hot Bi Ladies," "Women Who Obey Women," and so forth. (Dery 1994: 227)

The conversation in the room appears on the user's screen as text and the individual can enter into the conversation by typing the message at the bottom of the screen. It is similar to a telephone conversation except that multiple users can engage in a conversation simultaneously. The exchange is pure discourse—it is dependent on language and the language skills of the users. The rapidity of the conversation creates a dreamlike atmosphere as words and thoughts enter the users' imagination faster than they can be processed. In the process the individual becomes mesmerized, losing touch with the temporal world that has been ignored by the engaged imagination.

Sexual intercourse on the medium of the Internet is purely cerebral. Arousal is achieved through manipulation of the language of love and sex. Those who can master the discourses will achieve sexual satisfaction from the exchange. It is within this arena that women are equal to men and can assert their power and dominance.

Foucault argues in his book, *The History of Sexuality, An Introduction* (1978), that Western societies sought to gain control over an individual's sexuality by banishing its display from the public sphere. To this end, sexuality was reduced to discursive language, especially through church canon. Made visible as it was in the printed medium, individual sexuality could then be purified and controlled. Control in this case was in the hands of the church and other institutions. According to Foucault, "[T]hese discourses on sex did not multiply apart from or against power, but in the very spaces and as the means of its exercise" (Foucault 1978: 32). The church controlled the direction and expression of the individual's sexual life. Through this process, repressive mores such as those of Victorian society became canon, predicated on theological notions of sin and repentance.

As the centuries passed and the church began to lose its control over Western society, sexual discourse became more diffused throughout the institutions of science and politics. According to Foucault:

The secure bond that held together the moral theology of concupiscence and the obligation of confession (equivalent to the theoretical discourse on sex and its first-person formulation) was, if not broken, at least loosened and diversified: between the objectification of sex in rational discourses, and the movement by which each individual was set to the task of recounting his own sex, there has occurred since the eighteenth century, a whole series of tensions, conflicts, efforts at adjustment, and attempts at retranscription. . . . Rather than the uniform concern to hide sex, rather than a general prudishness of language, what distinguishes these last three centuries is the variety, the wide dispersion of devices that were invented for speaking about it, for having it be spoken about, for inducing it to speak of itself, for listening, recording, transcribing and redistributing what is said about it. (Foucault 1978:33–34)

In this arena the discourse of sexuality has bumped heads with the discourses of power, creating a sphere of openness in which any competent individual can define his or her own sexual persona. As the power of three major controlling bodies of social sexuality (canonical law, the Christian pastor, and civil law) have become more diffused in twentieth-century society, the individual has gained more room to negotiate the tension between the ideas of procreation and pleasure (Foucault 1978:37).

Discourse and power relationships help an individual to define his or her self-awareness. According to Allucquére Rosanne Stone, "Development of self-awareness takes place in a field that is already contoured by that invisible and impalpable structure called power. And while there is still plenty of mystery about how the self manages to emerge under these circumstances, there is a deeper mystery about how self and power mutually constitute each other" (Stone 1995:30). It is in the area between the formalized structure of language and texts and the interactive, computer-mediated text that a point of negotiation can begin. An individual who enters the space of the Internet to interact with others faces a unique opportunity to renegotiate the formal structures of power by engaging in leveled discourse. The pure discourse allowed on the digitalized screen and the anonymity afforded by the amorphous electronic links of the computer network allow for men and women to renegotiate and redefine sexual relationships. Net sex is empowering for both men and women because it allows sex to be freed from the physical and dwell in the intellect. At this level sex is free from the baggages of duty and family and becomes pleasure and fulfillment.

Net discourse is superior to other erotic discourses. The first advantage is that it is exchanged with another in a nearly simultaneous fashion. This exchange creates a type of common ground in which both participants become "agents." Brenda Laurel says of the notion of common ground: "It [sic] not only provides a superior representation of the conversational process but also supports the idea that an interface is not simply the means whereby a person and a computer represent themselves to one another;

rather it is a shared context for action in which both are agents" (Laurel 1991:4).

The second advantage of the medium is what it lacks. Absent from the discourse is the politics of the physical self. There is no physical voice, no inflection in the exchange. There are only words on a screen and a moving cursor that marks the progress of the exchange. Words in themselves are not political, they are purely denotative. And, according to Foucault, this type of sexual discourse traces the meeting line between body and soul following all of its meanderings (Foucault 1978:20). It is within the context of usage that the discourse gains power. The user of the discourse can manipulate this power. A woman in this medium is free to initiate or refuse the exchange, manipulate the flow of discourse, or passively enjoy the flow.

Net sex is devoid of the gaze because of the lack of a physical presence of the participants. Devoid of the judgment of the gaze a woman is free, anonymous, a vessel of words and discourse. The only limitation is set by the internalizing gaze, the preconceptions that are honed by her participation in the culture. This judgment can be overcome by confident engagement in the discourse. The negative reinforcement of the gaze is overcome because the physical is no longer the object of pleasure. A woman's sense of self-worth is reinforced by the pleasure her words evoke in the recipient. Even if he's faking an orgasm, how is she to know? The woman gains control through confidence with language. Confidence and competence at this level are equated with beauty. The ability to arouse another beyond the limitations of the body can be a liberating experience.

Empowerment of the woman is described by Shelagh Young as "a struggle against a form of power that makes individuals subjects, that causes individuals to conceive of themselves in a limited and limiting way" (Gamman and Marshment 1989: 183). Net discourse, at this juncture, frees the woman from subjectification. She becomes the giver of pleasure as well as the receiver; the proof of arousal lies in the reciprocal communication. She cannot give pleasure without tapping into another's pleasurable discourse, and she cannot receive pleasure if she does not allow another into her discourse. In this instance the field is level. Shared discourses operate with the same words and the same connotations, and must share the same context. Net sex is pure emotion expressed in words. What creates these emotions, creates the pleasure.

Because the mind is connected to a physical body, Net sex does have its sensory limitations. A kiss is still a kiss, no matter how it is temporalized, and it loses its potency in the translation from the physical to the literate. The sexual discourse of the Net is combined for most users with auto-stimulation or an offline physical relation. For some, masturbatory response can be fulfilling. This act of sexuality is empowering in itself. Control and manipulation of physical response remove the power of control that one partner has over another, freeing the body to respond to the mind. Offline physical coupling has in many cases been enhanced by online exchanges. Many couples have met and assumed real-time relationships as a result of Net sex encounters.

In many instances Internet exchanges act as a sort of story-telling and can become a type of text in themselves. Texts in this instance are didactic, aiming at a direct relationship with the receiver. According to Jorgen Bang, "The communication takes place on equal terms, though the sender may address his or her addressee like a teacher, from a position of greater knowledge, but always taking into account the assumptions of the pupils" Andersen, Holmqvist, and Jensen 1993:214). In the Internet environment, the texts become open as the each partner is impelled to participate in the direction of the action of the story in order to maximize his own or his partners' pleasure.

Michael Joyce, in his book, *Of Two Minds: Hypertext Pedagogy and Poetics*, has called the graphic, discoursed text found on the Internet and other channels "hypertext." According to Joyce:

Hypertext is, before anything else, a visual form. Hypertext embodies information and communications, artistic and affective constructs, and conceptual abstractions alike into symbolic structures made visible on a computer-controlled display. These symbolic structures can then be combined and manipulated by anyone having access to them. (Joyce 1995:91)

Hypertexts are created on and for the Internet, and they are used extensively on the World Wide Web. Through the power of the interconnected computer networks that form the net, these constructed texts are exchanged by readers and writers at a rapid pace. The reader/writer line is blurred as one user interacts with the other user to manipulate the story direction or other elements. For Joyce, "The dissolving of distinctions between writer and reader makes the hypertext a valuable tool for learning and information management as well as a revolutionary artistic medium" (Joyce 1995: 20). Practiced Net users combine their textual skills with graphic icons, sound, pictures, animation, and even video to create files designed to titillate their readers, or at least to attract their attention. The reader/receiver is then free to access any and all parts of the hypertext to peruse and manipulate according to her needs. For Internet users, hypertext creates a medium that is, according to Liestol, "anti-hierarchical and democratic" (Andersen, Holmqvist, and Jensen 1993:266). The free-flowing text combined with the anonymity of cyberspace can create an atmosphere of unrestricted imagination for both the author and the reader.

Three types of texts are generated by online encounters. Gareth Branwyn describes them as embellishment of real-world circumstances, creation of a pure fantasy scenario, and "tele-operated compu-sex," as when one party describes online what he or she would like the other party to do (Dery 1994:230). The key to the differing types of texts is the interaction and story-building between the users.

Branwyn provides an example of a multiuser online orgy, which in this case would be a type of pure fantasy scenario;

BethR types: "I'm climbing on top of Roger104, just as Roger104 is finishing sex with Nina5."

Roger104 might type: "Nina5 and I get so worked up, we roll onto the floor. As Nina5 falls off me, the always randy BethR, not missing a beat, climbs on top of me."

Then to tidy things up, Nina5 adds: "I begin to make out with BethR and to massage her breasts while she rides Roger104." (Dery 1994:230)

Branwyn's example illustrates the difficulty with multiuser sex, which is scrolling across the screen at a rapid rate; that is, the imagination and actions of the participants are faster than can be transmitted in the format. But it shows the give-and-take that occurs between the partners.

The next example, a combination of a fantasy scenario and embellishment of the real world, occurred between two users who met in a writers' discussion group.

From Evan-

What a splendid letter! And it is now 3:45 pm my time and 2:45 yours. I tried once to see if you were in UNIX but it said you were not connected. How little do they know? So far as I can tell you are very well connected and I can almost feel the vibrations when I read your e-mail. From what you say and your overall approach to cyber or cerebral (academic term) sex, I have no doubt we will be compatible and probably multi-orgasmic. . . . Normally when I give a cyber-massage I am naked under a robe after a shower. . . . I am truly glad that we have met. Mental rapport is vital for any kind of sex whether cyber or real. Without rapport, both are blah. Even now, I know I like your style and I am certain rapport will develop. (Internet exchange February 22, 1995)

From Cyndi-

E—so glad to talk to you on the telephone. You have a great voice, it gives me a better picture of you. Beard, voice like brandy, robe—this is an inflammatory picture—I want to taste all of you. Turn down the lights and dream of me, I'll be dreaming of you . . . the intensity of my passion makes me blush. (Internet exchange, February 26, 1995)

From Evan-
Dearest Cyndi,
I call you that after your most torrid description of a cyber-kiss I have ever received.

Believe it or not, you not only made me breathe hard but lower elements of my being became VERY VERY hard. To get even I am sending a poem "Under the Hood." As you can see it has nothing to do with automobiles. (Internet exchange, March 3, 1995)

From Cyndi

E—just like I imagined. Just how I like it. Anglo language of love is arousing to me. If I get offended by a word, I will let you know. My offensive mode is turned off when I am making love. I want you to know that last night I laid awake for hours after reading your poem. I have never been so turned on in my life. I realized much later that I did indeed experience an orgasm reading it. It was different than pure vaginal orgasm, unique. You have to remember that I read it after I kissed you—my mind was open to it. Even touching myself wasn't enough. And now I wake up and find those next beautiful messages from you. I feel like I have been making love for hours and hours. (Internet exchange, March 4, 1995)

This last example shows how the give-and-take build-up between the couple has formed a broader and deeper relationship that some users miss when they engage in the hit-and-miss format found on a "chat" line.

According to Branwyn the most common text-based sexual exchanges "mirror" real-time sexual encounters: "Participants begin with foreplay and progress through increasing levels of (spelled out) intensity ending with on-line orgasm" (Dery 1994:234). At all levels in the story-building/intercourse process the participants stand on an equal footing with their partners, exchanging pleasures in the form of dialogue with one another.

The smorgasbord of technological options on the Internet system offers users whatever forum they are most compatible with. Some users prefer a combination of textual exchanges coupled with telephone conversations. Some prefer exchange of graphical interface files (gifs), which are pictures digitalized and sent over the Net combined with textual exchange for gratification. Fax machines, computer scanners, copiers, CD-ROMs, and computer software are also available to enhance the user experience. Some users prefer pure textual exchange, but the possibilities for connections are endless and are limited only by ability and preference.

Advancing computer technology is rapidly blurring the lines between the physical and the machine. In literary genres produced in the Industrial Age, the question of the machine replacing the human has long been examined. In the Computer Age, as technology advances the reality of mechanical physical manipulation, it has become more than speculation.

Virtual Reality (VR) technology is a machine-induced reality that combines computer graphics with simulated bodily sensations. For VR experiences the user becomes technically connected to the machine through hardware extensions. This hardware generally includes a type of glove worn by the user, which is combined with a hood, helmet, and eyepieces.

This hardware does two things for the user. First, it detaches users from the reality of the environment by depriving them of visual and tactile stimuli present in real-time. VR technology immerses the individual in the environment created in and by the computer. Second, the hardware acts a receiver and translator of the electronic signals from the computer program, in much the same way that the television or movie screen receives and amplifies the signals. But in a much more personal manner, VR technology redefines the tactile, aural, and visual environment. Deprived of other distracting stimuli, the individual can almost "feel" what is being played out on the eyepieces. In this environment the individual can quickly lose touch with real-time. According to Mark Dery: "Using current developments as a springboard, one might imagine users in head-tracking 3-D goggles, a quadriphonic sound system embedded in the goggles' earpieces. As the user looks up, down, or from side to side, the computer's high-speed program animates the world—and its soundscape—accordingly, creating the illusion of a 360-degree, real-time hyperreality" (Dery 1994:7). VR technology has found wide adaptation by the computer game industry. VR "transports" the players into the environment of the game, making them feel less like passive players and more like active participants.

For computer sex, the future envisioned by aficionados of VR has users encased in full body stockings or suits that could detect and transmit the motions of the individual via the modem to others at the other end who are similarly attired. In the words of author Howard Reingold: "The inner surfaces of these suits would be covered with an array of intelligent senso-effectors—a mesh of tiny tactile detectors coupled to vibrators of varying degrees of hardness, hundreds of them per square inch, that can receive and transmit a realistic sense of tactile presence" (Dery 1994:7).

With this type of hardware, and coupled with olfactory stimulators, the only thing missing from the actual sex act would be the body fluids. All the partners engaged in the action could physically feel the sensations caused by the long-distance manipulations.

Net sex, which engages much of existing computer hardware, leads the individual more and more into the transcendent world defined by the imagination. In removing the body from the physicalness of real-time, the user can experience a type of death. This type of death has long been associated with sex. Claudia Springer provides this analogy in her essay, "Sex, Memory, Angry Women":

Sex is being replaced by computer use, which provides the deathlike loss of self once associated with sexual pleasure. Identifying with computers can be appealing on several levels in our fragmented postmodern existence. Vulnerable late-twentieth-century bodies and minds turn to electronic technology to protect themselves from confusion and pain. Fusion with computer can provide an illusory sense of personal wholeness reminiscent of the Lacaninan Imaginary: the fused cyborg condition erases the difference between the self and other. (Dery 1994:162)

Has the ultimate sexual/computer death truly liberated us, or has it just served to further isolate the individual? Mind coupling sexual encounters via computer-mediated bodies have long been the subject of science fiction and other writers from Aldous Huxley to Donna Haraway.

One question that comes to mind after reading the examples of Internet exchange is: Is Net sex just another form of pornography and victimization of women? This question has relevance when one considers the preponderance of men using the Internet and computer technology. In many discussion lists, the postings are done by men who have the technical expertise and the desire to spend time learning the intricacies of the computer. Most of the services and equipment that are used to create the computer environment is very expensive and can seem a waste of money for many women who put the needs of their families first. Men, after all, have created the structure and power relationships of both the social discourses and the Internet.

But cyberspace offers an anonymity for women that cannot be negotiated in many of the other electronic mediums. A woman can choose whether to disclose her identity in this format, but in doing so exposes herself to unwanted advances and harassment from males. Without the body, women become their discourse, and in Western society discourse carries with it the stigma of gender. But can female discourse really be identified and separated from the discourse of the male? This is the point of negotiation at which a woman can reassert her power by mastering a neutered discourse or by re-examining her own to eliminate its weaknesses and play on its strengths.

Many users are worried about exposing themselves to violence on the Net. Nelson Thrall, director of the Project McLuhan, asserts that violence is the hidden icon of the Internet. Thrall says that because electronic, visually oriented man is increasingly caught in an arena of simultaneous information that seems to defy rational and linear progression, he becomes more and more disassociated from his reality. In order to reaffirm his identity, disassociated man turns to the violence of language to reassert his power. In this process, the lesser participants are likely to be trampled. For Thrall, the Internet represents the wild and lawless West, where "women and children should get out of the way" (Thrall 1995). Many women would agree with Thrall's assessment, especially those who choose to keep silent for fear of being flamed for their incompetence. (Flaming is an electronic diatribe sent via e-mail to someone who breaks the rules of a particular discussion or community, an electronic tongue-lashing.)

This brings us back to the question of pornography, which differs fundamentally from Internet sex in two ways. The first difference is that pornography is a nonparticipatory medium of expression for women. The second difference lies in the power structure of pornography, which objectifies a woman within its discourse. Pornography is most often created by and caters to men. In this forum women have no control over their sexuality or its expression. Pornographic sex is not reciprocal. The process of objectification found in pornography serves the purpose described by Simone de Beauvoir, which is to "cut the woman off from her transcendence in order to offer her as prey to male desires" (de Beauvoir 1952:529). In this way the object serves the man's power by erasing the threat of independence.

Pornography is a perfect example of Foucault's idea of institutionalized language of sex that controls the individual in social space. Net sex, on the other hand, is predicated by mutual satisfaction and does not work if one party tries to control the imagination and sexuality of the other. The openness of the language in Net sex exchanges does not hide the sexuality of the participants; the language and the medium combined rather enhance and highlight the rituals that bring about pleasure. The questions posed by Teresa de Laurentis about identification, self-definition, the modes or the very possibility of envisaging oneself as subject become possibilities for redefinition in the Net (Pribram 1988:177).

As a caveat, the Internet has a long way to go before women will feel truly safe from male predation. Males have staked it out as a sphere of power based on their knowledge of technology. Online "rape" and offline harassment are real possibilities.

One widely publicized case of a University of Michigan student who wrote a rape-murder fantasy story about one of his classmates stands as a warning to those who would engage in Net sex fantasies (Lessenberry 1995). But the question remains, is the fantasy real? Would the student, Jake Baker, have acted out his fantasy? Or were his musings an example of pleasurable pornography that could not complete his arousal unless it was observed by others? The story was not given to the woman but exchanged between Baker and a third party via the Internet. Baker was arrested and charged with making a threat against an individual. Sick as the fantasy may be, repression of Baker's narrative impinges on the freedom of speech and thought sought by those who wish to gain empowerment and satisfaction from Net exchanges. The threat is not enough to erase the possibilities of expression afforded to women who can engage in the discourse.

CONCLUSION

Net sex is not without its limitations. The medium itself is ever-changing as new uses for the Internet are discovered daily. Regulation by governmental agencies and other regulatory bodies is an ever-present threat. Commercialization is controlling more and more of the free space in "Cyberia." Anonymity is not guaranteed for the users; they can be traced through their usage patterns. Usage patterns, or networks that the user accesses, are generally the site of engagement for the partners. In a semi-anonymous environment, one that is potentially regulated, it is hard to choose a likely partner. Blatant broadcast of one's intentions can be effective in certain situations. In other situations, members of a chat group or newsgroup discern compatibility through exchanges on various subjects, compatible interests, so to speak. From this point, partnerships are established and the users retire to a semi-private channel to engage in their relationship. In an unregulated arena there is no guarantee of privacy, the exchange can be downloaded (saved in a file or printed) and circulated in other medium. In a regulated environment the participants risk censorship. Increasingly, First Amendment laws and other laws governing written and pornographic materials are invoked to prosecute blatant violators of personal freedom. But because the information superhighway is a relatively new medium, there is little protection offered to the user.

The key to a successful relationship, in my opinion, is mutual consent. Mutual consent implies a sort of trust, and trust is a basis for a satisfying relation. Net sex offers excitement, risk, power, and cerebral fulfillment. It has a broad appeal to both women and men. Net sex is physically safe; the only virus that can be spread is a computer virus. Computer terminals can't procreate, but words can. One word leads to another and to another, creating a discourse but nothing more—no commitments, no attachments, no pressure. All computers have an off switch that is controlled by the user.

Net sex is a fantasy, one shared by multiple users, but nevertheless surreal. The transcendence of the temporal is the strength of the Internet. Pure exchange of ideas is the goal. In this world all the players are equal, especially those who revel in cerebral exchange. But fantasy carries a risk, the risk that threatens the real. The threat is that the fantasy is so far superior to the real that it will replace the real. Fantasy is addictive, as is the exercise of power. The exercise of extreme power opens the individual up to exploitation and annihilation.

The question then becomes: Does the woman want to enter this world? Are the shackles that hold us in reality-bound relations so onerous that we would throw them off for unmitigated freedom? Do we want to exercise our right to power in an equal forum as men? Dare we risk the pleasure of transcendence that exposes us simultaneously to annihilation of the soul? Net sex offers women the opportunity, the means, and the method to fulfill our sexual fantasies, a pleasure men have been enjoying for years through their use of their erotica. In my opinion, the power and the pleasure need to be examined and experienced. The only shadow I see on the horizon is that when men (and other less-liberated souls) find out how much we enjoy Net sex, they will find a way to limit our access to it.

REFERENCES

Andersen, Peter Bogh, Berit Holmqvist, and Jens F. Jensen. 1993. *The Computer as Medium*. New York: Cambridge University Press.

de Beauvoir, Simone. 1952. *The Second Sex*, trans. by H. M. Parshley. New York: Vintage Books.

Dery, Mark, ed. 1994. *Flame Wars: The Discourse of Cyberculture*. Durham, N.C.: Duke University Press.

Foucault, Michel. 1978. *The History of Sexuality Volume I: An Introduction*, trans. by Robert Hurley. New York: Vintage Books.

Gamman, Lorraine and Margaret Marshment, eds. 1989. *The Female Gaze: Women as Viewers of Popular Culture*. Seattle: Real Comet Press.

Joyce, Michael. 1995. *Of Two Minds: Hypertext Pedagogy and Poetics*. Ann Arbor, Mich.: University of Michigan Press.

Laurel, Brenda. 1991. *Computers as Theatre*. New York: Addison-Wesley.

Lessenberry, Jack. March 5, 1995. Cyberspace sex tale will test free speech. *The Blade*, p. B-1.

Pribram, Deidre, ed. 1988. *Female Spectators Looking at Film and Television*. London: Verso.

Lewallen, Auis. 1989. LACE: Pornography for women?, in Lorraine Gamman and Margaret Marshment, eds. *The Female Gaze: Women as Viewers of Popular Culture*. Seattle: Real Comet Press.

Radway, Janice. 1984. *Reading the Romance: Women, Patriarchy, and Popular Literature*, Chapel Hill, N.C.: University of North Carolina Press.

Rushkoff, Douglas. 1994. *Media Virus! Hidden Agendas in Popular Culture*. New York: Ballantine Books.

Stone, Allucquére Rosanne. 1995. *The War of Desire at the Close of the Mechanical Age*. Cambridge: MIT Press.

Thrall, Nelson. March 3, 1995. Violence is the hidden icon of the Internet. *Project MeLuhan*.

14

Embracing the Machine: Quilt and Quilting as Community-Building Architecture

Andrew F. Wood and Tyrone L. Adams

This chapter considers the use of the World Wide Web (WWW) as a protest vehicle that circumvents conventionally appreciated norms of communication, especially where marginalized (feminist) voices are concerned. We consider Kathy Daliberti's online reaction to the imprisonment of her husband in Iraq as a Web site that demonstrates how technology might be reappropriated, reshaped, and embraced as a tool for feminist liberation instead of captivation. Explaining and employing the "ironic-metonymic quilt" as a rhetorical framework by which our analysis unfolds, we then consider the home page as a space of rhetorical contest between human notions of public and private dimension. Last, the observations derived from this ironic-metonymic reading of the Daliberti Web site are discussed.

Technology is not an image of the world but a way of operating on reality. The nihilism of technology lies not only in the fact that it is the most perfect expression of the will to power . . . but also in the fact that it lacks meaning.
                            —Octavio Paz (b. 1914), Mexican poet, in
             Alternating Current, "The Channel and the Signs" (1967)

INTRODUCTION

It is becoming difficult to avoid the World Wide Web (WWW) as a topic in popular or scholarly discussion.[1] Once considered an experimental and elite medium for developmental research scientists, the WWW has recently exploded in popularity—presumably doubling the amount of information being made available every five months (Neobyte Media 1996). This embryonic form of computer-mediated communication (CMC) has, in its very short duration, spawned myriad research contexts, ranging from corporate organizational uses (Churbuck 1995) to archaeology (Gill 1995), journalism (Hearst 1996), theater (Istel 1995), and maintenance of self-esteem (Levy 1992). Therefore, it should come as no surprise that this maturing form of interaction is extremely attractive to communication scholars (Newhagen 1996; Spears and Lea 1994). In spite of the obvious, there remains relatively little exploration of the diverse ways in which the WWW might be understood on a theoretical level.

Given the widespread impact of this medium, with its unique ability to provide the means for mass communication to millions of people (Morris and Ogan 1996), the opportunity to expand theoretical boundaries is most intriguing. Informed by the assumption that theory-building necessarily challenges the ways in which dominant assumptions maintain power inequities, we propose that an examination of the ways in which the WWW creates a space for women to resist patriarchal constraints provides a good place to start closing the gap between theory and direct experience, thus diminishing the artificial obstacles between the academic and the actual. While there is a great deal of literature that addresses women's relationships with computers (McGaw 1987; Machung 1988; Smith and Balka 1988; Turkle 1988; Jansen 1989; Matheson 1992; Jensen 1995), there is little investigation into the emerging potential of the WWW to reshape that relationship.

Building theory on this bearing requires, we believe, an examination of the ways in which the WWW can reorient conventional assumptions about the relationship of women, machines, and a "sense of place." Further, this work rests on the assumption that machines in the modern era have been used to put women "in their place"—outside the public sphere of work, home alone. In this chapter, we contemplate Kathy Daliberti's online response to the imprisonment of her husband as a site in which the machine might be reappropriated, reshaped, and embraced. At this point, some background may be useful. In March 1995, David Daliberti and Bill Barloon were captured by the Iraqi government for illegally crossing its borders (Clayton 1995; Greenhouse 1995; Powell 1995). In her Florida home, Kathy Daliberti was forced by the U.S. government to play a passive role, waiting for information as the State Department failed to contact her for weeks at a time (Lancaster 1995: A7). Adding to her admitted frustration and anxiety, newspapers and television stories aired inconsistent reports of her husband's condition. In response to her lack of voice in a cacophony of conflicting information and tight-lipped diplomats, Daliberti created an online message to international media outlets and the U.S. and Iraqi governments—in the form of a Web site called the "Yellow Ribbon" home page.[2] We believe that this site provides a model of nonverbal, nonoratorical rhetoric that challenges traditional assumptions about computer-mediated protest.

Before understanding this challenge, however, a more fundamental issue must be addressed. A central theme discussed in this chapter is the articulation of what constitutes "home" on the WWW. In common parlance, many of us who use the WWW refer to sites as "home pages," imagining them to be spaces where we collect the multifaceted stuff of our selves. Even Daliberti's site is referred to as a home page. We believe that this idea of home requires a critique from a feminist standpoint—to unpack naturalized assumptions about public and private, and the machinery (semantic and otherwise) that structurally maintains that dichotomy. Certainly, we do not propose that Web sites should no longer be called homes. Neither, for that matter, do we suggest that Daliberti suffers from some false consciousness by using "home" as a referent to her Web site. The point we wish to make is that the WWW, by its nature, creates the space to interrogate gendered assumptions naturalized through architecture, such as the concept of home. In this chapter, we will explore a theoretical perspective useful toward the ironic reading of metonyms. From this perspective, we will attempt to reveal the limitations of the dominant perspective of the WWW from that of an alternative standpoint: the quilt and process of quilting.

THE IRONIC-METONYMIC QUILT

Geographic descriptors, those ways in which we organize abstract knowledge according to spatial terms, are subject to analysis of their metonymic assumptions. In *A Grammar of Motives*, Burke (1962) explains that metonymy—one of his four master tropes—constitutes a one-way road of deduction from quality to quantity. He illustrates this reduction by suggesting that a metonymy for the emotions might be "the heart." To the ends of definition, metonymy offers an efficient communicative mechanism. While a metaphor represents, metonymy reduces. To translate this into a computer-mediated context: The myriad ways that data might be approached, employed, and explained is metonymized into a singular image—the library, highway, or city, for example. Rather than represent all of the potential ways in which data might be organized, the constellation of meanings is reduced to a single perspective, defined according to dimensions that include access, purpose, and power relationship. Yet description of metonymy alone does not serve to unpack the ideological implications of a site. In his discussion of the ironic dialectic, Burke warns that "if you isolate any one agent in a drama or any one advocate in a dialogue, and see the whole in terms of his position alone, you have the purely relativistic" (1962: 512). Brummett (1994) expands on this concept when he states that careless use of metonyms results in a perspective based on stereotypical assumptions and lacking in analytical richness.

The theoretical turn of this chapter is to introduce an ironic-metonymic approach as a means of exploring the spaces of protest made possible in WWW sites. Burke (1962) writes that irony, with its integrative "development" of multiple reference points, fashions a meaningful whole in which "none of the participating 'sub-perspectives' can be treated as either precisely right or precisely wrong" (p. 512). Such an approach is appropriate in a computer-mediated context that allows the existence of multiple and overlapping spaces of meaning. This is because the ironic-metonymic analysis develops a critical vantage point through the engagement of two or more metonymic dimensions within the dominant geography of an artifact. This process requires (1) mapping out the points that form the dominant geography of a metonymy; and (2) realigning those reference points according to critical fissures in the text.

MAPPING HOME ON THE WWW

Our ironic-metonymic critique of the home emerges along three dimensions: isolation, control, and violence. The collection of physical and discursive structures that constitute the home is organized around discrete physical spaces and places that, for women, result in isolation. Shields (1991) claims that "geographical space is mediated by an edifice of social constructions which become guides for action and constraints upon action" (p. 30). For women, these guides and constraints include modernist assumptions that specialization found in the workplace-city require a private anti-space for rest and refinement. To be sure, the importance of such a locality to social life would suggest that life in the home is steeped in antitheses of political ideology. But that meaning is patriarchally censored through isolation. One who acts within a sphere of influence must be physically able to interact with others. The political space in which freedom might be found is bounded by institutionalized places—courthouses, airports, holy ground—far beyond the walls of home, separated by distance, mores, and cultural norms.

A second metonymic dimension found in the idealized, fictionalized "essential" home is control. Hayden (1981) believes that the modern suburban home was a man-made response to socialist and feminist-collectivist movements of the latter nineteenth century. Within this zeitgeist, women were socialized to manage the home according to a strict regimen of housework, defined by Delphy (1984) as "work done unpaid for others within the confines of the household or the family" (p. 90). Rather than enjoy the opportunity to mingle with other women in the communal activities of the agrarian society, the industrial woman serves as an isolated household manager surrounded by complex and powerful machines. Kramarae (1988) provides a historical support for this claim, describing how household clothes-dryers replaced clotheslines and home sewing machines replaced community sewing centers. As these machines enhanced the ability of women to accomplish their tasks, they simultaneously increased male-dictated expectations of quality and cleanliness and, as a result, decreased interaction with other women.

A third dimension to the metonymic home is violence. In their discussion of technology's impact on women in popular texts, Rushing and Frentz (1989) propose a means of understanding this phenomenon through their description of Prometheanism—the advance of technological progress—as a "masculine myth that tends to ignore values associated with the feminine" (p. 65). The Promethean evolution of the home in popular texts results in crippling isolation. In this environment, where standardized work replaced communal activity, the housewife "became more isolated from her husband, who now worked away from home; her children, who attended school all day; and, the rural social networks of kin and neighbors" (Hayden 1981: 13). Friedan (1963) describes how this structure led to millions of women seeking therapy through drugs and some even turning to suicide. Rosser (1994) points out that "this isolation has in turn permitted an astonishing rise in family violence and abuse" (p. 67). Indeed, Parker (1995) states that "more than two million women are physically abused each year" (p. 26). These statistics illustrate a larger message. While one may argue that the myth of the conventional wife in the typical suburban home no longer exists in actuality, the interconnected realities of isolation, control, and violence remain.

The metonymic qualities of home pages emerge from this concept's striking similarity to the physical home. The page-as-home is a "place" on the WWW, marked by an Internet address that can be "found" and "visited." Most often, this visiting is an isolated event, accomplished from a single location by a single individual. The multiplicity of visitors may be inferred by a "hit counter," which counts the number of times browsers download the hypertext-markup code that constructs the page. Yet, the experience of living at home on a computer, building a home page, and waiting for visitors is rather desolate. Despite recent developments in chatline technology, waiting for the hit counter to roll over another digit might be compared to waiting for someone to visit one's actual home, only to find that one must settle to hear knocking on the door. One can never open the door, for in reality, it doesn't exist. The computer is merely a window pointing more technology back in the user's face. In the webbed environment, the metonymic conception of home suggests operational isolation in a theoretical world of community.

The metonymic concept of control in the home page is more subtle. Within the isolated home page, one is subject first to the rigors of the code. For many, mastering the intricate nature of hypertext-markup language is a forbidding space composed of nonsensical commands and requirements. To be sure, there is a lot to appreciate in a language that provides cross-platform accessibility and a relatively approachable learning curve. Still, one may never simply create a home on the WWW. Myriad telephonic, linguistic, and cultural norms must be satisfied. The notorious penchant for Internet users to provide almost instant criticism to supposed mistakes found in electronic mail, newsgroups, and Web pages is, in this way, both reassuring and terrifying. That is to say, it's reassuring to know that another is always watching and potentially terrifying for the same reason.

A discussion of violence within the metonymic home need not play semantic games with the language associated with the WWW, such as "hit counts" and "crashes." It serves no purpose to review the many gendered assumptions built along with the hardware into every machine we use. Rather, it is useful to consider the interrelated nature of isolation and control that develops what we believe is a *de facto* culture of violence. Alone at home, waiting for unknown and unseen visitors, the page maintainer is subject to any number of threats, regardless of gender. Several years of "spamming," computer viruses, computer-mediated stalking, and the explosion of warnings against "unsafe computing" have worked to reinforce the assumption that our windows for viewing the outside world also provide access to its most insidious dangers. At the Mid-Atlantic Alliance for Computers and Writing conference on October 4–5, 1996, keynote speaker Gail Hawisher described how the process of representing visual images on the WWW leads to fear, especially among women. How, she asked, is a woman to know how her graphical image is being used by the institution sponsoring her Web site? In what other sites on the WWW might she find her name, image, or other personal information being used or abused by others? The infamous "Babes on the Web" (Toups 1996) site provides ample evidence of the ability for an individual home page to be misappropriated though the hypertextual linking process—literally epitomizing the potential for personal space within the home page to be surreptitiously violated.

WRAPPING THE HOME INSIDE THE QUILT

Having explored the ways in which the metonymy of home on the WWW can be analyzed along the rhetorical dimensions of isolation, control, and violence, it is necessary to consider an alternative means. Our selection of quilt is embedded in this chapter's feminist project: the assessment of ways in which technology—its semantic conceptualization and practical implementation—might be appropriated by marginalized groups and individuals. While quilts have traditionally fulfilled the basic human needs of warmth and protection, they are rarely recognized as objects of significant rhetorical statement. As Levy (1992) notes, mechanized production and standardization of the industrial age resulted in a cultural "scorn for the craft tradition of women's domestic arts" (p. 32). Despite the potential for quilts to write the intimate stories of families and communities, they are placed—and ignored—in the sphere of so-called "woman's work." Regardless, Orlofsky and Orlofsky (1992) note that quilts have recently begun to receive critical attention "for their strong contemporary visual qualities" (p. 86). Wahlman (1993) gives one example of this scholarship, noting that quilts provide a means of recovering the histories of African-Americans. Naturally, the stories told by historical quilts cannot be assumed to tell a single and definite narrative. Rather, as Williams (1994) suggests, the quilt and the process of quilting provide a medium and means to multiple interpretations, creating overlapping spaces of resistance.

However, the selection of quilt and quilting as metonyms is strategic (and, we hope, liberating) because of the craft's intrinsic qualities. The quilt serves the double purpose of addressing the place of marginalization by its traditional location in the home and creating the space for empowerment through its communal nature. The quilt is a product and process of creation, growth, and change. Rather than reduce a message to simple form, the quilt and the process of quilting provide a medium and means to multiple interpretations. In her description of the Names Project AIDS quilt, Elsley (1992) argues that the quilt "quite literally, invites a reading—the panels are the leaves of an enormous textile text . . . speaking its complex visual, verbal, and nonverbal language" (p. 189). It is of little surprise then that a popular and award-winning site on the WWW is an online version of the AIDS quilt (Memorial 1996). Quilts possess a communal potential by stitching together clusters of meaning beyond the individual contexts of the quilters. This will be demonstrated through an analysis of Daliberti's Web site along the dimensions of structure (quilt) and function (quilting). In this case, the quilt will be defined in ironic contrast to the metonymic reading of home provided earlier in the chapter. In response to the potential for isolation, control, and violence, we argue that quilt and quilting (as product and process) merge to create an environment of community, liberation, and safety.

The community of "Yellow Ribbon" evolves from its structure, as a collection of separate panels stitched together by "links." As with many quilts, each panel represents a unique idea. As with the physical process of quilting, Daliberti's page provides the means of communal expression. Unlike traditional uses of the electronic media, this use of computer technology empowers people who are otherwise unaffiliated with a power structure. Like the communal quilt, co-constructed in traditional "bees," Daliberti's Web site provides the opportunity to add one's own panel. By visiting Daliberti's site, one has the opportunity to jump to the pages of Congress members, write them letters, or read the letters they have sent and respond. Even the mere act of visiting contributes to the quilt's rhetorical growth. For several months, one panel—the tally of people visiting the site—changed constantly. On June 20, 1995, the most recent date in which statistics were offered, Daliberti wrote: "At 10:00 this morning (local time), there had been about 22,000 visits to the Yellow Ribbon. This translates to more than 113 thousand files accessed and roughly 315 megabytes of information transferred to more than 2400 different sites in 45 countries, including several locations in Kuwait" (Daliberti, Yellow Ribbon stats 1996).

This movement of files represents the patchwork of connections built between computers around the world to create a community of caring. As such, the text of Daliberti's Web site may be viewed as part of a larger "docuverse" that grows to link individual voices into a communal text (Landow 1992). The assumption that others are visiting the same place at the same time enhances a sense of shared context. Daliberti's use of context was established first by her page's statement of the time and date in Baghdad (currently inoperative). Through this strategy, Daliberti's site became connected to a real sense of place, which included her husband. Unlike the electronic mall described by Gumpert and Drucker (1992), the goal is not individual consumption but a communal production of a response to a tragedy felt by people around the world.

The liberation of "Yellow Ribbon" emerges from the sense of choice developed through the multitude of ways in which one may view the quilt. Using a WWW browser, the viewer is free to focus on individual panels in any order by choosing the links to be followed. In the hypertextual environment, links connect the various panels of the site. As with large physical quilts, such as the Names Project AIDS quilt, an abstracted "guide" to the panels is necessary. To be sure, this guide suggests a subtle means of control through its order and emphasis. However, as will be explored more fully below, the ability to follow one direction or the other (or another still) creates a space for resistance. In Daliberti's *Yellow Ribbon News* (1996) site, the visitor can select from a list of statements, press releases, and articles. The sense of liberation that emerges from choice responds to the isolation found in traditional uses of technology.

It must be recalled, of course, that Daliberti contributed a clear agenda to the overall construction of her Web site—developing a sense of control that was shaken by the imprisonment of, and lack of accurate information about, her husband. The purpose of her page was clear: in her April 14 post, Daliberti (1996) states, "I am using this home page to keep the world informed about my husband." This was no mere electronic billboard, however. Daliberti's goal was nothing less than to bypass the dominant gate-keepers and geographical borders of information. In a previous posting that is no longer archived, she stated: "I have every reason to believe that the comments we post here—unfilted [sic] by the news media—are reaching officials in the Iraqi government." In order to address the conflicting and inaccurate stories told by various news media, Daliberti used the site to provide an accurate and consistent view of her feelings and concerns: "As long as they are held captive, it would help the situation greatly if events were accurately reported. To that end, I'd like to restate some information that has been available, but not widely reported" (March 27, 1996, statement). Accurate or not, Daliberti discovered a structurally secured emancipation through the WWW that she could not find by simply waiting at home.

The safety of "Yellow Ribbon" comes from a sense that one can wrap one's self within a miniature world of connections and hidden spaces—to be seen or to hide. Freed from the isolating and controlling constraints of the structure, the quilt grows and connects, creating places of community on the very margins of power. Those who participate in its co-creation, even through the simple act of viewing, construct an alternative world—like the patches of a quilt that serve to recall distant times and places. William Gibson (1988) explores this theme with his description of the aleph, an approximation of the world's computerized data within a "single solid lump of biochip" that can be moved, placed, and infinitely repositioned (p. 154). In this description of the rhetoric of walking, de Certeau (1984) operationalizes this concept: "In the framework of enunciation, the walker constitutes, in relation to his position, both a near and a far, a here and a there" (p. 99). Thus, the world arises, unfolds, moves, and recedes through the deliberate actions of the user. Those spaces he or she visits might not be the places intended by their author or architects. Yet, they constitute, through their interconnections, some of the options defining the rhetorical space being explored.

As other individuals co-create the quilt, they influence its shape, message, and impact. Each new letter and new link alters the cluster of meanings, sometimes subtly, sometimes drastically. This is epitomized by our recollection of the use of date and time in the Daliberti site. While they did not change during our visits to the site, each subsequent visit reveals a new point of temporal reference. The fact that a similar shift takes place each time the physical AIDS quilt travels the country is significant. This phenomenon doesn't challenge the value of quilt or quilting as metonyms, but rather illuminates the potential of metonymic analysis. Unlike the reductionistic threat described by Burke (1962) and Brummett (1994), this metonymy enlarges with each application and sheds light on an increasingly complex set of undiscovered meanings.

CONTEXTUAL PARALLELISM: FRONTIERS AND THE MARGINALIZATION OF QUILT AND QUILTING

While understanding quilt and quilting absent the dominant ideological migration occurring alongside, if not due to, new information technologies supplies this chapter with the artifactual content required for our feminist ironic-metonymic analysis, it clearly falls short of explaining why isolation, control, and violence need be manifested altogether. Carveth and Metz (1996) provide some foundation for this when they explain that new information technologies exaggerate any given input dynamic—be it individual, social, organizational, or otherwise—through an amplification of motive (p. 72). This perspective holds that information technology enhances the rhetorical performance of that which it encounters; through technology, then, patriarchy begets a more influential patriarchy, feminism a more instrumental feminism. This is not to argue that philosophy is purified because of technology. However, it is to say that arguments are magnified, whatever their ingredients.[3] Garbage in, garbage out; quality in, quality out, as the maxims hold. Logically, to reason that ideology is not influenced by technology is to agree with Paz when he writes that "technology lacks meaning" (1967:13).

But, if technology amplifies and accelerates, as we believe it does, how does this phenomenon affect quilt and quilting? New frontiers, not so much unlike old frontiers, beg for the creation of order out of chaos (Fisher, Margolis, and Resnick 1996:11). When humans are confronted with the unknown, we intuitively explore, naming the unfamiliar, staking out rights, claiming territory (Carveth and Metz 1996:76). With all of the known earth having already been explored, excepting the voyage into inner space, which requires a significant amount of controlled equipment, the mass human expedition has taken a technological turn toward cyberspace. Into this new digital land, of sorts, we march forth bearing the traditional frontier psychologies of days long past, seeking innovation, invention, and resplendence, while exacting the motives of yesteryear (Pinkerton 1996: 458). We offer the communal WWW our known ideological champion, in bulk: capitalism. Heading into tomorrow, we employ our McLuhan-professed "rearview mirror" as a historical guide. This is the overarching capitalistic context in which sites like "Yellow Ribbon" and the "online AIDS quilt" must operate.

Over the past few years since WWW growth truly exploded in 1995, however, much has changed, not so much in what is available online (though this is indeed significant), but rather in terms of the process by which WWW pages are created. No longer are users required to learn the arcane syntax and intricate codes needed to produce information online. A generation of what-you-see-is-what-you-get (WYSIWYG) hypertextual editors can automatically translate, code, upload, and structure WWW home pages with as little precision and knowledge as it takes to operate a simple word processing utility. This truly democratizes the process of WWW frontiership, in the sense that almost anyone with a basic understanding of computer technology can create home pages. But, this development also objectifies the process of home page construction, for it is no longer considered a task of skill; it becomes relegated to the status of menial labor, arguably "woman's work." Ostensibly, this technological development carries extremely profound implications, for now, anyone with Internet access can be a contributing member of an ever-expanding, theoretically unlimited information community. Questions of Internet access-equity clearly remain, though, despite this software-assisted demystification of hypertext markup language.

Yet the new frontier that seems to be, is not in actuality. Home pages, and networks of home pages, no longer push the perimeter of the cyberspatial frontier. Home page construction is familiar territory. The powers of mind, higher-order cyberspatial processes, undoubtedly reign supreme (Dyson, Gilder, Keyworth, and Toffler 1994:28). Currently, virtual-reality markup language (VRML), interactive video conferencing, and asynchronous video-on-demand represent the envelope of innovation, the edge of what is known. Even seemingly advanced home pages offering audio and video streams are now considered pedestrian by elite digital explorers. Analogous to quilting in the pre-Industrial Revolution era, home pages in the pre-WYSIWYG editor period were handmade. Following the Industrial Revolution, however, this sewing art became automated; so has homepage construction. The object and process of quilt and quilting, akin to home page and home page construction, have both been reduced to subservience because the frontiers of knowledge and capitalism have expanded past their profitable utility.

CONCLUSION

On July 16, 1995, David Daliberti and Bill Barloon were released from captivity and the "Yellow Ribbon" was placed in an archival site. While the perspective of this chapter (equipment for living) makes determining the empirical "effectiveness" of Daliberti's WWW-based rhetoric problematic, it is clear that two significant areas of future study emerge from this analysis. The first concerns the concept of quilt as a protest mechanism. While we have chosen to concentrate on the ways in which quilting creates a sense of community, liberation, and safety, there remains a need to explore Daliberti's Web site more specifically as a protest against actions of the Iraqi government and the silence of American diplomacy. This perspective might draw from Williams' (1994) claim that quilters communicate toward an audience, but do not center their efforts with it. She notes that "quilts function to help the protesters develop, clarify, and reinforce their own ideas, making the protesters themselves a major audience for the quilts" (p. 36). This protest through community, as opposed to protest through confrontation, raises interesting questions about the nature of social influence in the electronic context. We believe that further research on computer-mediated protest would be useful. Particular emphasis might be paid to whether context is necessary or even possible in this frequently anonymous, asynchronous environment. Given that Daliberti used maps and time zones to contextualize her Web site, contemporary assumptions that the computer-mediated environment is relatively free of context cues might need to be revised.

A second and similar concern addresses metonymic criticism. Assuming the value of strategic metonymic selection, one might wonder about the utility of exploring the insights provided by multiple-metonymic analysis. Perhaps this would ensure the ironic detachment discussed by Burke (1962), who writes that irony, with its integrative "development" of multiple reference points, fashions a meaningful whole in which "none of the participating 'sub-perspectives' can be treated as either precisely right or precisely wrong" (p. 512). Rorty (1979) adds further support for this contention, noting that "once conversation replaces confrontation, the notion of the mind as Mirror of Nature can be discarded. Then the notion of philosophy as the discipline which looks for privileged representations among those constituting the Mirror becomes unintelligible" (p. 170). It might be fruitful to consider whether such a perspective, in which multiple metonyms are placed in a creative cluster, would add to the value of metonymic analysis in feminist criticism. This would create a mirror that reflects rather than reduces.

An ironic interplay between these two perspectives offers greater hope, not to (re)view the object under study by the critic, but to reveal textual spaces within dominant places that offer the potential for resistance. This approach is particularly useful for the critical analysis of WWW-based protest due to its focus on the relationship between text and spatial organization. This relationship brings to sharp relief an intriguing set of epistemological issues mirrored in the writings of William Gibson, popularly credited as the person who coined the term "cyberspace." In a recent book, Gibson (1988) describes the search for shape—representing cyberspatial data in a way that supports the dominant power structure. This shape defines the way knowledge can be known and employed. We suggest that shape refers to the rhetorical architecture of text and images that permits access, constrains activity, and ultimately determines the form of online interaction.

This exploration of Kathy Daliberti's response to the imprisonment of her husband has provided an empowering metonymic perspective on the strategy and meaning of her Web site. This approach examined the structure and function of quilting as metonyms that transcend male-oriented mechanisms of home. Further, this effort argued that the strategic selection of metonymy can avoid hyper-reductionism. In this process, the relationship between women and computer technology might develop more fully into one of emancipation. Rather than attempt to command an isolated (and isolating) machine, Daliberti illustrates the power of technologically mediated interaction—the heart of the modern generation of computers—to liberate through the creation of community.

NOTES

1. The World Wide Web Consortium describes the WWW in its background and history section as "the universe of network-accessible information, an embodiment of human knowledge" (*About the World Wide Web* 1996). The WWW was created by the European Laboratory for Particle Physics as a means for individuals to access information in textual and visual form in computer databases around the world. It is the fastest-growing part of the Internet—the network of computer networks. The WWW is based on hypertext, a system that allows a person to access files, pictures, sounds, and even movies stored on one or multiple computers.

2. Daliberti stopped updating "Yellow Ribbon" soon after the return of her husband. For some time, the page was not available through the WWW. Eventually volunteers began to maintain an archival site, located at http://www.swaninc.com/yellowribbon/ However, there is no assurance that the site will remain available to the online community.

3. We agree with Carveth and Metz (1996) that technology enhances, and perhaps even accelerates the rhetorical structures that frame meaning. However, this position is not without credible opponents, like Cliff Stoll, information technology consultant and author of *Silicon Snake Oil*, who believe that in a majority of the cases, technology overwhelmingly dulls human productiveness rather than spurring it (Gerstner 1996:19).

REFERENCES

About the World Wide Web. 1996. Online: WWW: http://www.w3.org/hypertext/WWW/WWW/

Brummett, B. 1994. *Rhetoric in Popular Culture*. New York: St. Martin's Press.

Burke, K. 1962. *A Grammar of Motives and a Rhetoric of Motives*. Cleveland: Meridian Books.

Carveth, R. and J. Metz. March 1, 1996. Frederick Jackson Turner and the democratization of the electronic frontier. *American Sociologist* 27:72–76.

Churbuck, D. November 20, 1995. So you want to be a web publisher? *Forbes*. p. 202

Clayton, W. E., Jr. March 18, 1995. 2 Americans held in Iraq for 4 days, officials say. *Houston Chronicle*, p. A1.

Daliberti, K. 1996. *March 27 Statement*. Online: WWW: http://www.swanine.com/yellowribbon/news/statement.950327.html

———. 1996. *April 14th Statement*. Online: WWW: http://www.swanine.com/yellowribbon/news/statement.950414.html

———. 1996. *Yellow Ribbon News*. Online: WWW: http://www.swaninc.com/yellowribbon/news/

———. 1996. *Yellow Ribbon Stats*. Online: WWW: http//www.swanine.com/yellowribbon/news/stats.current.html

de Certeau. M. 1984. *The Practice of Everyday Life*, trans. S. Rendall. Berkeley, Calif.: University of California Press.

Delphy, C. 1984. *Close to Home: A Materialist Analysis of Women's Oppression*. Amherst, Mass. University of Massachusetts Press.

Dyson, E., G. Gilder, J. Keyworth, and A. Toffler. 1994. A Magna Carta for the knowledge age. *New Perspective Quarterly* 11 (September):26–35.

Elsley, J. 1992. The rhetoric of the NAMES project AIDS quilt: Reading the text(ile). In E. S. Nelson, ed. *AIDS: The Literary Response*. New York: Twayne Publishers, pp. 187–203.

Fisher, B., M. Margolis and D. Resnick. 1996. Breaking ground on the virtual frontier. *American Sociologist* 27 (April):11–20.

Friedan, B. 1963. *The Feminine Mystique*. New York: Dell Publishing.

Gibson, W. 1988. *Mona Lisa Overdrive*. New York: Bantam Books.

Gill, D. W. J. 1995. Archaeology on the world wide web. *Antiquity* 69 (September): 626–30.

Gerstner, J. 1996. An interview with cyber-skeptic: Cliff Stoll. *Communication World* 13 (June):19.

Greenhouse, S. March 18, 1995. Iraq holding 2 Americans seized near Kuwaiti border. *New York Times*, p. A3.

Gumpert, G. and S. J. Drucker. 1992. From the agora to the electronic shopping mall. *Critical Studies in Mass Communication* 9(2):186–200.

Hayden, D. 1981. *The Grand Domestic Revolution: A History of Feminist Designs for American Homes, Neighborhoods, and Cities*. Cambridge, Mass.: MIT Press.

Hearst, A. 1996. Can the paperless magazine make it? *Columbia Journalism Review* (January/February):15–16.

Istel, J. 1995. Media: Stage presence in cyberspace. *American Theater* (December): 75–76.

Jansen, S. C. 1989. Gender and the information society: A socially structured silence. *Journal of Communication* 39:196–215.

Jensen, K. January 8, 1995. A woman's place? In cyberspace. *Atlanta Journal Constitution*, p. G1.

Kramarac. C. 1988. Talk of sewing circles and sweatshops. In C. Kramarae, ed. *Technology and Women's Voices: Keeping in Touch*. New York: Routledge and Kegan Paul, pp. 147–60.

Lancaster, J. May 7, 1995. Visit to Iraq prison bittersweet for wives, comfort to husbands. *Austin American-Statesman*. p. A7.

Landow, G. P. 1992. *Hypertext: The Convergence of Contemporary Literary Theory and Technology*: Baltimore: Johns Hopkins University Press

Levy, H. F. 1992. *Fiction of the Home Place*. Jackson Miss.: University Press of Mississippi.

Machung. A. 1988. 'Who needs a personality to talk to a machine?' Communication in the automated office. In C. Kramarae, ed. *Technology and Women's Voices: Keeping in Touch*. New York: Routledge and Kegan Paul, pp. 62–81.

Matheson, K. 1992. Women and computer technology: Communicating for herself.

In M. Lea, ed. *Contexts of Computer-Mediated Communication*. New York: Harvester Wheatsheaf, pp. 67–88.

McGaw, J. A. 1987. Women and the history of American technology. In S. Harding and J. F. O'Barr, eds., *Sex and Scientific Inquiry*. Chicago: University of Chicago Press pp. 47–77.

Memorial Quilt. 1996. Online: WWW:http://www.aidsquilt.org/quilt/

Morris. M., and C. Ogan. 1996. The Internet as mass medium. *Journal of Communication*. 16(1):39–50.

Neobyte Media. 1996. Online: WWW:http://www.neobyte.com/web.htm

Newhagen, J. E. 1996. Why communication researchers should study the Internet: A dialogue. *Journal of Communication* 46(1):4–13.

Orlofsky, P. and M. Orlofsky. 1992. *Quilts in America*. New York: Abbeville Press.

Parker, V. F. 1995. Battered. *RN* (January):26–29.

Paz, Octavio. 1967. The channel and the signs. *Alternating Currents*. Mexico City: Siglio Veintiuno Editores.

Pinkerton, J. 1996. The new paradigm. *Vital Speeches* 62 (May):57–62.

Powell, E. L. March 19, 1995. Baghdad says it seized 2 Americans at border. *Washington Post*, p. A31.

Rorty, R. 1979. *Philosophy and the Mirror of Nature*. Princeton: Princeton University Press.

Rosser, P. 1994. There's no place like home. In J. Frueh, C. L. Langer, and A. Raven, eds. *New Feminist Criticism: Art, Identity, Action*. New York: HarperCollins, pp. 60–79.

Rushing, J. H. and T. S. Frentz. 1989. The Frankenstein myth in contemporary cinema. *Critical Studies in Mass Communication* 6(1):61–80.

Shields, R. 1991. *Places on the Margin: Alternative Geographies of Modernity*. New York: Routledge.

Smith, J. and E. Balka. 1988. Chatting on a feminist computer network. In C. Kramarae, ed., *Technology and Women's Voices: Keeping in Touch*. New York: Routledge and Kegan Paul, pp. 82–97.

Spears, R., and M. Lea. 1994. Panacea or panopticon? The hidden power in computer-mediated communication. *Communication Research* 21:427–59.

Stoll, Clifford. 1996. *Second Thoughts on the Information Superhighway*. New York: First Anchor Books.

Toups, R. M. 1996. *Babes on the Web*. Online WWW: http://www:toupsie.com/2.0 BABE.html

Turkle, S. 1988. Computational reticence: Why women fear the intimate machine. In C. Kramarae, ed., *Technology and Women's Voices: Keeping in Touch*. New York: Routledge and Kegan Paul, pp. 41–61.

Wahlman, M. S. 1993. *Signs and Symbols: African Images in African-American Quilts*. New York: Studio Books.

Williams, M. R. 1994. A reconceptualization of protest rhetoric: Women's quilts as rhetorical forms. *Women's Studies in Communication* 17(2):20–44.

Index

Advanced Research Projects Agency, Department of Defense, 104
Americans with Disabilities Act (1990), 50–51
Apple Computer, 160
Atwell, Robert, President of the American Council on Education, 162

Bandai Digital entertainment, 160
Barloon, Bill, 220
Bolter, Jay David, 124
Bureau of Labor Statistics, 164

Center for Social Organization of Schools, 146
Communicative style, 186
Community networks, 41
Community of yellow ribbons, 225–227
Computer-mediated communication, 185–186, 188
Computer-mediated conversation, 24
Contact zone, 125
Culture symbols, 86
Cyber age, 122
Cyber discourse, 3
Cyberghetto, 2, 6

Cyber philosophers, 124
Cybersex, 3
Cyberstealth, 3
Cybertopia, 2

Daliberti, David, 220
Daliberti, Kathy, 219, 220
Dawson, Michael, 84
Deutsch, Karl, 174
Diffusion of Innovation Theory, 89
"Double day," 21
Durkheim, Emile, 86

Easton, David, 174
Electronic commerce, 8
Electronic red-lining, 6, 35
Emancipatory technology, 6
Ethnic minority model, 173

Female Gaze, The, 205
Foster, John Bellamy, 84
Foucault, Michel, 126, 172, 207

Gates, Bill, 84, 122–123
Geertz, Clifford, 86
Gender bias, 23

Gerbner, George, 85
Gingrich, Newt, House Speaker, 83
Government Accounting Office, 138
Graphic, Visualization, & Usability
  Center, The, 159
Great equalizer, Internet as, 15–18, 29–
  30, 83

Herring, Susan, 126, 186–187
High-Performance Computing Act
  (1991), 110
Human Capital Theory, 39

Information Age, 33, 39
Information apartheid, 6–8
Information poor, 28
Information red-lining, 29
Information superhighway, 29
International Association for Evalua-
  tion of Education Attainment, 144,
  147
Internet sex, 206
Inter-relay chat, 206
Ironic-metonymic dimension, 222

Landow, George, 124
Lanham, Richard, 124
Libertarians, 54
Los Angeles Gay and Lesbian Center,
  181

Male-centric, Internet as, 7
McLuhan, Marshall, 85, 124, 126
Megabyte University, 188
Morrison, Toni, 124

Names Project AIDS quilt, 225–
  226
Negroponte, Nicholas, 124
Net sex, 209, 213, 215–216
Network wizards, 159
Nielsen Media Research, 159

Office of Education Research and
  Improvement, U.S. Department of
  Education, 142
Ong, Walter, 126
Operation Restore Hope, 68
Operation Uphold Democracy, 68

Parallel structural strategies, 41
Pew Research Center, 88, 95
Postman, Neil, 85

Queer Cyber Center (QCC), 171–176

RAND, 67, 159
Reasonable accommodations, 53
Rheingold, Howard, 84

Stone, Allucquére Rosanne, 208
System-changing strategies, 42

Technological literacy, 36
Thrall, Nelson, 214

Universal service, 56–57
Usenet, 189–190

Virtual communities, 3–6, 50

About the Editor and Contributors

BOSAH EBO is a professor in the Department of Communication at Rider University, in Lawrenceville, New Jersey. He teaches and writes on international communication, communication ethics, and media and popular culture. His publications include "Media Diplomacy and Foreign Policy: Toward a Theoretical Framework," in *News Media and Foreign Relations*, edited by Abbas Malek, and "War As Popular Culture: The Gulf Conflict and the Technology of Illusionary Entertainment," in the *Journal of American Culture* 1995.

TYRONE L. ADAMS is an assistant professor of speech communication in the Division of Arts and Languages at the University of Arkansas at Monticello. He is the editor of the *American Communication Journal*, an online publication of the American Communication Association. Previously, he was a fellow with the International Center for the Advancement of Political Communication and Argumentation (ICAPCA).

CHARLENE BLAIR is assistant director of graduate resources in the Graduate College Professional Development Program and a doctoral candidate in American culture studies program at Bowling Green State University. Her research interest is in gender and cyber-culture.

MARK BORCHERT is a doctoral student in mass communication at the University of Colorado, Boulder. He is completing his dissertation, which examines communication policy, new technologies, and deaf and hearing-impaired persons in America. He also is conducting research related to the information superhighway at CableLabs, a research consortium of cable television system operators in the United States, Canada, and Mexico.

REBECCA CARRIER is an assistant professor of journalism at California Polytechnic, Pomona. Her work focuses on media studies, in particular the social and political effects of mass media globalization.

META G. CARSTARPHEN is a faculty member in the Department of Journalism at the University of North Texas in Denton. She was awarded a research fellowship by the Poynter Institute for Media Studies to conduct a year-long study on how journalists are changing the way they use race in their reporting and writing. Her 1995 article, "New Media Literacy: From Classroom to Community," was published through the Family Literacy Center of the ERIC Clearinghouse on Reading, English, and Communication.

KEVIN CROWSTON is an assistant professor in the School of Information Studies at Syracuse University. He was a founding member of the Collaboratory for Research on Electronic Work at the University of Michigan and of the Center for Coordination Science at Massachusetts Institute of Technology Sloan School of Management. His current research focuses on new ways of organizing made possible by the use of information technology.

MORTEN G. ENDER is an assistant professor of sociology and peace studies at the University of North Dakota, Grand Forks. His paper, "Social Presence Theory, Military Families, and the Comparison of Old and New Media," received the 1996 Elise M. Boulding Paper Award from the Peace and War Section of the American Sociological Association. His current research examines the use of the Internet for chain referral sampling.

ERICKA KAMMERER is a doctoral candidate in computer information systems at the University of Michigan School of Business Administration. Her research is on the role of personal narrative in the social construction of virtual communities. She is a partner in the Reston Consulting Group, and develops health care services computer simulation models.

NADINE S. KOCH is an associate professor in the Department of Political Science at California State University, Los Angeles. She received a Ph.D. in American politics from Ohio State University. She is an outside consultant on a project funded by the Annenberg Center for Communication Studies to create the Community Queer Cafe in Los Angeles. She and her colleagues are studying the impact of the Internet on the gay and lesbian community.

JACQUELINE JOHNSON LAMBIASE is a lecturer in the Department of Journalism at the University of North Texas in Denton. She is a doctoral candidate in humanities (rhetoric/composition and American studies) at the University of Texas at Arlington, finishing her dissertation, "Surfing Past Traditional Media: The Internet's Impact on the Fourth Estate."

JOHN G. McNUTT is an assistant professor in the Graduate School of Social Work at Boston College. He has presented numerous papers at conferences and published in journals, including *Journal of Volunteer Administration* and *Journal of Social Work Education*. He co-edited a book, *The Global Environmental Crisis: Implications for Social Welfare and Social Work*, in 1994.

JAMES L. McQUIVEY is a graduate fellow and a doctoral candidate at Syracuse University's S.I. Newhouse School of Public Communication. He has worked in film and video production, public relations, and management consulting. His research interest is new media technologies with a focus on the use of the Web as a medium for advertising.

ELVIN MONTERO is a master's degree candidate at the Annenberg School, the University of Pennsylvania. He also is the national president of Lamda Pi Eta, the national undergraduate honor society. His research focuses on the Internet and computer-mediated communication.

JOHN C. POLLOCK teaches in the Communication Studies Department of the College of New Jersey in Trenton. He received his Ph.D. from Stanford University and previously was a corporate communications researcher at AT&T. His newest book, *Newspapers, Public Issues and Public Policy: City Characteristics and Social Transformation*, was published by Hampton Press in 1997. Partial funding for the research for his chapter was provided by a Faculty and Institutional Research and Sabbatical Leave (FIRSL) grant and Phi Kappa Phi Student-Faculty Research Award, both at the College of New Jersey.

PAULETTE ROBINSON is the founder and president of EdOnline, and educational technology consulting firm in Laurel, Maryland. She is also a doctoral student at the University of Maryland, College Park, where she is studying curriculum and instruction and instructional technology. She is particularly interested in the effective integration of computers into the classroom.

H. ERIC SCHOCKMAN is the associate director of the Center for Multiethnic and Transnational Studies at the University of Southern California. He is a political scientist from the University of California specializing in urban/state, politics/ethnic, sexual, and racial politics. He also has served as an administrator and consultant to the California State Legislature and Los Angeles City Council for over a decade.

DAVID R. SEGAL is Distinguished Scholar-Teacher, professor of sociology and of government and politics, director of the Center for Research on Military Organization at the University of Maryland, College Park. He is also a faculty associate at the Center for International and Security Studies at Maryland (CISSM). He was a Distinguished Visiting Professor of sociology at the United States Military Academy, West Point. His books include *Peacekeepers and Their Wives* (1993).

ALECIA WOLF received a master's degree in business administration in 1985 from the University of Texas at Tyler, and is currently a student in humanities at the University of Texas at Arlington. She presented "Gendered Use of Emotions on the Internet" at the Arlington Humanities Colloquium in April 1996.

ANDREW F. WOOD is a doctoral candidate at Ohio University. He is interested in feminist, postmodern, and architectural research. Previously, he served in the Navy as a broadcast journalist.

ISBN 0-275-95993-7

EAN

9 780275 959937

HARDCOVER BAR CODE

DATE DUE

DEC 1 5 2002			